This book is made available in part by a generous gift from the Dale Hull Memorial Fund through the Lomax Church of Christ.

His Table
2025 Devotional Guide

thejenkinsinstitute.com

HIS

TABLE

ISBN: 9798300340063

Published by:
The Jenkins Institute
thejenkinsinstitute.com

Logo & Cover Design:
Dale Jenkins

Editing & Interior Layout:
Joey Sparks

Order additional copies of this resource at:

thejenkinsinstitute.com/shop

or

tji@thejenkinsinstitute.com

We dedicate this book to those who prepare, serve, and help make our weekly observance of the Supper without distraction.

Thank you for all you do to serve the Lord and His People.

Table of Contents

HIS FINAL WEEK: MONDAY

HIS FINAL WEEK: TUESDAY EVENING

HIS FINAL WEEK: WEDNESDAY

HIS FINAL WEEK: THURSDAY - THE LAST SUPPER

HIS FINAL WEEK: THURSDAY 10:30 PM-1:00 AM

HIS FINAL WEEK: FRIDAY MORNING

HIS FINAL WEEK: FRIDAY 9:00 AM -12 NOON

HIS RESURRECTION: SUNDAY

HIS PEOPLE

With Thanks

A project of this size takes a lot of humble servants. Over 100 ministers and 50 elders helped in making this material come to life. We are thankful for them all. We hope you'll write notes of appreciation to some of them as the material blesses your life.

We are thankful for our friend, Joey Sparks. He sees our projects through to the end and puts up with our (Dale's) constant irritation about when it will all be done. He handles our formatting and helps with editing.

We are thankful to congregations who purchase copies of this book to aid their members in their growth and for individuals who gift this book to others.

We're thankful for you and pray this book blesses your life.

Most of all, we thank the Lord who loves imperfect people and reveals his faithfulness to them. All glory and praise for this work goes to Him.

How to Use This Book

In 2016, a small group of preachers organized a weekly devotional and study guide, resulting in *One Word*. TJI has been honored to continue publishing similar editions. Gratefully, *His Table* is now the seventh weekly devotional guide we have published.

This year's edition is special in that it draws us nearer to the Lord's Table. The topics for each week's devotionals come from Jesus' week leading up to his crucifixion, concluding with His resurrection and the church's practice of communion.

There are several ways to use this devotional guide. You might just read it a section a day each weekday for the year. It might be that each member of the church will have a copy and you all will be reading and growing together. It might be a book you'll use for a class, a small group, or some other Bible study group. With each lesson, there is a related Scripture reference and a fitting action prompt. We encourage you to make the most of these to apply these sacred truths.

The most notable difference this year is that at the beginning of each week, you will find "Table Meditations" written by elders from congregations all across the country. Use these on Sundays to help you focus on our Lord during communion.

There is also a digital version you can have if you would rather read it on a device. In some churches, the preacher will use the sermon companion that goes with this devotional guide and preach his lessons around the theme for this year.

All materials can be ordered at *TheJenkinsInstitute.com*.

Foreword

The final week of the ministry of Jesus was filled with many activities. There was much that Jesus wanted to do and say in those last days before the cross, both with His apostles and the leaders of the nation of Israel. In noting what Jesus did and said during that final week, we should remember that the Jews calculated time with a new day beginning at six o'clock in the evening.

Most believe that the final week began for Jesus on Friday, "six days before the Passover" (John 12:1), when He traveled with his apostles to Bethany where He enjoyed the hospitality of His friends, Martha, Mary, and Lazarus, and where He was anointed by Mary (John 12:2-11). On Saturday (the Jewish Sabbath) Jesus observed a day of rest. On Sunday ("the next day," John 12:12), Jesus made His "Triumphal Entry" into Jerusalem and returned to Bethany. On Monday ("the next day," Mark 12:12), Jesus entered Jerusalem and cleansed the Temple. On Tuesday ("in the morning," Mark 11:20), Jesus experienced the great day of questions, and it was "two days" before the Passover (Mark 14:1). Wednesday must have been a day of rest for Jesus since we have no recorded activities. On Thursday, the observance of the Passover took place on "the first day" of the Paschal week "when they sacrificed the Passover lamb" (Mark 14:12). On that day, Jesus came together with His apostles and instituted the Lord's Supper, saying that the unleavened bread represented His body and the fruit of the vine represented His blood offered on the cross for our sins. He presented Himself as "our Passover" (1 Corinthians 5:7) and said, "Do this in memory of Me" (Matthew 26:26-28). The first-century church did this (Acts 20:7), and I want to believe that every Sunday from then until now has found faithful brethren coming together to observe the Supper in memory of Christ. This volume contains five devotionals (one per day of the week), written by preachers of the gospel, connecting us to these events.

As you read the following pages, you will also find fifty-two articles, all written by men who serve as elders in the church, which will help you to prepare each Sunday to take of the Supper as you remember the death, resurrection, glorification, and the coming again of Christ.

Our thanks to Jeff and Dale for compiling these thoughts for our edification.

Jay Lockhart

Tyler, TX

HIS
PROPHECIES

Table Meditation
Scripture: Ephesians 1:9-10

It is difficult to imagine the depth and breadth of God's love for us. Consider that God formulated a plan before the beginning of time that included the sacrifice of His one and only Son. He died for us because we failed to submit to His perfect love and will.

He created us with free will, but in doing so, we often yield to our will rather than His will. Through the centuries, man has disobeyed God's commands, resulting in hardship and heartbreak. Even though we are unfaithful, God is always faithful, waiting with open arms for us to answer his call.

On our own, we can never reach the state of perfection that God desires for us. Therefore, in His wisdom, He created the perfect sacrifice that would cleanse and purify us so that we might be wholly acceptable to him. That sacrifice called for Christ to come in the flesh and live among us, being tempted and tried, scorned and hated, shedding His blood on the cross so that we may be made holy, someday joining God in heaven to glorify Him forever.

In God's plan, He gave ALL for us! As we take this bread and this cup, let us consider if we are giving our ALL to Him!

MONDAY
A Snake in the Grass
Today's Scripture: Genesis 3:15; Ephesians 6:11-12

Have you heard the idiom, "a snake in the grass"? According to Dictionary.com, it can refer to two things: "a treacherous person, especially one who feigns friendship" or "a concealed danger." The idiom was first used by the poet Virgil in 37 B.C. in the line, "You boys that pick flowers and strawberries near the ground, run away from here, a cold snake hides in the grass" (Grammarist.com). It refers to those who manipulate and deceive others to get what they want and is a term that fits well in the background of the text we focus on this week, Genesis 3:15.

Genesis 3:6 records the introduction of sin into God's creation and the curses God hands out on the serpent, Eve, and Adam. God curses in the reverse order of how the culprits are mentioned in Genesis 3:12-13, beginning with the serpent in Genesis 3:14-15. Jesus identifies this snake in John 8:44 as the devil who was "a murderer from the beginning." From the beginning of creation, this serpent has been one who will use half-truths or whole lies to tempt and manipulate humanity. His work is described in passages like 1 Peter 5:8, 2 Corinthians 4:4, 2 Corinthians 11:14, and Revelation 20:10. He has always been a "snake in the grass" when dealing with humanity.

The serpent works in manipulative and deceptive ways to destroy our walk with God with each other. Ephesians 6:11-12 makes plain that our fight is not against one another but against the one who schemes against us. Adam and Eve faced the serpent and fell. Today, believers have all that the Bible reveals to help avoid his deceptive and manipulative ways.

Today, I will…commit to be aware that the serpent is an active agent working in our world.

TUESDAY
The Fight Is On
Today's Scripture: Romans 7:13-25

On September 1, 2007, the Georgia Tech Yellow Jackets rolled into South Bend, Indiana, to play the Notre Dame Fighting Irish. The pregame speech by Georgia Tech chaplain Derrick Moore is one of my favorite motivational speeches of all time. The climax is Moore telling the team a phrase his middle school coach used to tell him. It goes, "We gonna fight until we can't fight no more. We gon' lie down, bleed awhile. And then we are gonna get up and fight some more." He repeats this again and again. Every time, I find myself getting worked up with his words. They capture so much of what we believers live in our daily walk against the serpent.

The curse that God places on the serpent in Genesis 3:15 includes the reality that there will always be enmity between the offspring of the serpent and the offspring of Adam and Eve. This enmity was seen in the deception of Eve in the garden (Genesis 3:1-8), and it continues today between the serpent's forces of evil and those who belong to God. Paul teaches us that enmity is the name of the game between believers and the serpent (Romans 7:13-20). We "lie down and bleed awhile." However, the promise throughout scripture is that there is victory when believers "get up and fight some more" with the one who has won the victory over this serpent (Romans 7:24-25; see also 1 John 3:8; Romans 16:20; Hebrews 2:14).

For the record, Georgia Tech won that game, defeating Notre Dame by 30 points.

Today, I will… encourage others with the truth that, while at times we may fail God due to the ongoing nature of our fight with the serpent, we can continue to fight knowing that Jesus has decisively won the victory for us.

WEDNESDAY
Head Over Heel
Today's Scripture: 1 Corinthians 15:20-28

Any trauma surgeon would say a head injury is much more serious than a foot injury. Foot injuries can be serious, but when the brain is involved, the results can be life-altering. If the person survives, brain injuries impact the injured, family members, and caregivers. It is much easier to deal a fatal blow by striking the head than a foot.

Genesis 3:15 tells us that the enmity between the serpent's offspring and Eve's offspring will result in a series of strikes. The serpent's offspring will strike and bruise the heel of the offspring of Eve. The offspring of Eve will strike and bruise the head of the offspring of the serpent. "Bruise" is an adequate translation of the verb, but the location of the bruise makes all the difference.

Scholars debate whether or not this passage explicitly talks about what Jesus has done through the cross and resurrection or whether this passage refers to the ongoing struggle between humanity and the forces of evil. No matter the view we hold (or whether both can be true in the text), we must know that the advantageous bruise is on the heel and not the head. 1 Corinthians 15:20-28 portrays Jesus doing the bruising by "destroying every rule and every authority and power. For he must reign until he has put all his enemies under his feet" (1 Corinthians 15:24b-25, ESV). Paul's imagery perfectly describes what Genesis 3:15 predicted. The serpent continues to strike today (1 Peter 5:8), but Jesus has dealt the decisive and fatal blow.

Today, I will... remember the decisive blow Jesus has delivered to satan, and I will remind those struggling that his victory is certain.

THURSDAY
More Winning than Losing
Today's Scripture: 1 Corinthians 15:54-58

When people fight one another, there is usually a clear winner. Children gathering around a playground fight happily share who they believe to be the winner once the fight ends. The same goes for world conflicts: there are winners and losers. What happens when we are unsure who won the fight? It is easy to think that the continual fighting between the offspring of the serpent and the woman in Genesis 3:15 will lead to a draw. The serpent's efforts seem to be winning. Look at the Western world and its continued decline in the Christian faith. However, we see his efforts thwarted by the growth of the faith worldwide in places like China, India, and Africa.

Throughout Scripture, the images of Genesis 3:14-15 are seen in multiple victories.

- At the throne of David, God promises that his offspring will be established forever (2 Samuel 7:12; Psalm 89:3) and that those who stand before them will be crushed under their feet (Psalm 89:23; 2 Samuel 22:39).

- Enemies of the King will "lick the dust" like the serpent (Psalm 72:9; Micah 7:17).

- With God's help, satan will be crushed by believers (Romans 16:20).

These images remind us that what God promised the serpent in Genesis 3:14-15 is already a reality. At the end, the serpent will experience his ultimate defeat (Ephesians 1:20-23; 1 Corinthians 15:24-28). There may be times when it seems the serpent is winning, but the ultimate victory belongs to Christ (1 Corinthians 15:54-58).

Today, I will… know that, while it may appear at times that the serpent is winning, we know God's victory is greater.

FRIDAY
The Snake-Crusher Will Win
Today's Scripture: Revelation 12

I love to read Bible story books to my children. My four-year-old asks for them, and I am happy to oblige. These books supplement our regular in-home and Bible class studies. One book that I love is called *The Biggest Story Bible Storybook.* While it is not Scripture, Kevin DeYoung presents stories from the Bible in a way that connects them to Jesus Christ. In the second story, "The Fall," based on Genesis 3, DeYoung refers to Jesus as the "Snake Crusher." I love this image. In coming to save us from our sins, Jesus has crushed the serpent who has plagued humankind since the beginning.

While Genesis 3:15 can be read about the enmity between humanity and the spiritual forces of evil, it can also be seen as what some call the "protoevangelium" or "The First Gospel." This would mean it is the first instance in scripture that points to the serpent's ultimate defeat by Christ. While I believe both ideas are evident, Revelation 12 shows Genesis 3:15 as pointing to the work of Christ. Revelation 12:9-11 assures us that Jesus is indeed the "Snake Crusher." This text also includes that those with Christ will stand victorious. Let us never miss this great truth when we gather together to celebrate the work of Christ on the cross.

Today, I will…thank God that Jesus is the "Snake Crusher."

Table Meditation
Scripture: John 10:17-18

Today, as we partake of communion, I want us to think about the various moments of suffering that Jesus endured for us:

- He was betrayed by one of his chosen apostles.
- He prayed in such agony that his blood was mixed with sweat. Jesus had full knowledge of what he was about to go through. He pleaded with the Father to let this cup pass, but alas this was the plan of salvation from the beginning of time.
- He was put through multiple trials involving physical assaults.
- He was spat upon.
- A Roman soldier beat Him with a whip containing bits of bone and metal, ripping the flesh from His body.
- After this, He was forced to carry His cross to Calvary until He collapsed from exhaustion.
- Nails were driven into the wrists and feet of our Lord.
- The cross, with Jesus nailed to it, was raised up and dropped into the hole prepared for it—oh, the pain that must have caused!
- He hung on that cross, suspended between heaven and earth for some six hours.
- To breathe, He would have to lift himself up using those nails and then slump back down again when the pain became unbearable. He repeated this each time He needed to breathe.
- Jesus went through a separation from God the Father because he became the sin offering for us.

No one took His life, He freely gave it for us, for salvation, to make atonement for our sins.

Praise God this is not the end of the story.

He rose victorious from the grave!

The Precious Christ—His Power

Today's Scripture: Isaiah 53:1

Our devotional thoughts for the Lord's Table this week are from Isaiah 53. The book of Isaiah is called the Fifth Gospel by some because it has 66 chapters (as the Bible has 66 books), and the final 27 chapters deal with the Messianic Age (as the New Testament has 27 books). This week, we focus on Jesus the Messiah as the Precious Christ. Peter uses the word "precious" 7 times, but most significantly to the Precious Christ (1 Peter 2:6, citing Isaiah 28:16). What makes Christ precious? We will note His power, His posture, His pain, His payment, and His place—all from Isaiah 53 and all representing His preciousness.

In verse 1, Isaiah directs us to His power because it is the arm of the Lord (Yahweh) who will cause His incarnation (John 1:14). This verse is cited in John 12:38 and Romans 10:16 by John and Paul. As Jesus reveals the work of "the arm of the Lord," Isaiah repeats a phrase he used in 51:9. The coming Christ will come not only from God's arm, but He will have limitless power. He will demonstrate power to heal the sick, cast out demons, raise the dead, and heal the leper (Matthew 10:8). He will even read minds (Mark 2:8). So, did the Roman nails hold Jesus to the cross? Absolutely not. If He wished, He could have jumped off the cross and said, "What else have you got?" (John 10:18).

However, humanity's freedom of choice dictates that not all will believe (i.e., "Who has believed?"). My human choice can override all the evidence for Jesus being the Messiah because my own selfishness is very powerful.

Today, I will…prepare to take of the Supper by focusing on His power and my submission to Him.

The Precious Christ—His Posture
Today's Scripture: Isaiah 53:2-3

Imagine a king from an earthly perspective. What images come to mind? Maybe a throne, regal clothing, servants to command, opulent living, having every desire immediately fulfilled. Jesus came as King, but none of these images applied to Him. He will meet no Messianic expectations common to first-century Israel. Have you ever overlooked a lost object because you were looking for an object of a different size, color, or form? This represents many first-century Jews who were looking for the wrong Messiah.

Notice the posture of the Messiah about whom Isaiah prophesied in the eighth century B.C. He grew up as a normal child (Luke 2:52) in the dry region of Nazareth. Divinely intentional. Jesus was not ugly, but there was nothing physically exceptional about Him (v. 2). I used to wonder, "Where did Mary put the halo of Jesus when she was bathing Him?" The Renaissance images are all wrong. Jesus did not glow, He did not have a halo, and He was not physically handsome. However, He does represent me—a common man with common needs. He understands my plight, although without sin (Hebrews 4:15). Even the New Testament is written in "koine" Greek—the Greek of the marketplace.

Yet this same Jesus will be despised by many (v. 3). Isaiah 49:7 had previously spoken of the nations rejecting the Messiah. Without this level of hatred from "the nations," Jesus would never have been crucified, and we would still be in our sins. Jesus came from sorrows (remember the circumstances of His birth), and He knew sorrows like no one on earth has ever known. The Hebrew text of "hiding faces" could be either that the Messiah will hide His face from others or that others will hide their faces from Him. Can it be that His sorrows that we envision in His Supper could bring joy and peace to me? It can—but it is up to me.

Today, I will…appreciate that the precious Christ assumed his humble posture so that I can be saved (Philippians 2:5-9).

WEDNESDAY
The Precious Christ—His Pain
Today's Scripture: Isaiah 53:4-5

I suppose that these two verses from Isaiah 53 are the two most commonly used verses by men introducing our thoughts for the Lord's Supper. Maybe we focus on His pain so often because we need to focus on our pain. Recently, I have had trouble with one of my sciatic nerves. Pain demands your attention and challenges you to focus on anything else. However, wouldn't it be superfluous to endure pain if it could be avoided? That is exactly what Jesus, the precious Christ, did for us all. Through his pain, he bore the iniquities of us all as a surrogate for our own pain and as a scapegoat for our own sins.

Matthew 8:17 sees Isaiah 53:3 reflected in the many people healed by Jesus, including Peter's mother-in-law. The irony is that we esteem Him stricken and afflicted (Isaiah 53:4) even though it is *our* sins that are causing the affliction (Psalms 69:26). The concept of the "piercing" of the Messiah should occupy much thought. Isaiah prophesies it, and the prophet Simeon continues it when he first sees Jesus as a baby (Lk 2:35). Zechariah 12:10 also tells us the Messiah will be pierced. I wonder if Mary thought of Simeon's prophecy when she saw the soldier thrust his sword into the side of Jesus (John 19:34). The magnanimity of the unrighteousness of this occasion leads to our righteousness only through Jesus (Romans 4:25).

The paradox of His open wounds is that they give us peace and healing (Isaiah 53:5; 1 Peter 2:24). This reality should entertain our thoughts and hearts as we partake of the Lord's Supper. Unless the Lord's Supper is personalized, we engage in a meaningless ritual (Matthew 15:8-9). Everything imposed on Him was because of me. His pain should have been my pain. His stripes were my stripes. His torment should have been my torment.

Today, I will…focus on the pain of the precious Christ by appreciating that God sent His Son to willingly endure pain that rightfully belonged to me.

THURSDAY

The Precious Christ—His Payment

Today's Scripture: Isaiah 53:6-9

Today, we focus on the payment of the precious Christ taught in Isaiah 53:6-9. What should be the payment for one who lost all the flock of sheep? Israel's straying is prophesied in Jeremiah 50:6, 17; 1 Peter 2:25. Sheep are pretty stupid; that's why a strong shepherd is needed to control them. I have seen the dependence of sheep on the shepherd in the fields of Palestine. Because of the sin of each one of us, Yahweh lays on the Messiah that which should be laid on us (2 Corinthians 5:21; Colossians 2:14). Even in the depth of his oppression and affliction (Isaiah 53:7), He did not open His mouth. During His trials, Jesus appeared twice before Pilate. The first time, He admitted that He was the King of the Jews. The second time, He remained silent (Matthew 26:63; Mark 14:61; John 19:9; and 1 Pet 2:23). This silence is deafening to all who know that Jesus could have removed Himself from this suffering. He was as innocent as a newborn lamb (Jeremiah 11:19; Acts 8:32).

How much did it cost? The payment for our salvation was steep, even unpayable. Only Jesus could pay the price. Yet to pay the price, He had to be cut off from the living by dying on the cross between two wicked men. He died the death of criminals, appearing dishonorable and associating with the wicked (Isaiah 53:9). However, two rich men, Joseph of Arimathea and Nicodemus, took Jesus from the cross. Nicodemus was rich because poor people did not make it to the Sanhedrin. Rich men wanting the body of Jesus is one of the rare events recorded in all four gospels (Matthew 27:57-60; Mark 15:42-46; Luke 23:50-53; John 19:38-42). Even immersed in violence, Jesus did not sin, nor did He die with guile in His heart (Isaiah 53:9). Incredible.

Today, I will…focus on the payment of the precious Christ by seeking to understand His payment and striving to surrender to Him more completely.

The Precious Christ—His Place
Today's Scripture: Isaiah 53:10-12

Is the sacrifice going to be worth it? I am sure this thought has crossed your mind. What does the Messiah get after enduring the cross? Isaiah tells us about the place of the precious Christ that he enjoyed on earth and that he now enjoys in heaven. However, the process of getting there was tough. Our sacrifices pale in significance to what Jesus had to endure.

The phrase "the will of the Lord (Yahweh)" is prominent. The will of the Lord will crush the Messiah; yet the will of the Lord will prosper in His hand (Isaiah 53:10). The will of the Lord can bring you peace, but sometimes it can frighten or crush you—especially when your prayers for health and healing are not answered in the way you wanted. The will of the Lord can be ideal (2 Peter 3:9), it can be contingent (i.e., one may or may not accept God's salvation; 1 Peter 1:22), or it may be final (Matthew 25:31-46). The problem is—how can we tell the difference? Jesus asked if He could be alleviated from the suffering of the cross—if it be the *will* of God, but He knew He had a path to follow (John 17:3).

I used to tell my students that our righteousness could only be "borrowed," not owned (Romans 4-5, "justification by faith"). I illustrated it as someone shooting at a target. If he or she hits it every time, right in the center, then that person is said to be "righteous." What hope do I have of such perfection (Romans 3:23; 6:23)? If I can be saved only through His righteousness, only through faith, then is it something I can earn? Of course not—but He earned it for me. I am "counted" as being righteous, and His righteousness cancels my debt and clears my sin-debt with God (Acts 13:39; Romans 4:3-5). However, I in no way earn my salvation.

Am I not grateful that He will divide His "portion" with me (Isaiah 53:12; Philippians 2:9)? Because His soul was poured out in death when He was considered a transgressor, He now has become my perpetual intercessor.

Today, I will…exalt Christ because of His place as King of Kings and Lord of Lords—my precious Christ.

HIS TEACHINGS

Table Meditation
Scripture: 2 Corinthians 5:17-19

In Middle Eastern culture, there is a traditional form of reconciliation that spans many, many generations. It is known as "sulha" [صلحا]. While there is no direct, single-word equivalent for this word in English, in its most literal sense, it is commonly translated as "They made peace." Sulha is a traditional method of conflict resolution throughout the Arabic world. During sulha, the two parties in opposition are brought together over a meal by a mediator to reconcile their differences.

Echoes of the sulha concept can be found in Psalm 23:5, which states, "You prepare a table before me in the presence of my enemies."

It is neither accidental nor incidental that we gather around the table as a family of believers on the first day of each week to remember Christ. We remember His sacrifice and the blood debt He paid to reconcile us with God the Father. Like the prodigal son in the parable of the Forgiving Father in Luke 15, as sinners, we are openly defiant of God's will and in opposition to His purpose. Christ enters our lives to expunge our past sins and reconcile us to a right relationship with our heavenly Father. As we partake of the bread, which represents Christ's body, and the cup, which represents His life-giving blood, let us focus our minds and our hearts on who Christ is, what He has done for us, and the reconciliation He has affected between us and our heavenly Father.

MONDAY
It Was Destroyed
Today's Scripture: John 2:19

Isaiah prophesied that the suffering of God's Servant would be horrific. We sometimes overlook the statement that the Servant's "appearance" would be "so married" that it would be "beyond human semblance" (Isaiah 52:14). So when Jesus used the phrase "destroy this temple" in John 2:19, there is no way He was understating it.

It is easy to picture a building being destroyed. Each of us has seen a building completely ruined through storms, neglect, or intentional action. Maybe you have watched videos of huge structures—such as an outdated baseball stadium or a now-unsafe high-rise building—being intentionally demolished. Then, maybe you have seen pictures of the rubble remaining where that huge structure once stood. You might be able to make out a part of the old scoreboard or a few windows, but the building is now unrecognizable.

That is what Isaiah prophesied about Jesus when He would go through the sufferings involving the cross. Just as the Jewish temple would be reduced to rubble, so the body and face of Jesus would be made to be unrecognizable through the suffering He endured. Movies, plays, artwork, and TV shows have all tried to portray Jesus on the cross, but none have likely been fully accurate as to just how "unhuman" He looked by the time He took His last breath.

While "destroyed" is a word we rarely use of the body of Jesus, it is the one He used. He was physically destroyed. That alone should cause us to think more deeply when we consider reflecting on the table of the Lord.

Today, I will...try to not "sanitize" the picture of Jesus on the cross, but will remember that He was destroyed...for me.

TUESDAY
46 Versus 3
Today's Scripture: Isaiah 52:13-15

When asked for a sign, Jesus gave the sign of the temple. He stated, "Destroy this temple, and in three days I will raise it up" (John 2:19, ESV). The people, we are told, were shocked by His words and connected them to the length of time it had taken to construct the temple, 46 years. And now Jesus is saying He will raise it from rubble in just three days?

It is easy to get into the minds of the people because they saw the grandeur of the temple. They knew the background. And Jesus intentionally used the imagery of the temple. So let's not be hasty in saying they were ignorant, especially at this fairly early point in Jesus' ministry.

That said, the people's response does reveal something of human nature, and it can even reveal itself when we gather around the Lord's Table. The Lord gave us physical elements to partake of during communion. Stated bluntly, we eat crackers and drink grape juice. Those are physical things, and common ones at that. As the Jews were familiar with the temple, we are familiar with these two common items.

As such, we must think and concentrate deeply. If we are not careful, we can quickly eat and drink and not get past the physical nature of the emblems. Our minds can focus on the taste ("This grape juice is bitter this morning.") or the logistics ("What do I do with the cup when I'm done?"). Then we are like those who could not think beyond the physical nature of the temple of Jerusalem.

But we must! If we are going to take the Lord's Supper as God commanded, our minds must focus not on the physical aspects of communion but on the deeper spiritual meaning of what we are doing.

Today, I will…focus my attention on the spiritual aspect of the Lord's Supper instead of the physical and logistical aspects of it.

WEDNESDAY
"I Will Raise It Up"
Today's Scripture: 1 Corinthians 15:26

From the beginning of His ministry, Jesus—both specifically and in more opaque ways—said that the cross was coming. As His ministry unfolded, He would become more explicit with His apostles.

In John 2, however, He made a statement that would only make sense after the fact. "Destroy this temple, and in three days I will raise it up" (John 2:19, ESV). While the people did not understand the meaning yet, the wording is extremely significant. Jesus did not say, "It will be raised up," and He did not say, "I will play a part in raising it up."

Instead, He clearly stated, "I will raise it up." Even if the people did not understand it yet, Jesus was staking the claim that He would overcome death. In Himself—in His own Divine power—He would defeat the last enemy, death (cf. 1 Corinthians 15:26).

Consider this claim. It is as audacious a claim as possible. It would be very audacious to say that one could raise the dead. But to claim that you, yourself, would raise yourself? It is as bold of a claim as one could ever make. Yet, here is Jesus, near the beginning of His ministry, making just such a statement.

One main objective in reading the Gospel narratives is to follow that claim through. If Jesus made any claim, including this one, and did not fulfill it, then He is not Divine. However, praise the Lord; He fulfilled every claim, including this most audacious one. He is Lord!

Today, I will…be in awe of the audacious claims that Jesus made and fulfilled, including overcoming death.

THURSDAY
If They Only Knew
Today's Scripture: John 1:1-5

The Jews listening to Jesus made the historically accurate claim that it had taken 46 years to build the temple. That is a very long time, indeed. So, for Jesus to claim that, if that temple was destroyed, He would raise it in a mere three days seemed unfathomable.

Through John's pen, the Holy Spirit makes sure that students of Scripture grasp the message: "But He was speaking about the temple of His body" (John 2:21, ESV).

However, let your mind think for a few moments about Jesus's power. If the people listening to Him on that day had been able to understand who was speaking, this would not have been an audacious claim in the least!

After all, just one chapter earlier, as John opened his account of the Gospel, he had described Jesus as "the Word" (1:1) and made it clear that He was the Creator. "All things were made through Him, and without Him was not any thing made that was made" (John 1:3, ESV). We cannot fathom what it means that Jesus was the agent through whom everything was created.

That being true, whether Jesus had been talking about the temple of His body—which He was—or the actual structure of the temple, to raise it up in three days would have been child's play! To state the obvious, for One who is truly almighty, three days was plenty of time to accomplish what the people thought would be impossible if given many, many years.

When we eat the Lord's Supper, part of what we remember is that this One who had all power allowed Himself to be utterly shamed and overwhelmed. He had the power to end it all—to destroy everyone around or to perform a miracle from the cross that proved clearly that He was who He claimed to be. But the all-powerful One took it for you and me.

Today, I will…stand in awe of the almighty power of Jesus. I will be humbled that the all-powerful One allowed Himself to be overwhelmed and crucified for my sins.

FRIDAY
The Temple
Today's Scripture: Luke 22:19

The picture of Jesus describing His body as the temple is one that is rich with meaning. The temple was the place where the Jews worshiped. It was the place in which God's presence dwelt via the mercy seat. It had a giant veil to protect the way to the Ark of the Covenant. It was a symbol of national pride.

And Jesus used that to describe Himself. Hebrews regularly points to the fact that Jesus took away the old law, but the book also gives us some concept of the ways in which Jesus is a better reality of all those things in the Old Testament. Whatever we read about when we consider the tabernacle and later the temple, Jesus perfects them all.

But here in John 2, Jesus makes that clear of the temple structure itself. The place of worship. The centrality of this structure to the gathering of God's people. The joy and pride it conjured up among God's people. All of those would be true of Jesus Himself, making it no longer a physical structure that matters, but the person of God the Son.

The Lord's Table should bring that to mind. We often describe it as "gathering around the table." That is true, but it is true because of the One whom we are gathering to remember. He is the "place" now. He is the One who brings joy and pride to God's people. It centers on Him, which is why He said—and so many of our tables engrave the words for us to focus on—"Do this in remembrance of Me" (Luke 22:19, ESV). We gather because of Him, and we gather to honor Him.

The temple could never, and did not, last. Though awe-inspiring, it was a physical structure and would fall. Jesus "is the same yesterday and today and forever" (Hebrews 13:8, ESV). May we focus on Him when we gather.

Today, I will…consider Jesus as the center of worship and the reason I gather with my fellow Christians.

Table Meditation
Scripture: Ephesians 1:7

I love the rewards of hard work, but I also enjoy things that are easy or free. There's an old saying, "There's no such thing as a free lunch," that indicates you can't get something for nothing.

As I think of the free gift of salvation mentioned by Paul in Ephesians 2:8 (ESV)—"For by grace you have been saved… it is the gift of God"—it just seems too easy. My mind usually goes to the Old Testament where individuals were trying to earn and deserve their salvation. We know that plan doesn't work out if you aren't perfect, but it still seems to be popular among many today.

Something so valuable shouldn't be free and easy to obtain. There should be a large cost to cover all our sins. We should have to live a life with very little sin, totally dedicated to God in everything we do, think, and say.

Here's the problem with that thought…it takes perfection to reach heaven, and that's not possible for humankind. Knowing this, Jesus followed God's will and went to the cross on our behalf. He is the perfect sacrifice for all of mankind who believe and are obedient to Him. Ephesians 1:7 says, "In him we have redemption through his blood, the forgiveness of our trespasses, according to the riches of his grace" (ESV).

Why is salvation so easy to receive and called a "gift of God?" Salvation is easy for us because it was hard for Him! (Matthew 27:28-31).

MONDAY
He Who Came Down from Heaven
Today's Scripture: John 6:33-35

When the Israelites came out of Egypt and embarked on their journey to the promised land, they found it impossible to forage and hunt for food. In the Sinai desert, there is no food and no water. The people instinctively grumbled and complained. Their displeasure was targeted at Moses and God. They cried out, "Would that we had died by the hand of the LORD in the land of Egypt, when we sat by the meat pots and ate bread to the full, for you have brought us out into this wilderness to kill this whole assembly with hunger" (Exodus 16:3, ESV).

God, as He has done so many times before, provided for His people despite them being completely unworthy. God made bread—called manna (meaning "what is it?")—rain down from heaven (Exodus 16:4). The nation of Israel continued to gather this bread from heaven daily (except on the Sabbath) until they entered into the promised land nearly 40 years later. Fast forward 1,500 years, and Jesus feeds the 5,000 (John 6:1-14). Jesus encourages the people to believe in Him as the one the Father had sent. The people refer back to the sign of manna and ask Jesus, "Then what sign do you do, that we may see and believe you? What work do you perform? Our fathers ate the manna in the wilderness; as it is written, 'He gave them bread from heaven to eat'" (John 6:30-31, ESV).

Jesus did not point to Moses or the manna, but instead to himself as the true bread of God: "For the bread of God is he who comes down from heaven and gives life to the world" (John 6:33, ESV). The true bread of God that gives life to the world is not the bread collected on the dusty ground of the Sinai desert but the precious body of our Lord, which is represented by the unleavened bread we partake of around the table of the Lord's Supper.

Today, I will…read John 6 and note every time Jesus references His body and blood.

TUESDAY
He Gives Life to the World
Today's Scripture: John 6:1-14

Except for the resurrection, the feeding of the 5,000 is the only miracle that is mentioned in all four Gospel accounts (Matthew 14:13–21; Mark 6:31–44; Luke 9:12–17; John 6:1–14). John's account of this feeding sets up the entire chapter. They had come a long way to hear Jesus on the shore of the Sea of Galilee: it was late in the day, and they had not eaten anything. Jesus fed the multitude of 5,000 men (likely thousands more, including women and children) with just five loaves of bread and two fish. The people are amazed at the incredible ability of Jesus to give food. They are so overcome with joy and hope that they look to take Jesus by force and declare him to be the true king for which the nation of Israel had been eagerly awaiting. Jesus slips away in the night and walks on the Sea of Galilee to meet up with the disciples. The people realize that Jesus has left, and they race to track him down. Upon finding Jesus, they request that He feed them again to meet their physical needs.

They are focused on the physical and temporal, just as we so often are today. Jesus redirects their focus to seek the spiritual and eternal. As humankind, we all have physical and temporal needs that must be met. But more importantly, we have spiritual and eternal needs that can only be met by the bread of heaven. "Jesus then said to them, "Truly, truly, I say to you, it was not Moses who gave you the bread from heaven, but my Father gives you the true bread from heaven. For the bread of God is he who comes down from heaven and gives life to the world" (John 6:32-33, ESV).

This bread does not give caloric sustenance—it gives eternal life!

Today, I will…take time to thank God in prayer for sending Jesus to meet my spiritual needs to provide eternal life.

WEDNESDAY
Give Us This Bread Always
Today's Scripture: John 6:58

In John 6, after feeding the 5,000, Jesus tells the crowd that He is the bread that has come down from heaven, which gives life to the whole world (John 6:33). There is no limit to His power. He fed them all. There were 5,000 men there (and thousands more, including women and children). Jesus tells them he has the power to feed not only thousands upon thousands but the whole world! And the crowd responds by demanding, "Sir, give us this bread always" (John 6:34). They had previously "eaten their fill" (John 6:12, ESV). Eating until you were satisfied in the ancient world was a rare luxury. Throughout most of their existence, they ate until what they had was gone. Yet when they were fed by Jesus, every man ate until he was full, and there was extra left over.

One can empathize with their desire to always have access to this extraordinary state of satisfaction. In asking for continual access to this bread of life, the crowd spoke better than they realized. They wanted one source of complete nutritional fulfillment, which would take away the need to find sustenance elsewhere.

Jesus will tell them later that He and He alone is the source of true fulfillment. He is the source of abundant life (John 10:10). He is the source of eternal life (John 3:16). "This is the bread that came down from heaven, not like the bread the fathers ate, and died. Whoever feeds on this bread will live forever" (John 6:58, ESV).

May we feed on this bread and say as they did but with a clearer understanding: "Lord, give us this bread always."

Today, I will…stop looking for fulfillment and abundance in the things of this world and instead find my true sustenance in the bread which came down from heaven.

THURSDAY
Never Hunger, Never Thirst
Today's Scripture: Revelation 7:16-17

A water main in the town where I live recently broke, shutting down access to water for the better part of a day. The grumblings on social media and local community internet pages were out in full force! Having fresh, clean water anytime you please by simply turning on the faucet was taken away for less than 24 hours, and the citizenry was panicked in near revolt!

The majority of us today would find it extremely difficult to live in the ancient world where the comforts of life were non-existent and the necessities of life, such as food and water, were not abundantly plentiful and readily available—let alone guaranteed. The time and energy needed to obtain and cook food was astronomically higher than it is today.

So when Jesus fed this great multitude (out of practically nothing), the people wanted Jesus to keep on feeding them day after day. They said to him, "Sir, give us this bread always." Jesus said to them, "I am the bread of life; whoever comes to me shall not hunger, and whoever believes in me shall never thirst" (John 6:34-35, ESV).

The apostle John heard Jesus utter the phrase "shall not hunger… never thirst" along the sea of Galilee as Jesus taught people to understand His identity, authority, and power over their lives. But it was not the last time the apostle John heard this phrase. He would hear it again decades later in his heavenly vision: "They shall hunger no more, neither thirst anymore; the sun shall not strike them, nor any scorching heat. For the Lamb in the midst of the throne will be their shepherd, and he will guide them to springs of living water, and God will wipe away every tear from their eyes" (Revelation 7:16-17, ESV). I wonder if John thought back to the Lord making that very promise beside the sea of Galilee (John 6:35) and hearing it fulfilled while looking at the heavenly crystal sea (Revelation 4:6). God is indeed faithful (1 Corinthians 1:9)!

Today, I will…have peace knowing that God is faithful and I can put my complete trust in "His precious and very great promises" (2 Peter 1:4).

FRIDAY
I Am the Bread of Life
Today's Scripture: John 6:35, 48, 51

In the gospel of John, we find the seven "I am" statements. Here in John 6, Jesus stresses on three separate occasions that He, and He alone, is the Bread of Life (John 6:35, 48, 51). Bread was a word that, of course, could refer specifically to bread. But the term also could be used as a general reference to all food. Jesus does this in the model prayer when He instructs us to pray, "Give us this day our daily bread" (Matthew 6:11, ESV).

Jesus is not saying that He is literally bread. He is the true source of man's life. When satan tempted Jesus to turn stones into bread, Jesus rebuked him by quoting, "It is written, "'Man shall not live by bread alone, but by every word that comes from the mouth of God'" (Matthew 4:4, ESV). And Jesus Himself is "the Word [that] became flesh and dwelt among us, and we have seen his glory, glory as of the only Son from the Father, full of grace and truth" (John 1:14, ESV). Now that Christ, the Bread of Life, has come, He has become the life source for all humanity. Every spiritual blessing is in Christ, and outside of Christ there are no spiritual blessings (Ephesians 1:3). What a privileged blessing it is to be in Christ and a part of His body (1 Corinthians 12:13; Ephesians 4:4).

The people of God are reminded of this every time we gather together during the Lord's Supper to partake of the Lord's body represented in the unleavened bread. The night before our Lord's sacrificial death, he instituted the Lord's Supper in the upper room and forever linked himself with bread: "And he took bread, and when he had given thanks, he broke it and gave it to them, saying, "This is my body, which is given for you. Do this in remembrance of me" (Luke 22:19, ESV). Every Lord's Day, when Christians gather to partake in the Lord's Supper, they proclaim to themselves, their spiritual family, and the world, "Jesus is the Bread of Life."

Today, I will...rejoice and praise God that Jesus is the Bread of Life.

Table Meditation
Scripture: Romans 8:37-39

The world asks, "Why does a God of love allow bad things to happen to good people?" Before answering, consider:

- Romans 3:23, "for all have sinned and fall short of the glory of God." (ESV)
- 1 John 1:8, "if we say we have no sin, we deceive ourselves." (ESV)
- Ecclesiastes 7:20, "there is not a righteous man on earth who does good and never sins." (ESV)

So, the better question is, "Why does God allow good things to happen to bad people?"

Romans 8:37-39 tells us that despite our sin and rebellion, it is God's deep and unconditional love that allows good things to happen to us. John 3:16 tells us that God so loved the world that he gave his one and only Son to save us from our sins.

Perspective. The world sees death as the end. We see death as a beginning.

Fast forward to Judgment Day. Because God is just, he *must* punish sin. Sins will be exposed, and wrongs made known. As he scrolls down the Book of Life to find our name, what appears? A blank space, blotted out, white as snow? An asterisk saying, "see Jesus?" Maybe a stamp "debt paid".

Jesus died to atone for our sins. Not only that, but we are clothed in His righteousness. The very righteousness of God. Why? Because he loves us. The story of Jesus is too good to be true, but it is true.

Perspective. It is not about us this morning—it is about Jesus.

MONDAY
Nourished by God
Today's Scripture: John 6:48-50

Focus on God's provisions. God, the greatest parent, supplies our deepest needs.

It is estimated that worldwide there were 368,000 babies born every day in 2023. And according to the Centers for Disease Control and Prevention, in 2021 and 2022 more than 10,000 children were born in the U.S. every day. That's a lot of stork deliveries! As the due dates approach, many parents are thinking about getting everything ready: is the crib ready? is the nursery prepped? do we have the necessary supplies? Good parents want to make sure they are prepared to provide everything their new baby will need to thrive, and hopefully, this concern for seeing our children thrive never goes away.

When God looks down upon us, what does He see? What emotions does He feel? Surely there is this same type of concern for providing what we need to thrive. Christ once remarked that if good human parents know how to provide what is necessary for their children, how much more does the Father above know how to provide (Luke 11:13)?

But the greatest need humanity has, and which God is willing to supply, is an avenue for spiritual life and flourishing. Jesus stated, "I am the bread of life. Your fathers ate the manna in the wilderness, and they died. This is the bread that comes down from heaven, so that one may eat of it and not die" (John 6:48-50, ESV). With these words, He was pointing to Himself as the greatest gift that humanity could receive—the bread of life. And this was supplied willingly by a loving God. With our history of wrongdoing—both personally and universally—people need an avenue for forgiveness and direction for righteous living. We need a Savior.

We don't need to climb into the reaches of heaven to find this solution, nor must we descend to the depths in search of it (see Romans 10:6-8). The solution, salvation through Jesus, is readily available. The Gospel says the Lord has readily supplied what we need so that we do not die; instead, we can flourish in our relationship with our Creator. Thanks be to God!

Today, I will...listen to the words of Jesus more fully and let His Word guide my life. I will make sure that I am cleansed by His blood and am ready to live with Him forever.

TUESDAY
Testament of Love
Today's Scripture: John 6:51

Focus on Christ's love and sacrifice. No one should doubt their value in God's sight.

During the American Revolution, the colonist Nathan Hale, working for the cause of the Continental Army, was arrested in New York City by the British for espionage. Following the standard treatment for captured spies, the twenty-one-year-old Hale was hanged. Among his last remarks before his execution, he is reported to have uttered the words, "I only regret that I have but one life to lose for my country." For his actions and the selflessness expressed in such words, he has been lauded as a hero ever since.

Self-sacrifice on behalf of others, whether individuals or a larger cause, has always inspired people by its noble and gallant spirit. The epitome of such self-sacrifice is Jesus Christ. He once remarked, "Greater love has no one than this, that someone lay down his life for his friends" (John 15:13, ESV). And He did this very thing. Not only was He the master teacher and the master exemplar, but He was also the master sacrifice, yielding His utmost at Calvary. He knew this was part of His mission, leading Him to say the following: "I am the living bread that came down from heaven. If anyone eats of this bread, he will live forever. And the bread that I will give for the life of the world is my flesh" (John 6:51, ESV).

The Lord was no stoic figure marching with a stiff upper lip to the cross, barely fazed by what He was experiencing. Rather, He asked for an alternate plan in the Garden of Gethsemane (Mark 14:35-36) and was strengthened by an angel during His distress rather than being relieved of His mission (Luke 22:43-44). He cried loud cries, accompanied by groanings and tears. He still went to the cross (Hebrews 5:7-9). This love-driven display is the most remarkable expression of self-sacrifice ever witnessed. He gave His life "for the life of the world" (John 6:51, ESV).

Today, I will…lift my voice and thoughts in prayers of gratitude for this declaration of divine love. I will be as committed to my relationship with the Lord as He has been to me.

The Best Meal Ever Offered
Today's Scripture: John 6:55

Focus on true health. Worldly thinking emphasizes the physical.

Within the last decade, there has been significantly increased concern for physical health and well-being manifested in many ways. Gym memberships continue to rise; more people are adopting healthy lifestyles designed to improve quality of life and extend one's life span. But one of the most significant ways people have promoted healthy living is their diet. Our vocabulary has expanded to include words like vegan, vegetarian, gluten-free, foodie, gourmand, super-food, artisanal, and clean-eating. Concern for healthy eating and care for our bodies is commendable. But what is the most important food? It might surprise you.

Jesus once said, "Truly, truly, I say to you, unless you eat the flesh of the Son of Man and drink his blood, you have no life in you. ... For my flesh is true food, and my blood is true drink" (John 6:53, 55, ESV). How strange this must have sounded to His listeners, knowing God's prohibition about eating blood (Genesis 9:4; Leviticus 17:10; Acts 15:20). And no one suggests the Lord was advocating cannibalism. Instead, He was symbolizing His person and sacrifice, which would be nourishing in a way that no super-food could match. He was not speaking of literally consuming His body and blood; He was speaking of learning about, taking advantage of, and assimilating all that He offered in His sacrifice. It is akin to the blessedness of those who "hunger and thirst after righteousness" (Matthew 5:6).

Just as He spoke to the woman at the well about the living water (John 4:10), here He encourages listeners to be spiritually fed and nourished by what He has done by giving Himself at Calvary. How important is His sacrifice to me? How essential is it for my health and well-being? Too often, people are concerned with their physical situation and give little thought to their spiritual health, but Jesus' sacrifice was meant to be our greatest gain.

Today, I will...feed my soul by feasting and meditating on God's Word and by living in imitation of His Son, Jesus.

THURSDAY
The Real BFF
Today's Scripture: John 6:56

Focus on the relationship shared with Christ. Every person should have a strong relationship with God

I confess it is a challenge to keep up with abbreviations, especially the ones emerging from our younger generations. But one that has been universally embraced is the abbreviation "BFF," or "Best Friends Forever." We even have forms of this abbreviation—someone is our "bestie!" Our BFFs are typically persons with whom we share likes and dislikes, with whom we go through the ups and downs of life, and with whom we are tied so closely that they can almost be like a second self. But our "besties" can also change: someone exceptionally close to us in our teens may not be as close later when life plans diverge. Or a new BFF like a spouse comes along, taking that special spot in an unmatchable capacity.

But there is one BFF that should never change, someone with whom we are so close that the bond can never be broken or replaced. That closest figure needs to be Jesus. He promised, "Whoever feeds on my flesh and drinks my blood abides in me, and I in him" (John 6:56, ESV). These are intimate words. They are relational words. They promise the closest of ties.

What does it mean to "abide in Jesus" or have Him "abide in us"? It is the dearest of relationships in which both parties are in harmony with one another, enjoy the company of one another, and travel the same path. In John 15:4-5, Jesus spoke with His apostles concerning bearing much fruit, i.e., being productive and effective workers in His kingdom as long as they abide in Him. Just a few sentences later, the Savior indicated that abiding in His love is linked to following His commandments (John 15:10). And in John 17:21, amid His prayer to the Father, Jesus prayed for His followers to have a tight fellowship with one another and with God Himself. These are the concepts tied up in the words of John 6:56—if someone is willing to take part in the life offered by Christ, they become linked to God and God's people in the most special way.

Today, I will…cherish the fellowship I have with the Lord above all others.

Where Are You Headed?
Today's Scripture: John 6:54

Focus on the eternal life made available. Christ wants all to be tied to Him and be resurrected to life

The patient was terminally ill and requested a visit by the hospital chaplain. During their conversation, the patient asked the chaplain, "What is heaven going to be like?" The other man hesitantly admitted, "I don't know. I'm not sure I even believe in heaven." As unbelievable as this sounds, it was an actual discussion that was reported in a national newspaper. How sad that in the most desperate hour, a chaplain had no help to offer.

What would Jesus have said differently were He in the chaplain's shoes? Would He have described heaven using words from Revelation chapters 4 and 5? Or maybe chapters 21-22? Without a doubt, He would not have been uncertain about the life to come. During His conversation about eating and drinking His flesh, Jesus explicitly pointed to life after death when He promised, "Whoever feeds on my flesh and drinks my blood has eternal life, and I will raise him up on the last day" (John 6:54, ESV).

Though we do have a wonderful relationship with God while on earth, it will be richer and more enjoyable to be with Him in heaven for eternity (2 Corinthians 5:6-7). Jesus knew that His sacrifice was the means of providing for that possibility. Hence, He offered Himself freely. The "feeding and drinking" is a figurative way of saying that we are sustained by loving Him, depending upon Him, and following Him. In short, He sustains us as we march toward eternity, and then He welcomes us to the heavenly home. Thoughts about the life to come and our communion with the Lord in heaven are not intended to be vague or vapid. Instead, a person should look forward to the eternal life Jesus makes possible. We should long for the final resurrection and the great reunion that God's people will experience.

Today, I will…celebrate the relationship I have with God that extends from now into eternity. I will not allow anything to jeopardize my walk with Him and my arrival in heaven.

Table Meditation
Scripture: Isaiah 53:7

We sometimes hear stories when a person was wrongfully accused and incarcerated, and many years later, with new evidence, is released. Family and friends are overjoyed, but years of society thinking the accused was guilty is hard to overcome. This person's name continues to carry the burden of guilt for many people despite the reversal.

If you were accused of something you did not do, would you defend yourself? What if you were wrongly accused of something and it required you to be tried in a court of law, which could cause your name to be severely tarnished? For the people I know, the answer is very plain—they would do everything in their power to clear their name and ensure that true justice is reached.

However, there is one man that I know who is the exception to this and we read about Him in Isaiah 53:7 (ESV):

> He was oppressed, and he was afflicted,
> yet he opened not his mouth;
> like a lamb that is led to the slaughter,
> and like a sheep that before its shearers is silent,
> so he opened not his mouth.

The man is Jesus Christ. He was accused of crimes he did not commit, brought before a rushed trial, convicted, and sentenced to immediate and public death by crucifixion. We should take note that "he opened not his mouth." He could have easily defended himself or called a legion of angels to come to His rescue, yet just like a lamb led to the slaughter, our Jesus "opened not his mouth."

Each week, we gather as Christians to commemorate the death, burial, and resurrection of our Savior Jesus Christ. My challenge to you is to remember that Jesus had a choice, and He chose to be silent and endure the unjust punishment on our behalf so that we could all live in eternity with Him.

MONDAY
Martha
Today's Scripture: John 12:2

"Martha served." These two words from John 12:2 indicate the heart of Martha. The Lord was present, and she desired to serve Him and His disciples. She was a person of action. Luke says, "Martha was distracted with much serving" (Luke 10:40, ESV). Martha is often criticized for being too busy in contrast to Mary, who sat at the feet of Jesus, but this is an unfair accusation. Jesus did not criticize Martha for being too busy but expressed concern that she was "anxious and troubled about many things" (Luke 10:41, ESV). He also reminded her that Mary had made the right choice to sit at His feet and listen to Him. Sometimes, we are busy when we need to be still. This was a lesson that Martha needed to learn.

Do you have the heart of a servant? Jesus said that it is more blessed to give than to receive (Acts 20:35). The greatest blessing in giving is the act of giving itself. Only when we empty ourselves of self can we be filled with Christ. A beautiful song states: "Make me a servant, Lord, make me like you."[1] Jesus is our example of servitude. The apostle Paul wrote:

"Let each of you look not only to his own interests, but also to the interests of others. Have this mind among yourselves, which is yours in Christ Jesus, who, though he was in the form of God, did not count equality with God a thing to be grasped, but emptied himself, by taking the form of a servant, being born in the likeness of men. And being found in human form, he humbled himself by becoming obedient to the point of death, even death on a cross" (Philippians 2:4–8, ESV).

While Martha needed to be reminded of what was most important, she demonstrated the need for a servant's heart. She desired to serve Jesus.

Today, I will…examine myself to ensure I have a servant's heart.

---

[1] "Make Me a Servant," Jimmy and Carol Owens, 1978.

TUESDAY
Lazarus
Today's Scripture: John 12:2

"So they gave a dinner for him there. Martha served, and Lazarus was one of those reclining with him at table" (John 12:2, ESV). Imagine what it would be like to be Lazarus at that moment. At the table with Jesus! Lazarus knew what it was like to go to the Hadean realm and return to this life. He had been dead for four days! At the command of Jesus, he had returned to this life and came forth from the tomb where he had been laid (John 11:38-44). Even before his resurrection, Lazarus was very close to Jesus. When Mary and Martha, the sisters of Lazarus, sent word to Jesus of his illness, they said: "Lord, he whom you love is ill" (John 11:3b, ESV). Now, Lazarus, whom Jesus loved, is alive and well at the table with Jesus!

Can you imagine the conversation between Lazarus and Jesus during dinner? Here was a man who had died and been resurrected to life at the table with the man who had raised him from the dead! In addition, Jesus was about to die and be resurrected himself! He was about to experience what Lazarus had just experienced. Of course, Jesus' death would be much more agonizing, and His resurrection would have much more impact. The two men had much to talk about. It is reasonable to expect that one thing Lazarus said was, "Thank you, Lord, for giving me life!"

As Christians, we gather at the Lord's Table each Sunday to commune with the Lord and each other. The word "communion" is translated from *koinonia*, the same word we translate as "fellowship." When we take the communion, we have fellowship with Christ in His death. As Christians, we were once dead in our sins. We died to sin as we were buried in baptism, to be raised to a new life in Christ (Romans 6:4).

Today, I will…prepare to come to the table with Christ saying, "Thank you, Lord, for giving me life!"

WEDNESDAY
Mary
Today's Scripture: John 12:3

"Mary therefore took a pound of expensive ointment made from pure nard, and anointed the feet of Jesus and wiped his feet with her hair. The house was filled with the fragrance of the perfume" (John 12:3, ESV). What devotion! Mary realizes she is in the presence of royalty and, more than that, deity. This is no trivial act. The nard with which Mary anoints Jesus was made from a plant in India and was very expensive. Judas states the value as 300 denarii. A denarius is generally understood as one day's wage for the common man. Therefore, the perfume Mary anointed Jesus with was worth about one year of work based on a five-day workweek. Mary held nothing back in expressing her devotion to her Lord.

It was customary for guests to be offered water to wash their feet. The host who wanted to honor his guest would wash his guest's feet. The miles of daily walking in dirty conditions while wearing sandals made this gesture even more meaningful. Mary went well beyond the expectations of a good hostess. Jesus was not just her guest. He was her Lord! She paid Him the homage rightfully due. Judas, in stark contrast, was blinded by his greed and indignant at her gesture. He claimed the precious substance should have been sold and the money given to the poor. Jesus, however, recognized the true value of Mary's act, saying, "Leave her alone, so that she may keep it for the day of my burial" (John 12:7, ESV). This tribute to Jesus was not only for the day of His burial but for all time as a monument to His glory and evidence of Mary's devotion.

When you come to the table to commune with Christ, do you honor Him? Do you pay Him the homage and devotion He is due? The life you have lived through the week will be your "perfume" to demonstrate to your Lord the devotion you offer Him.

Today, I will…give careful thought to how my day demonstrates my devotion to Jesus.

THURSDAY

Judas

Today's Scripture: John 12:5

How could he do it? What evil could have invaded his heart to bring him to these depths? Jesus had selected Judas to be one of His apostles. He had seen Jesus show compassion on the socially rejected. He had witnessed Jesus healing the sick, lame, and blind. He had watched Jesus return love for the evil He had suffered. He knew who Jesus was! What depths of depravity could cause him to betray Jesus for a few pieces of silver? The account of Jesus at dinner with Mary, Martha, and Lazarus (John 12:1-8) sheds some light on the sin that had taken root in the heart of Judas. When Judas saw Mary anoint Jesus' feet with a very expensive ointment, He did not appreciate the sacrifice of homage to Jesus. He said, "Why was this ointment not sold for three hundred denarii and given to the poor?" (John 12:5, ESV). John reveals that Judas did not care for the poor but that he was a thief and would steal money from the moneybag with which he was entrusted. The Lord had trusted him, but he violated that trust.

Judas allowed his pride and greed to blind him and allowed satan into his heart. Once he had given his heart to the devil, there was no limit to which sin would take him. Sin will take you further than you want to go, keep you longer than you intended to stay, and cost you more than you thought you would pay. Sin is no game! It results in spiritual separation from God. Sin invades our hearts through our desires. When we give in to that desire, sin brings spiritual death.

When we come to the table to commune with the Lord, it is an opportunity for each of us to examine our hearts (1 Corinthians 11:28). Let us come to the table with penitent hearts that seek God's holiness. The blood of Jesus we commemorate washes us and makes us pure in God's eyes.

Today, I will…dwell upon the forgiveness and patience of God and eliminate the pride and greed in my own heart.

FRIDAY
Jesus
Today's Scripture: John 12:2-8

Jesus visited with His friends at a dinner held in His honor (John 12:2-8). They did not realize it, but He would soon be hanging on a cross at Golgotha. As He looked around the table, he gazed upon the sight of dear friends and faithful disciples. He could see Martha bustling about and serving as she so often did. He loved Martha for her heart of service. Then there was Mary, the devoted disciple who clung to every word He spoke and adored Him as her Lord. The fragrance of the expensive perfumed ointment with which she had anointed His feet still hung in the air. Lazarus was reclining near him at the table—his dear friend Lazarus, who had died and whom Jesus had brought back from death. The fact that Lazarus was alive and present was a monument to the undeniable truth that Jesus was indeed the Son of God!

Many people surrounded them who had come to see the Lord and the one who He had resurrected from the tomb. For this reason, the chief priests and Pharisees were scheming to kill them both. Also in that crowd were some who would turn against Him, and He knew who they were. There was Judas. Jesus loved him, but He could see that satan had a grip on his heart and that Judas would betray Him. Jesus knew that very soon He would suffer horrible torment at the hands of the Roman soldiers. He would die on the cross but overcome death as He would be resurrected to life. This is why He had come. This was His mission.

Shortly before this dinner, when Lazarus died, Jesus had told Martha, "I am the resurrection and the life. Whoever believes in Me, though He die, yet shall he live" (John 11:25, ESV). Jesus died so that we might live for eternity. He rose from the grave, bringing victory over death, sin, and Hell.

Today, I will…contemplate the hope that I have in Jesus.

Table Meditation
Scripture: 1 Corinthians 10:16-17

During the earthly ministry of Jesus, He often engaged in what is referred to as "table fellowship." Jesus would go into someone's house, enjoy a meal, and leave them with a spiritual lesson. Jesus had table fellowship with both friends and foes.

For example, Jesus dines with Simon the Pharisee (Luke 7:36) and with Martha and Mary (Luke 10:38). Table fellowship was more than just a meal to Jesus. It was an opportunity to form a relationship, to meet people where they were the most comfortable, and to reveal to them the personal side of Jesus. Some of the best lessons we learn from Jesus involve "table fellowship." Who can ever forget the lesson Jesus left at the house of Martha in Luke 10:42, "But, one thing is needed; and Mary has chosen that good part, which will not be taken away from her." (NKJV)?

Every first day of the week, every Christian engages in "table fellowship" with Jesus. In Matthew 26:26-29, Jesus institutes what has come to be known as the Lord's Supper (1 Corinthians 11:20) or communion (1 Corinthians 10:16-17). This is not a common meal but a spiritual feast. It is "table fellowship." I once heard the late brother Winfred Clark explain that the Lord's Table is the longest table in the world, for it brings every Christian from every part of the world together with Jesus. That is unity. What an awesome thought!

May we value the lesson of "table fellowship" the communion brings us every Lord's Day!

41

Goodbyes & See You Laters
Today's Scripture: John 16:16-18

The Upper Room in Jerusalem must have been tense. This Passover was different than previous ones—the significance of the meal, betrayal among the group, and now this talk of Jesus going away. The winds of foreboding change were swirling in this room. Was this the breaking up of this company of friends? And how would you begin to say goodbye to the One who brought all of you together to follow Him?

But Jesus does not say goodbye; He says, "See you later." Just because an expression is cliché does not make it untrue. Jesus even uses the phrase "a little while" to show that their sense of separation from Him would be temporary. This whole discourse in the Upper Room (John 13-17) has a sobering and comforting tone. "You will no longer see Me" is an impending reality they need to know. But "again a little while and you will see Me" is where the story is truly headed.

When Christians gather on the Lord's Day to eat the supper Jesus instituted in that room, we each arrive with a life narrative full of change, questions, tension, relationships in flux, and uncertainty about the future. But reflecting on Jesus' journey through the cross, the tomb, and the open tomb provides grounding for our own life narratives. The Lord's Table is a place that reminds us that our overall story is not defined by our life experiences of the moment. For all my uncertainties and tensions, fellowship with my Lord and with His people is an unending certainty. Each time I leave the Table for a little while and go through my weekly trials, I do not have to tell my fellow Christians, "Goodbye." I tell them, "See you later." Even death is not a goodbye for the Christian.

Today, I will…eagerly anticipate the next time I "see" the people of Jesus at His Table. It will only be a little while.

Ascended but Present
Today's Scripture: John 16:16-18

A classic comedy-type scene is the young man who has double-booked himself. He has dates with two women at the same time on the same night, and the women are unaware of his conflicting situation. He tries to go back and forth between tables at the restaurant to spend time with each lady, but he ends up getting caught in the end because he can only be present at one table at a time.

You have probably experienced moments when you wish you could be in two places at the same time. Our current mortal bodies do not allow it. So how do we make sense of Jesus saying that He is "going to the Father" (John 16:17, ESV) and "going to prepare a place" (John 14:2, ESV), yet He also says, "I will not leave you as orphans; I will come to you" (John 14:18, ESV) and "I am with you always, to the end of the age" (Matthew 28:20, ESV)? Can He be present in Heaven at the right hand of the Father and here on earth with us at the same time?

Remember that Jesus now has a resurrection body of glory. The fullness of deity still dwells in Jesus' ascended body (Colossians 2:9), where "the man Jesus Christ" is the one mediator between God and men (1 Timothy 2:5, ESV). He has brought the full experience of humanity to Heaven with Him and therefore holds all things in Heaven and earth together (Colossians 1:17, 20). He is the bridge between the human and divine, between Heaven and Earth. One day we will see Him again in bodily form when He comes in judgment. Until then, He shares His presence with us through His Spirit. Yes, the Holy Spirit is also called the Spirit of Christ (Romans 8:9; Philippians 1:19; 1 Peter 1:11). He fills our hearts and our church community with the presence of Christ. And one of the main ways we spend time with Christ is through His Supper.

Today, I will…think of the Lord's Supper as a connection between Heaven and Earth—how God has chosen for us to spend time with the resurrected and ascended Jesus.

Reading of Reality
Today's Scripture: John 16:20

The 1980 Winter Olympics hold a prominent place in American sports history because of the "Miracle on Ice." The Soviet Union had won 5 of the prior 6 Olympic Gold Medals for ice hockey. They were the heavy favorites to win again in 1980 and had already crushed the American team 10-3 in an exhibition earlier that year. But in the medal round, the U.S. team pulled off an all-time shocker by upsetting the Soviets by a score of 4-3 on their way to taking the Gold Medal. It was a monumental moment in the Cold War. The 2004 film *Miracle* captures the exuberant celebration across America, including broadcaster Al Michaels' memorable call, "Do you believe in miracles? Yes!" But the film also shows how distraught the Soviet players and coaches were. They reacted with horror, for nothing but disgrace was to be attached to them at home. Even with silver medals, none of the Russian players turned their medals in to have their names inscribed on them. They were too ashamed.

It is amazing how the same event can produce such drastically different reactions. Unfathomable joy and horrific pain at the same time.

The world interprets an event very differently than the way a disciple of Jesus does. We look at the same occurrence but through different lenses. Jesus said the world would rejoice at His death while His disciples would weep (John 16:20). The tables were turned a few days later with the news of Jesus' empty tomb. What is wise to the world is foolishness to God, and what is truly wisdom from God is seen by the world as foolish (1 Corinthians 1).

The Lord's Supper produced similar divergent reactions. The Roman world of non-Christians looked at the practice of Christian communion with puzzlement, skepticism, and offense. It sounded to many like drunkenness, gluttony, maybe even cannibalism. Their lenses did not allow them to see the wonders of what Jesus instituted.

Today, I will…look upon the Lord's Table as a place of joy, as a place of real meaning. I will pray for those of the world to have their eyes opened to the reality of the treasures of the Lord's Table.

THURSDAY
Birth Pangs
Today's Scripture: John 16:20-22

As a male, I do not claim to approximate the pain of birthing a child. I can only go by the testimony of my wife and other mothers who have gone through the experience. The closest thing males may experience is the passing of a kidney stone. But delivering a kidney stone produces no life. There's only the relief of pain so that life can resume as it was before. Delivering a child, albeit with great pain and risk in a fallen world, produces a precious baby boy or girl who overwhelms the pain with joy. And life now has a new quality since it is shared with one more beautiful human.

Birth pangs are a powerful image in Scripture for suffering which ends with joy and new life. They are a reminder of the curse of our brokenness (Genesis 3:16) but also of the promise that our brokenness is temporary. New life is on its way. Jesus knew that His trials and crucifixion would be a time of excruciating suffering for Him. But He is also concerned about the shock, fear, and grief that His followers would face while watching the events unfold. He knew that the birth pangs of that weekend would end with new life emerging. The tomb would deliver a resurrected Jesus. And those who beheld Him would experience joy that would extinguish their pain.

One of the directions we look when we come to the Lord's Table is FORWARD: "You proclaim the Lord's death until He comes" (1 Corinthians 11:26, ESV). Romans 8:22 says, "The whole creation has been groaning together in the pains of childbirth" (ESV). Everything experiences the curse of sin and death. Then Romans 8:23 says, "We wait eagerly for adoption as sons, the redemption of our bodies" (ESV). We look to the final coming of Jesus because all the tombs will be opened, and He will deliver us from birth pangs to new life. We will be resurrected in His likeness. And we will have the fullness of eternal joy.

Today, I will…know that my experiences of suffering are real and have been experienced by Jesus. But, like His suffering, my suffering is also temporary and not worth comparing with the glory that is to be revealed (Romans 8:18).

No One Will Take Your Joy
Today's Scripture: John 16:22

Earlier in the Gospel of John, Jesus described Himself as a good shepherd who guards His sheep. And He contrasts this shepherd with a thief. He says, "The thief comes only to steal and kill and destroy. I came that they may have life and have it abundantly. I am the good shepherd. The good shepherd lays down his life for the sheep" (John 10:10-11, ESV). So who is the thief? Well, satan is an obvious answer. He works through deception to attempt to steal what is good and true and life-giving from us. And he has conditioned many people to use the same tactics on others. The thief could come from many directions —it is anyone or anything that attempts to steal our joy. But Jesus says He laid down His life so that we would have a more abundant life. And if we allow Him to shepherd us, nothing will rob us of that joy.

Jesus speaks of "joy" six times in His Upper Room Discourse (John 15:11; 16:20, 21, 22, 24; 17:13). And He emphasizes His desire for His followers' joy to be full or complete. And if we go back to the shepherding image of John 10, that joy is experienced within the fold of fellow sheep who have submitted to the protection of the good shepherd.

When we commune with one another on the Lord's Day, we share joy. Yes, we share the gravity of sacrifice made for us. But we focus on the outcome of the sacrifice and share the shepherd's feast together in a place where no one steals our joy. The Lord is a shepherd who prepares a table for us in the presence of our enemies (Psalm 23:5), meaning we can securely share an overflowing cup of life while the things that want to rob us of joy wait outside with no entrance.

Today, I will...rejoice that Jesus is alive and that He grants me abundant life. I will approach the coming Lord's Supper this Sunday with the joy of Christ in my heart. And I will share that joy with my fellow sheep.

HIS FINAL WEEK
SUNDAY

Table Meditation
Scripture: 1 Corinthians 11:26-29

Sometimes, people ask, "Why do you take the Lord's Supper every Sunday?" Peter said we should be ready to give an answer to anyone who asks us why we believe what we do or do what we do (1 Peter 3:15). We observe this memorial because the Lord asks us to do it to remember Him. We do it every Sunday because early Christians observed it weekly (Acts 20:7; 1 Corinthians 11:26-29; 16:2). Often, these questioners will ask, "Doesn't taking it every Sunday lead to boredom?" The strange thing is, some of those churches that don't partake of communion every Sunday never seem to get bored taking up a collection every week.

This brings up a worthwhile thought. We should be concerned about something so important to our relationship with the Lord becoming boring. If we sit during the Lord's Supper and have our minds anywhere else but on the Lord's body and blood, it can become boring. To keep it from becoming boring, we should first prepare our minds to partake of the bread and fruit of the vine (1 Corinthians 11:27-29). When partaking of the bread, remember it represents the Lord's body which was tortured for our sins. When we partake of the cup, we need to remember it represents His blood, which He poured out for the salvation of our souls.

Will you pray with me as we observe the bread and fruit of the vine remembering the Lord's body and blood?

The Lord Has Need of You
Today's Scripture: Luke 19:28-34

Luke's gospel focuses on Jesus' journey to Jerusalem. In Luke 9:51, the text states that the days drew near for Jesus to be "taken up," referencing His atoning work to be completed in Jerusalem. So, he "set his face" to go towards Jerusalem, a phrase that describes Jesus' resolute attitude and focus. Jesus was a man on a mission. Ten chapters later, Jesus enters the outskirts of Jerusalem and comes to Bethany and Bethphage on the Mount of Olives. Upon arriving, he sent two of His disciples into the village to secure transportation into the city. They were to untie a colt upon which no one ever sat and bring it to Jesus (Luke 19:30). Understandably, the owners questioned the disciples, and the disciples responded, "The Lord has need of it" (Luke 19:34). The owners gave it to the disciples.

The Table of the Lord is an opportunity for regular, spiritual examination. For example, during the Lord's Supper, we are instructed: "Let a person examine himself, then, and so eat of the bread and drink of the cup" (1 Corinthians 11:28, ESV). As we examine our lives, many thoughts come to our minds. Mistakes we made over the past week, areas where we need to grow, and our hopeless state without Jesus are just some of the ideas that might grab our attention. We may think, "Why does God want someone like me?" To this thought, Scripture responds, "The Lord has need of you." You see, examination is not just a time to reflect upon our failures but also a time to consider ways we can serve the Lord. Reflecting upon His goodness motivates us to serve faithfully all of our days (see Luke 5:11). Never underestimate your contribution to Christ's kingdom in your community. The Lord has need of you!

Today, I will…examine my relationship with God and reflect on ways I can serve the Lord and remember that my life has value to Christ and His church.

TUESDAY
Songs of Praise for the Savior
Today's Scripture: Luke 19:35-40

The Mount of Olives was a significant place in the Gospels. Jesus preached there concerning the destruction of the temple and His return. He prayed there as the events of the Passion weighed upon His shoulders. In Luke 19:35-40, the physician records yet another significant event upon its slopes, the triumphal entry of Jesus. Our Savior came into Jerusalem with an entry fit for a king—rightly so because He is the King of kings. He rode upon an unridden colt. The people laid their garments on the ground and praised him, saying, "Blessed is the King who comes in the name of the Lord! Peace in heaven and glory in the highest!" (Luke 19:38). What a scene this entry must have been to behold! It caused such a stir the Pharisees exhorted Jesus to rebuke His disciples. Christ responded, "I tell you, if these were silent, the very stones would cry out" (Luke 19:40). When God is present, all creation cannot help but worship.

When we come to the table of the Lord, we reflect upon Christ's death, burial, and resurrection and praise God for His willingness to save sinful humanity. As we take the symbolic elements, our hearts should be filled with joy and gratitude because of the salvation wrought through Christ's atonement. We love and praise Him not because of *what* he does for us but because of *who* he is. He is the focal point of our life and worship. The crowds on the Mount of Olives understood this and were moved to praise Him. The same should be said for us. Remember what Paul wrote to the Corinthians, "Thanks be to God for his inexpressible gift!" (2 Corinthians 9:15).

Today, I will…reflect upon Christ—His person and work—and praise Him.

WEDNESDAY
The Heart of Jesus
Today's Scripture: Luke 19:41-44

When was the last time you felt a deep sense of lament? We often experience this when we face significant losses—a financial setback, a broken relationship, the passing of a loved one, and so on. In the Gospels, we see Jesus deeply lamenting over Jerusalem, not because of its physical state but because of its spiritual condition. In Luke 19:41-44, Jesus was moved to tears as he entered the city. He foresaw the impending judgment on this city, and He knew they would not heed anyone's warning (Luke 19:43-44). The Romans would lay siege to Jerusalem and eventually destroy it. The city would never be the same, and it was their own doing.

It was more than the physical destruction that made Jesus lament over Jerusalem. It was their spiritual state and the loss of their souls. Jesus made it clear that a person's soul is more important than anything in this world (Matthew 16:26). In the coming chapters, Jesus proceeded to pronounce judgment and call them to repentance, but they refused to repent. Remember, Jesus' mission is to preach the gospel and seek and save the lost (Luke 4:43; 19:10). Jesus' mission reveals His heart. He desires all men to be saved (1 Timothy 2:4; 2 Peter 3:9).

When you come to the table of the Lord, know that Jesus wants good things for you as he did for Jerusalem (James 1:17). This type of "good" is different from what you find in worldly pursuits. It blesses you spiritually and seeks your eternal benefit (Ephesians 1:3). Communing with Christ strengthens your faith, renews your mind, and gives you a purpose for living. If you seek to be a living sacrifice, you must commune with Christ daily. Then others will see Christ living in you (Galatians 2:20), and His desires become your desires (Psalm 37:4).

Today, I will…find time to commune with Christ through Scripture and prayer. I will seek to have a greater appreciation for the eternal good things he provides for me.

THURSDAY
Losing Sight of the Savior
Today's Scripture: Matthew 21:12-13

There are only a few times in Scripture where Jesus responded in aggravation, much less anger. In Matthew 21:12-13, Jesus entered the temple and witnessed something that angered him. His Father's house of worship, a place of profound reverence, had been corrupted. In righteous anger, Jesus drove out those who were making the temple a "den of thieves" (Matthew 21:13). In Mark's account, he adds that Jesus would not allow anyone with merchandise to pass through the temple (Mark 11:16). One Jewish source stated that doves and other sacrificial animals were being sold in the temple at inflated prices (*M. Ker.* 1:7). After he made havoc on the temple complex, he convicted them with Scripture quoting Isaiah 56:7, "My house shall be called a house of prayer." In this passage, Isaiah commends those who keep the covenant with the Lord, both Jew and Gentile alike. Through their sinful practices, the Jews broke the covenant and lost sight of the purpose of the temple. God pronounced His judgment through Jesus' actions and convicting words.

It is easy to lose sight of our purpose when engulfed in self-centered endeavors. The temple served as a place of worship and reflection. But, they forgot its purpose and used it as a means to meet an end. It is easy to respond, "How could they do such a thing?" without realizing we might behave similarly. It is easy to lose sight of Jesus' atoning work on the cross in daily life. It is easy to not make decisions in light of God's grace and mercy bountifully given to us (Ephesians 2:4-5). When we come to worship, we are focused on everything else but the reason we are there. In His divine wisdom, God gave us a weekly reminder. The Lord's Supper is a time to refocus and remember our purpose.

Today, I will...strive not to lose sight of Jesus' atoning work on the cross and focus my life on Jesus.

FRIDAY
The Passion of Jesus
Today's Scripture: Matthew 21:14-17

As the story progresses in Matthew 21, we have a scene that is unique to Matthew's gospel. God's presence enters the temple through Jesus, and He begins a healing ministry. This was a fitting purpose for God's house and stands in contrast to the marketplace it had become. The blind, lame, and afflicted came to Him to be made whole. God's house was a place of healing and hope for the first time in a considerable amount of time. Children began to praise Jesus, saying, "Hosanna to the Son of David" (Matthew 21:15, LSB). The situation caused the chief priests and scribes to become indignant. They wanted it to stop immediately. It is a sad commentary on their spiritual state. Instead of being filled with praise and joy, they were only interested in their self-centered goals.

This scene reminds us of two faith-building principles. First, God seeks to make us whole. Jesus entered the temple, and those who needed healing flocked to Him. These people came to God's house hopeless because of their state in life. They left, however, renewed, hopeful, and filled with purpose after experiencing a measure of God's grace that would foreshadow what was to come. Often, we come to the table feeling helpless and hopeless. Please understand that Christ seeks to make us whole by forgiving our sins and instilling in us joy and hope, which is inexpressible and full of glory (1 Peter 1:8).

Second, sin can blind us to what God is doing right in front of us. The chief priest and scribes were not interested in God's work. They were interested in maintaining power, honor, and wealth. They were blinded to what God was doing in their midst. Thus, they responded with anger and sought to control the situation (Matthew 21:16). Sin hardens our hearts and keeps us from taking a seat at the table of the Lord.

Today, I will…examine my life and bring anything keeping me from serving the Lord to Christ, asking Him to forgive me.

HIS FINAL WEEK
MONDAY

Table Meditation
Scripture: John 6:35

> "I thank my God upon every remembrance of you, always in every prayer of mine making request for you all with joy, for your fellowship in the gospel from the first day until now..." Philippians 1:3-5 (NKJV)

Over the years, we use different things to help remind us of special people or events. You may have a souvenir like a snow globe, a pennant, a bumper sticker, or a photo.

"Remembering" was important to the Apostle Paul as he prayed for the church at Philippi. Remembering is also central to Christian worship as the church assembles on Sundays. Jesus, however, is very specific in what he teaches us to do to remember Him. Rather than a physical object that could become an object of idolatrous worship, Jesus instead uses a meal to be consumed.

In many cultures, the sharing of a meal has deep meaning, namely, the sharing of life. I must eat to live. Thus, when I share my food, I am sharing "life." In the memorial supper, the Lord's Supper, we remember Jesus literally sharing his life with us. More than sharing, He gave his life for us, a perfect sacrifice to provide for the forgiveness of our sins.

> "And Jesus said to them, "I am the bread of life. He who comes to Me shall never hunger, and he who believes in Me shall never thirst." John 6:35 (NKJV)

MONDAY
Zeal for Your House Will Consume Me
Today's Scripture: John 2:17

Hiroo Onoda was a Japanese soldier in World War II stationed on Lubang Island in the Philippines. When the war ended in 1945, Onoda refused to surrender and continued to attempt to hold the island for Japan. He continued his mission until 1974 when he was finally convinced that the war had ended! Even though he mistakenly fought in vain for almost 30 years after Japan surrendered, Hiroo Onoda is a wonderful example of being zealous for a cause. Zeal is defined as "eagerness and ardent interest in the pursuit of something: fervor" (Merriam-Webster Online). Even though his zeal was wasted, Hiroo Onoda was certainly eager and ardent in his pursuit of Japanese victory.

When Jesus was in Jerusalem during the beginning of his ministry, he noticed the temple (God's house) being misused by moneychangers and merchants to make a profit and take advantage of worshippers (John 2:13-22). This so offended Jesus that He made a whip out of chords and drove the offenders and their livestock out of the temple. His disciples later remembered the Scripture that said, "Zeal for your house will consume me" (Psalm 69:9; John 2:17). Jesus indignation at the misuse and abuse of God's holy temple, coupled with his action to correct the misuse and abuse by driving out the offenders, certainly shows how zeal for God's house had consumed Him.

The New Testament calls the church "God's temple" (1 Corinthians 3:16-17), "a spiritual house" (1 Peter 2:5), and "the household of God" (1 Timothy 3:15; 1 Peter 4:17). Jesus was not merely zealous for a building made of stone. Jesus was so zealous for his father's house, the church, that He "...gave himself up for her" (Ephesians 5:25). He quite literally purchased the salvation of the church with His own blood (Acts 20:28).

Today, I will...prepare to partake of the Lord's Supper on Sunday. I will remember the zeal that Jesus showed by giving His life for the salvation of God's spiritual house, His church.

TUESDAY
His Disciples Remembered
Today's Scripture: John 2:17, 22

"Memorial Day…is a day to honor members of the military who were killed in service, both during deployments overseas or in training and service in the U.S." (*military.com*). Memorial Day is a very special holiday for many. Cemeteries are decorated with American flags. Red poppies are often worn. Families get together to attend parades commemorating the fallen or to eat together to remember loved ones who died serving in the Armed Forces. This holiday, and all that surrounds it, is to help those still living to remember the sacrifice made by others for the country.

Jesus cleansed the temple in John 2:13-22. When He was overturning the moneychangers' tables and driving out the livestock merchants, He said, "Take these things away; do not make my Father's house a house of trade" (John 2:16, ESV). When questioned about His authority to do this, He responded, "Destroy this temple, and in three days I will raise it up" (John 2:19, ESV). After both statements, John writes the words "His disciples remembered" (John 2:17, 22, ESV), signifying that after Jesus' death, His disciples recalled these events and statements and understood their meaning more fully.

The Lord's Supper is an occasion where it should be said of us, "His disciples remembered." Jesus tells us regarding eating the bread, "This is my body, which is for you. Do this in remembrance of me" (1 Corinthians 11:24, ESV). He tells us regarding drinking the fruit of the vine, "This cup is the new covenant in my blood. Do this, as often as you drink it, in remembrance of me" (1 Corinthians 11:25, ESV).

Today, I will…remember what Jesus has done for me. I will remember His life that he gave for me on the cross so that I could enjoy freedom from sin.

WEDNESDAY
Communing in a Worthy Manner
Today's Scripture: Mark 11:17

Roseanne Barr holds the dubious distinction of "singing" the worst rendition of the National Anthem that has ever been sung before a baseball game. On July 25, 1990, before a San Diego Padres baseball game, Roseanne proceeded to sing off-key and make several lewd/crude gestures mimicking baseball players. This caused a great deal of outrage, even earning a rebuke from the President of the United States. Roseanne took something considered sacred by many, the national anthem of the United States, and turned it into something common, even crude. Many felt this demeaned what America stood for and what many Americans had died to protect.

Jesus felt indignant when he saw that God's holy temple had been turned into a place of commercial business. The merchants who cheated the worshipers made him even more indignant. Jesus said, "Is it not written, 'My house shall be called a house of prayer for all the nations?' But you have made it a den of robbers" (Mark 11:17, ESV). His indignation prompted him to overturn their tables and drive them out. Jesus refused to condone how men had made what was holy—God's temple and his worship—into something common and crude.

The Corinthians had the same problem with the Lord's Supper. They had turned a very holy act of worship, communing with Jesus and his church, into something common and crude (1 Corinthians 11:17-34). They made Lord's Supper into their own supper by refusing to allow some Christians to participate while others feasted so much they became drunk (1 Corinthians 11:20-21). What should have been a holy and unifying act of worship, instead was reduced to a crude party resulting in division. As we partake of the Lord's Supper every week, let us remember the sanctity and holiness of it.

Today, I will…remember the death of Jesus Christ and understand that this sacred act of worship brings me closer in my fellowship with Him and other Christians.

THURSDAY
Thanksgiving
Today's Scripture: John 2:19

The first Thanksgiving holiday was celebrated in Plymouth, Massachusetts in November 1621. Following their first successful harvest in the New World, the pilgrims invited their Native American neighbors to a feast in celebration. This feast was designed to remember the hardships they endured during their first winter in Plymouth and to thank God for blessing them with a bountiful harvest before they entered their second winter. Hence the beginning of "Thanksgiving."

After driving out the moneychangers and the merchants from the temple, Jesus was asked who gave Him the right to do that. He responded, "Destroy this temple, and in three days I will raise it up" (John 2:19, ESV). Jesus was not speaking of the physical temple, but the fact that he would raise himself from the dead (John 2:21-22). Before that, however, Jesus' physical life would end on the cross.

The Lord's Supper is designed as a memorial of the death of Jesus Christ. Jesus' death on the cross was His supreme sacrifice for an unworthy mankind (Romans 5:6-8). He was given by God as a sacrifice because of His great love for sinful mankind (John 3:16). Without this sacrifice, sinful man would have no hope for forgiveness and salvation (1 Peter 1:18-19). This should elicit in us a strong feeling and expression of thanksgiving. The prayers before eating the bread and drinking the fruit of the vine should express thanks to God for these emblems and what they represent: the body that died and the blood that was shed for us (Luke 22:19-23; 1 Corinthians 11:23-26).

Today, I will…remember the death of Jesus with thanksgiving, knowing the tremendous sacrifice He made for my salvation.

FRIDAY

Take These Things Away

Today's Scripture: John 2:16

I once knew a family that found two large snakes in different places in their new home, on the same day, soon after they had moved in. One snake even attempted, unsuccessfully, to strike the wife. She very firmly informed her husband that, while he could choose to live where he wanted, she and their children would not live in the home until it was free from snakes and measures were taken to ensure that no more snakes could enter. The husband promptly removed all the snakes and blocked off all entry points!

When Jesus saw how God's temple had been polluted and corrupted by the money changers and merchants, He overturned their tables and drove them out, saying, "Take these things away" (John 2:16, ESV). He also said, "'My house shall be a house of prayer,' but you have made it a den of robbers" (Luke 19:46, ESV). Jesus recognized that God's house needed to be a place free from the pollution of sin and fit for sincere, pure worship of God.

When we partake of the Lord's Supper, we must ensure that our lives are free from the pollution of sin. Paul writes, "Let a person examine himself, then, and so eat of the bread and drink of the cup" (1 Corinthians 11:28, ESV). This is not to say that we must be perfect or cannot partake of the Lord's Supper if we sinned the week prior. It means that before we partake of the Lord's Supper, we must examine our lives and make sure we are living a godly life (1 John 1:7). Paul says again, "Let us therefore celebrate the festival (Lord's Supper), not with the old leaven, the leaven of malice and evil, but with the unleavened bread of sincerity and truth" (1 Corinthians 5:8, ESV).

Today, I will...ensure that I am living the right kind of life so that when I partake of the Lord's Supper, I honor the Lord and His sacrifice (1 Corinthians 11:27-32).

HIS FINAL WEEK
TUESDAY MORNING

Table Meditation
Scripture: Matthew 22:36-40

Symbols help us remember. The rings on our fingers help us remember the love between spouses. The cross is one symbol that is truly meaningful to Christians. It's a symbol of gruesome death, and yet, it's a symbol of the greatest demonstration of love. In John 15:13, Jesus says, "Greater love has no one than this, that someone lay down his life for his friends" (ESV).

We can also see the cross as a symbol of the two greatest commandments. When Jesus was challenged by the Pharisees, a lawyer asked Jesus this question from Matthew 22:36-40 (ESV):

> *"Teacher, which is the great commandment in the Law?" And He said to him, "You shall love the Lord your God with all your heart, and with all your soul, and with all your mind. This is the great and foremost commandment. And a second is like it, You shall love your neighbor as yourself. On these two commandments depend the whole Law and the Prophets."*

The cross was made of two wooden posts. The vertical post points upwards to heaven—a reminder to love the Lord your God. The second post points horizontally as a reminder to love our neighbors—those on our same level of humanity.

The symbol of the cross can be summed up in one word: Love.

MONDAY
Fruitful
Today's Scripture: Mark 11:19-25

Jesus' authority was fruitful, in contrast to the jealous and fruitless religious leaders of His day.

The Greek noun *exousia*, translated as "authority" or "power," appears 45 times in the Gospels, including ten times in Matthew, eleven in Mark, sixteen in Luke, and eight in John. Jesus' authority is often mentioned in the context of His teaching (Matthew 7:29; Mark 1:22, 27; Luke 4:32), forgiving sins (Matt 9:6, 8; Mark 2:10; Luke 5:24), or His general authority (Matthew 28:18; Luke 4:6; John 10:18; 17:2).

The Temple leadership was barren. Despite all God had done to prepare them through His word, there was still no fruit. The Jewish leaders frequently questioned Jesus' authority, as shown by their constant question, "By what authority are you doing these things, or who gave you this authority to do them?" (Mark 11:28, ESV; cf. Matthew 21:23; Luke 20:2). In an ironic parable of action, Jesus challenged the fruitlessness of the Jewish leaders by cursing the fig tree.

As Jesus was entering Jerusalem from Bethany, He saw a leafy tree without figs (Mark 11:12-14). At that moment, Jesus cursed the tree, saying, "May no one ever eat fruit from you again!" After cleansing the Temple, Jesus and the apostles returned to Bethany. The next morning, Peter noticed that the fig tree had withered from the roots up (Mark 11:20-21). Jesus used this as an opportunity to encourage Peter and the other apostles to have the kind of prayerful faith that could move mountains. The fruitless fig tree symbolized the fruitless leaders of Jesus' day.

Disciples of Jesus must recognize that no one can match His authority. Only Jesus could bear the perfect fruit that the leaders of His day failed to produce. Only Jesus could pay the price for our sin. Only Jesus can be the focus of our faithful remembrance as we gather around the table on the first day of the week.

Today, I will…seek to bear fruit like Jesus, while faithfully submitting to His authority.

TUESDAY
Responsive
Today's Scripture: Matthew 22:1-14

We are not worthy to be in the Lord's house, but He has invited us to a feast. "All things are ready, come to the feast!"

Jesus told three consecutive parables to the Jewish leaders who challenged His authority: the two sons (Matthew 21:28-32), the patient landowner (21:33-46), and the gracious king who hosted a wedding feast for his son (22:1-14). Jesus sought to compare "the kingdom of heaven" to a wedding banquet where most of the invited guests were unwilling to participate.

A patient king sent his servants a second time to remind the guests that the feast was ready to eat, but the invited guests either ignored the king's invitation or abused those he had sent to remind them (Matthew 22:4-6). Who could imagine treating the king in such a dishonorable manner? The wrathful king responded by sending his armies to burn their cities since the guests who had been invited to the banquet "were not worthy" (Matthew 22:8). Instead of canceling the event, the king then sent his servants to invite everyone they could find. Luke adds that "the poor and crippled and blind and lame" were all welcomed as well (Luke 14:21). Soon, the banquet hall was filled with those who accepted the king's invitation. Imagine how excited and overwhelmed many of these guests were to be in the banquet hall of the king. Yet because one man came to the banquet without the proper attire, he was bound and cast into the outer darkness (Matthew 22:11-13). All the other guests were allowed to share in a feast hosted by the king because those who had first been invited had refused his invitation.

Many of us have stood still through many invitation songs. We have gotten used to hearing about what God has prepared for us. Perhaps even the Lord's Supper has become a time when we fail to remember how much our gracious and patient God has offered us.

Today, I will…continue to respond to the King's invitation to share in His banquet with gratitude and enthusiasm.

Charitable
Today's Scripture: Matthew 22:36-40

When Jesus was asked about the greatest commandment, He responded with two verses that include the same verb: LOVE.

This was a difficult time in Jesus' public ministry. As the cross loomed nearer, His opponents asked more questions to try to condemn Him (Matthew 22:15, 18). Again and again, they were left speechless by the authority of a teacher unlike anyone they had ever encountered.

Perhaps the Pharisee, seeing an opportune time to ask a question since Jesus had just silenced his political rival, was looking to promote himself. Matthew tells us that he was asking the question to "test" Jesus (Matthew 22:35). The lawyer probably already had an answer in mind when he asked Jesus, "Teacher, which is the great commandment in the Law?" (ESV). The text does not give the impression that Jesus hesitated at all when He quoted Deuteronomy 6:5, saying, "You shall love the Lord your God with all your heart and with all your soul and with all your mind" (Matthew 22:37, ESV). Many of Jesus' hearers would have been pleased with this answer. This was the heart of the law and a part of the *Shema* that many recited frequently in their devotion to God.

But Jesus did not stop there. While we should love God first as the "great and foremost commandment," Jesus added a second one like it when He quoted Leviticus 19:18, "You shall love your neighbor as yourself" (ESV). Jesus stated that the whole Old Testament could be summarized by these two commandments (Matthew 22:40). How easy was it for some of God's people to neglect one another in the name of being allegiant to God?

Church history is full of examples of one group mistreating another because they claimed to be obeying God even in their abuse! In Jesus' day, some failed to care for their parents by claiming to obey God (Mark 7:9-13), while later others abused the privilege of taking communion together as one body (1 Corinthians 11:17-22). We love God and one another. We commune with God and our brothers and sisters. We seek to offer salvation to the lost just like Jesus (Luke 19:10).

Today, I will…refuse to neglect the brother or sister I am sitting with at the Lord's Table because I claim to be too focused on Jesus.

THURSDAY
Reverent
Today's Scripture: Matthew 23:5-12

Appearances can be deceiving. There is danger in seeking to advance yourself rather than Christ.

Jesus' rebuke of the scribes and Pharisees in Matthew 23 is one of the most stinging indictments of religiously minded people in all of Scripture! These blind guides were guilty of setting themselves up as the authorities of God's standards. Their pride blinded them from seeing their own hypocritical habits as they accused Jesus of wrongdoing. In Matthew alone, the religious officials accused Him of blasphemy (Matthew 9:3), associating with tax collectors and sinners (9:11), failing to require His disciples to fast (9:14), working by the power of satan (9:34; 12:24-26), violating their Sabbath traditions (12:2, 10), disregarding the handwashing tradition of their elders (15:1-2), and operating without proper authority (21:23-24). For all these reasons, the scribes and Pharisees wanted to arrest and kill Him (12:14; 26:4; 27:20).

Jesus quickly saw through the irreverence of His accusers. These men, who denied the authority of Jesus, were willing to work with the power of wicked leaders like Caiaphas, Pilate, and Herod to destroy Him. Later, it was even by "the authority of the chief priests" that Saul would work to persecute Christians (Acts 9:14; 26:10, 12). The scribes and Pharisees had evil hearts and empty habits. They sat in the chair of Moses in the synagogue but did not follow Moses (Matthew 23:2-12). They demanded that their hearers practice religious observances that they refused to live out. They put on a good show, wore garments that got attention, and did activities that got praise. They demanded honorable titles that belonged only to Christ. They were irreverent.

Woe to those who disrespect the One with real authority. When we gather around the Table of the Lord, we are mindful that He is the host. We revere Him as the One who gave His body and blood. We do not accuse Him of wrongdoing but rather reverently honor Him.

Today, I will…speak and act in ways that are reverent because of what Jesus has done, is doing, and will do for me.

FRIDAY
Balanced
Today's Scripture: Matthew 23:23-24

Obedience to God matters, but God has defined some aspects of our faithfulness as "weightier" than others.

In His rebuke of the scribes and Pharisees in Matthew 23, Jesus called them out for their imbalance. They were giving 10% of everything they owned to God, including their mint, dill, and cumin (Matthew 23:23). At first glance, it seems they should be commended for such attention to detail, but in doing so, they neglected "the weightier matters of the law," including justice, mercy, and faithfulness. In their imbalance, they became "blind guides" who choked on gnats (how much of these spices should we devote to God?) while swallowing camels (should we care about the people around us?).

It's easy to marvel at the imbalance of failed leaders, yet when I seek to assess my own walk with Christ, what do I see? Do I care about people like God cares about them? Am I more like the forgiving father who longs to be reconciled (Luke 15:20) or the older brother who is more concerned about his reward (Luke 15:29-30)? Paul reminded us that when we have success, it is because God gave the increase (1 Corinthians 3:6-7). There are many good things Christians can be involved in and celebrate, but at times, doing the good things can take our focus off the best things. Do we love our to-do list more than we love the lost?

This is acutely experienced in our communing around the Lord's table. At the table, we are reminded of what matters most. Jesus, the perfect Lamb of God, gave Himself for us. His body was pierced, and His blood was shed so that all may have life. There are other experiences and points of doctrine that are also important, but our connection with the Lamb matters most. He was killed for us and was raised on the first day of the week.

Today, I will…seek to sort out the camels and gnats in my thinking to focus on and minister to the things that matter most to God.

Table Meditation
Scripture: 1 Corinthians 11:27

Just before Jesus was about to be arrested, put on trial, and crucified, He took a moment while in the upper room to establish an important reminder. There was little time left for Jesus to give instructions about what was coming or what would be required of his disciples. Yet, with the brief time he had left with them, Jesus instituted the Lord's Supper.

For Jesus to spend some of his last moments on the Earth establishing the memorial ought to cause us to realize the importance of the Lord's Supper. When we assemble, every part of worship is important and commanded. The partaking of the Lord's Supper should have an elevated importance, considering that we are commanded to partake in a worthy manner. We need to use this time to make togetherness a priority. Taking the Lord's Supper as a family should bring a feeling of unity and common love with our brothers and sisters in Christ. We have all probably seen the illustration of a beautiful fire burning in a lovely fireplace. We understand that we can see the picture, but we can't feel the warmth that it provides to those in its presence. The pandemic seems to have given some the feeling that online worship is just fine. There are instances where it may provide an avenue to worship due to illness, but it never replaces the warmth and feeling of that in-person fellowship and warmth of being together.

The Lord's Supper does not lose its significance when it is taken weekly. The action of taking the Lord's Supper is about discipline. This is the same discipline mentioned in Colossians 3:2 when we are reminded to "set your mind on things that are above" (ESV). Then, in 1 Corinthians 11:27, taking the Lord's Supper in a worthy manner is discussed. The reality is that we are all unworthy sinners. However, God's grace and mercy allow us to be able to walk in a worthy manner, as seen in Ephesians 4:1 and Philippians 1:27. The phrase "unworthy manner" in 1 Corinthians 11:27 is translated as "unworthily" in the KJV. By taking unworthily, we are not discerning the Lord's body and blood as seriously as a Christian should.

There are challenges to partaking of the Lord's Supper in our worship. We can be distracted. Parents have a hard challenge when raising little ones; I'm sure that the Lord understands the obstacle that active children present to young parents.

This part of worship is also a maturing process. Most of us can remember the first time we observed communion. It was a new and novel experience that we looked forward to. No doubt, as young converts, we could not appreciate the depth of the ultimate sacrifice that grows each time we partake. There are memories I have of my mother and dad as I observed their examples. My father would be in prayer and reading scripture, and my mother was always in deep meditation. She would press the palm of her hand to try to focus on the nails piercing the flesh of our Savior.

The focus is faithfulness in our service and realizing the sacrifice made for us. God's abundant grace and mercy were poured out to us by the amazing sacrifice of His Son. We should not only reflect on this sacrifice but rejoice at the amazing nature of our Lord and Savior in that He wants us in Heaven with Him.

Setting Up the Table of Surrender
Today's Scripture: Mark 12:28-40

The incident involving "the widow's mite" is not a minor passage in Mark's gospel. It is a short passage about a seemingly insignificant gift that ends up mirroring the greatest gift of all. It is obviously powerful. We can learn a lot about the opportunity to be part of God's table from this brief paragraph in Mark 12:41–44. I want to first consider some context leading up to the episode.

In Mark 12:28-34, Mark describes the scribes who asked Jesus about the greatest commandment. You are likely well aware of Jesus' all-encompassing answer. Jesus' response pointed to complete devotion of self to God's purposes, for He gives all that we have.

Then, in Mark 12:35-37, Jesus recalls the prophecy that all things would be placed under the feet of the Christ. The fulfillment of that prophecy would necessitate the sacrifice from the Christ, as well. When we come to the Table of the Lord, we remember the One who loved us too much to cling to His position. This is a different picture than the verses just before our main text about "the widow's mite." In Mark 12:38-40, Jesus describes a group more concerned with the benefits and pretense of position. These are not men who would quickly surrender those things.

By comparison, the table to which we are invited is all about surrender. Now, Mark will show the reader a picture of surrender. I hope it will bless your week.

Today, I will…identify and surrender anything keeping me from what redemption deserves.

TUESDAY
Jesus Sits Opposite the Treasury
Today's Scripture: Mark 12:41

Today's thought opens with a scene we may quickly believe is easy to picture. Mark 12:41 says that Jesus sat down opposite the treasury and watched people putting money into the offering box. The idea is not just that Jesus noticed but that he watched. Jesus does a purposeful thing. Don't just observe the physical position the Lord took on that day in the temple, but also the ironies of that position when we come to commune with him.

First, Jesus sat by the treasury as one whose very being was the essence of a giver. This certainly rings true as we come to commune with Him and each other on the Lord's Day. The gift of Christ Jesus is a regular reminder that we could not earn the invitation to commune with Him. God cannot be out-given. In Luke 6:38, Jesus said, "Give and it will be given to you. Good measure, pressed down, shaken together, running over, will be put into your lap" (ESV). The fact that we are invited to the Lord's Table at all reminds us that God is the ultimate giver. Jesus, God in the flesh, sat opposite the treasury to watch that day. Can you imagine? This observer was qualified to judge what He was seeing!

Secondly, Jesus truly sits as "opposite" the spiritual position of those whom He watched. Remember, when we come to His table, we are there because of the truth found in 2 Corinthians 5:21, where Paul reminds us, "For our sake, He made Him to be sin, who knew no sin, so that in Him we might become the righteousness of God" (ESV). The giver knew no sin, and we commune with Him!

Today, I will…thank God for taking on my sin!

WEDNESDAY
Out of Our Poverty!
Today's Scripture: Mark 12:42; Revelation 3:17

We have already looked at the position of Jesus observing the gifts brought to the treasury. In the next verse, we see a great contrast. In the midst of others coming in great pride and wealth, a humble and poor widow approaches. The Lord sees her. He sees a woman poor in material goods but wealthy in understanding.

Many view gifts to God with clouded considerations, comparisons, and perceived unfairness. Christians are to consider who they were without His salvation compared to who they now are in Him. In Revelation 3:14-17, John writes to the church at Laodicea, whom God has considered "lukewarm." Some might consider that a life that is simply "going through the motions" rather than being "on fire" for the Lord. They feel as though they are rich and in no real need at all, but the reality is the opposite, being "wretched, pitiable, poor, blind, and naked" (ESV). What a contrast! This poor widow understood those same realities. She possessed limited material goods. She was likely still grieving the death of her husband and would have been more socially obscure compared to the other givers. Despite these difficulties, she would do something the Lord would praise and use to teach the disciples.

When we approach the table of the Lord, we approach it as a contrast. We approach in great wealth spiritually but not by our own means. We can come as humble, thankful, as well as confident. Why? Because, as Paul described to the Ephesian church, our God was rich in mercy. He took dead people and made them alive again (Ephesians 2:4-6). Thank you, Lord!

Today, I will…remember how God saved me out of my spiritual poverty!

Value Rooted in Sacrifice
Today's Scripture: Mark 12:42-43

Jesus was sitting by the treasury, observing the means, manner, and motive of various gifts brought to the temple. Some were materially and socially blessed, and some were not, including a poor widow who brought a tiny fraction of a day's wages. This would have seemed "flippant" to some. Jesus saw something else and called His disciples to Him. He might have seemed only observant at first, but he was defining true discipleship, faith, and even himself.

The message Jesus gave the disciples could, on the surface, seem questionable. After all, Mark states clearly that some gave large amounts. Yet Jesus, in saying this woman had given more than all others, was not referencing monetary value but of the heart. Her gift amount alone did not signal her faith before Jesus, but her sacrifice did. I recall these words from Scripture, where in 1 Samuel 16:7, the Lord told Samuel that while man looks on the outward appearance, our God "looks on the heart." The heart is the great equalizer. Eternity will reveal that the kingdom of God was full of people vastly different from one another. God brings together the outward measurables of age, color, economic status, talents, personality, and more. The one common trait of those in eternity is a selfless and singular faith that, as Paul says in Philippians 3:8, counted everything else as "loss" and "rubbish."

The poor widow of Mark 12 mimics the description of Jesus in Philippians 2:1-8. The widow brought her gift unconcerned with what was left over. She demonstrated faith in God's care. Paul reminds the Philippian church how Jesus gave it all to save man, demonstrating faith in His Father's care. When coming to the Lord's Table, we entrust all to the Savior whose sacrifice gives us immeasurable value.

Today, I will…remember my real value is rooted in Jesus' sacrifice.

FRIDAY
Made Sufficient
Today's Scripture: Mark 12:44; Matthew 5:3

"My Only Hope Is You" is a very simple song that Christians can sing to find life's peace. Making that brief statement reveals our basis for many decisions. In closing out the episode of the poor widow of chapter 12, Mark recalls the words of Jesus, stating that she had put in "all that she had to live on" (Mark 12:44, ESV). If her gift came with words, those may very well have been, "My only hope is you."

In Matthew 5:3, Jesus began the beatitudes with these words, "Blessed are the poor in spirit." The Lord is referencing the felt insufficiency of the soul. It is not a bad thing to recognize my spiritual poverty when left to my own goodness or worldly gratification. However, too many struggle to accept that. Jesus once encountered a rich young man struggling to find the path to the most important thing (Mark 10:17-27). Jesus knew the problem. The young man was holding on to material things and went away sad. Both Jesus and the apostles taught that true freedom is found in giving up that which one thought could be held onto. The poor widow of Mark 12, who gave all she had, is not usually called "the wise widow," but it would be an accurate description!

At the table of the Lord, we remember a Savior who gave from his wealth of position and authority and still gave it all. Some may say the poor widow who gave it all at least didn't have much to lose. While in one perspective, that may be true, she understood the limited power of a "here and now" focus. At the cross, Jesus understood trust in His Father as well as an eternal focus.

Today, I will…pray that I go "all in" on God's promise.

HIS FINAL WEEK
TUESDAY EVENING

Table Meditation
Scripture: 1 Corinthians 11:28

Here we are to partake of the Lord's Supper, just as we do every Sunday. It's part of our worship; we do this over and over each week. Certainly, this could become something ordinary or mundane. Have we allowed our busy lives to rob the focus and joy that we have in taking this Supper? If we're not careful, we could take these emblems without considering them for what they truly mean.

How can we take the "ordinary" out of the Lord's Supper so that it brings new meaning and joy? Make this a personal time to reflect upon our lives. We can focus on this past week. Did we have perfection? Did we do everything right? Certainly not! Paul said that we should examine ourselves and be honest with ourselves (1 Corinthians 11:28; 2 Corinthians 13:5; Galatians 6:4). This is the time to look inwardly and understand Christ's sacrifice on the cross and how that impacts us personally—today, right here, and right now. His sacrifice allows for our sins to be remembered no more. This is the "worthy manner" in which we should partake. It's very personal, and this brings us great thanksgiving and joy!

Consider these lyrics:
Every time I kneel to pray I open up my heart to my Lord
Every time I close my eyes I feel the sweet embrace of my Lord
Every time I see a child I see the gentleness of my Lord
Every time I watch a storm I know the awesome power of my Lord

I don't know why so many things seem to get in the way of seeing my God's glory
But I try every day to see and thank Him for all the things He's given me
Every time I see the cross![1]

This morning, let's slow down our lives and thoughts. Don't allow anything to get in our way. Let's all "see the cross!"

---

[1] Organ, Philip. "Everytime." Here To Him Music, 1994.

Who?
Today's Scripture: Matthew 24:1-14

Journalism is built on getting to the facts by answering basic questions. Those questions usually begin with one of six words: who, what, where, when, why, or how. As we consider Matthew 24 and 25 this week, we will gaze through the lens of five of those words.

The "Who?" question is answered in the first word of Matthew 24: Jesus. From His genealogy in Matthew's opening chapter, His profound remodeling of the old law in the Sermon on the Mount, His miracles, and the prophecies of what was to come, it has always been about Jesus. John's gospel makes it clear that Jesus existed in the beginning, long before the time He became flesh (John 1:1, 14). He is eternal. Paul tells us that He is of utmost importance. "For I decided to know nothing among you except Jesus Christ and him crucified" (1 Corinthians 2:2, ESV).

In this account, there is a second "Who:" us. Although Jesus is not speaking to us directly, His warnings about the end of the age still hold true. We will fall into one of the two categories He describes. "The love of many will grow cold. But the one who endures to the end will be saved" (Matthew 24:12b-13, ESV). Will we be the many whose love grows cold, or will we endure? My prayer is that we will be the latter.

And when we endure, it is amazing what happens. "And this gospel of the kingdom will be proclaimed throughout the whole world as a testimony to all nations, and then the end will come" (Matthew 24:14, ESV). Are you proclaiming the gospel every week? This is not a guilt trip about evangelism. It is a reminder. According to Paul, you are proclaiming the gospel every Sunday. "For as often as you eat this bread and drink the cup, you proclaim the Lord's death until he comes" (1 Corinthians 11:26, ESV).

Today, I will…proclaim the gospel of Jesus in word and action.

TUESDAY
What?
Today's Scripture: Matthew 24:29-31

We have access to incredible technology in the palms of our hands. I have an app on my phone that can track the International Space Station. As I write this, it tells me that tomorrow at 4:32 AM, it will appear 27 degrees above the horizon as a white dot moving east across the sky and disappear 3 minutes and 45 seconds later. It is accurate every time.

Sometimes, while I watch that white dot travel across the sky, knowing it is about to disappear, I think of the apostles at the beginning of the book of Acts. As Jesus ascended into heaven and out of their sight, they still stood there staring into the sky so intently that they did not realize that visitors had come with a message. "Men of Galilee, why do you stand looking into heaven? This Jesus, who was taken up from you into heaven, will come in the same way as you saw him go into heaven" (Acts 1:11, ESV). That is the "What?" of today's message: Jesus is coming back.

His apostles might have expected Jesus to return in their lifetimes. The early church appeared to expect that as well. Peter writes to people who might have even wondered why He was taking so long to return. "But do not overlook this one fact, beloved, that with the Lord one day is as a thousand years, and a thousand years as one day. The Lord is not slow to fulfill his promise as some count slowness, but is patient toward you, not wishing that any should perish, but that all should reach repentance" (2 Peter 3:8-9, ESV). The nearly 2000 years since have only been as a couple of days to God.

In communion, we continue to proclaim His death and his return. "For as often as you eat this bread and drink the cup, you proclaim the Lord's death until he comes" (1 Corinthians 11:26, ESV).

Today, I will…eagerly and patiently anticipate His return until He comes.

When?
Today's Scripture: Matthew 24:36-25:13

A couple of years ago, my son asked me to order something for him from Amazon. After I received a shipping confirmation, I let him know what day it would arrive. As soon as he got up that morning, he asked me when the package would get to our house. The day was not enough. He wanted to know the exact time. We live in a world that is like that. If I order a pizza online, I can track the process from order to oven to the delivery vehicle. If I paid for an extra service with my son's shipment, we could have followed the delivery truck on a map to our house.

The answer to the "When?" question in Matthew 24 is probably the most difficult to accept. We do not know when Jesus will return. No human does, but there is One who knows. "But concerning that day and hour no one knows, not even the angels of heaven, nor the Son, but the Father only" (Matthew 24:36, ESV). We may not know when, but we know the One who does. Since we do not know when we have to stay ready.

I grew up in a part of the country where we had hurricanes, and I currently live in Tornado Alley. In both places, I have learned to be prepared. We had a box of hurricane supplies on the Gulf Coast, and we have a tornado shelter today. In both situations, it is too late to prepare when the storm has arrived. But in those situations, there is usually some kind of warning. Our warning came almost 2000 years ago: "Watch therefore, for you know neither the day nor the hour" (Matthew 25:13, ESV). We cannot wait for another warning to sound.

When we take the bread and the cup each week, we do it to remember what Jesus has done for us. God gave us reminders, so we can be ready.

Today, I will...live without regrets, ready for His return.

How?
Today's Scripture: Matthew 25:14-30

Over the years, I have heard a phrase countless times in worship services: "separate and apart." Most of us know the words that follow: the Lord's Supper. For the sake of convenience, congregations frequently have the weekly offering after the Lord's Supper. The person leading the prayer wants to create a dividing line between the Lord's Supper that has just been eaten and the contribution that is to follow. Although the two are separate, we should not underestimate the importance of stewardship. In the Parable of the Talents, our use of resources is related to God's judgment.

In the New Testament, a talent is a measurement of money. In our present-day language, it refers more to gifts and abilities. For this reason, we frequently hear this parable referenced to encourage us to use the skills God has given us. Using our skills for God is a biblical teaching, but this parable is actually about resources. The three servants treat what they have been entrusted with quite differently, and the one who stewards his money poorly is condemned. The reasons for his poor stewardship might hit a little too close to home. He thought the master was harsh, and he was fearful.

Even faithful Christians might question God when things are not going well. We might be fearful and want to take control. When it comes to financial matters, we might be frustrated by how much wealth others have or fearful of how we will get by if we give too much. Like the one-talent servant, that might reveal our fears and how we see God. Paul echoes the spirit of this parable. "The point is this: whoever sows sparingly will also reap sparingly, and whoever sows bountifully will also reap bountifully. Each one must give as he has decided in his heart, not reluctantly or under compulsion, for God loves a cheerful giver" (2 Corinthians 9:6-7, ESV). In the Lord's Supper, we remember what He gave. That is how we see Him and why we give.

Today, I will…give generously and fearlessly.

FRIDAY
Why?
Today's Scripture: Matthew 25:31-46

Several years ago, our family spent a spring break in Seattle, Washington. While walking from lunch at McDonald's toward the Space Needle, we passed by a man sitting on the street with a sign asking for money. I have to admit that I did not even notice him. I was thinking about where our two boys were, where we were heading next, how much more expensive the food was than I expected, and probably plenty of other things, too. I did not see him. But my youngest son did. He wanted us to go back to McDonald's and buy some food for him.

How many people do we overlook? We might be busy. He might be different. We might have judged why she is in the predicament she is in. We might convince ourselves there is nothing that we can do. Would we ignore or walk by if it was Jesus Himself? Obviously not, but Jesus values these people just as much.

In this parable about a King, his servants, and the needy, the servants do not understand the King's assessment of their service to Him. He explains, "And the King will answer them, 'Truly, I say to you, as you did it to one of the least of these my brothers, you did it to me" (Matthew 25:40, ESV). Conversely, when I walk right by a man on the street in Seattle, I have ignored Jesus.

Why does it matter how we treat those who are less fortunate? We should treat them well because we follow the example of our Lord and His compassion. This parable provides a second unexpected answer: judgment. Here, we see Jesus separating groups based on their service. Let's not forget that baptism is the beginning of our walk, not the finish line.

Today, I will...be aware of people, love them, and serve them as Jesus would.

HIS FINAL WEEK
WEDNESDAY

Table Meditation
Scripture: John 15:13-15; John 19:25-27

One of the blessings of life is a "best friend," someone who really "knows" you. Someone to confide in, laugh with, and enjoy life together. Bob Gray was "that friend" for me, and when he was killed in Vietnam, I was devastated with grief. The sadness of his funeral and the image of his grief-stricken widowed mother will forever be in my heart.

When I prepare for the Lord's Supper, I often think of another friendship. I see John and Mary standing near Jesus' cross—John holding her tightly, doing his best to console her as they watched Jesus in agony, enduring hours of unspeakable pain and suffering. What were they thinking as they gazed upon Him with hearts bursting with grief?

John, the disciple Jesus loved, was looking up at his best friend, his teacher, and his hero. Mary was looking at her Son with memories only a mother can have. Both were in utter despair, powerless to help.

Then Jesus, with His dying breath, speaks words of love and comfort. He charges his mother to embrace John as a son and his friend to care for her as his own. That moment, recorded by John, is just a glimpse of the compassion of Jesus... even on the brink of death.

Yet, as Jesus cared for His best friend and His mother, He cares for all His disciples, calling us His friends. He willingly became the sacrifice for our sins. The blood he shed on the cross still cleanses us today.

MONDAY
He Knew What Was Coming
Today's Scripture: Matthew 26:1-16

Jesus said to His disciples: "You know that after two days the Passover is coming, and the Son of Man will be delivered up to be crucified" (Matthew 26:1). Can you imagine knowing that your death is coming and knowing full well all of the details concerning your death? I would assume most of us would have fled and lived somewhere where we could stay hidden. But not our Lord! He stayed in Jerusalem, celebrated Passover with His apostles, and initiated the Lord's Supper to remind all of us about what He did for us.

Jesus knew Judas was going to betray Him. He knew the method by which He would be killed. He knew the numerous laws that would be broken to kill Him—arrested without a true warrant, tried at night, and false witnesses. Our Lord knew what was coming, yet He went through with it. He died for you and me.

Every Lord's day, we gather around the table to focus on Him and what He did for us. We think about what He knew going into His crucifixion. Jesus took His stand against sin, injustice, and false leadership. He stayed where He knew they could find Him. Our Lord did this without the guarantee that anyone would care about what He did "…but God shows his love for us in that while we were still sinners, Christ died for us" (Rom. 5:8). Such thoughts are unfathomable.

Today, I will… contemplate the evil that took Jesus to the cross. I will get on my knees and thank Him for going through what He went through for me. I will prepare my heart, mind, soul, and body to take the Lord's Supper not just as I sit in the pew, but every day.

TUESDAY
Conspiracy
Today's Scripture: Matthew 26:1-16

There are a lot of wild conspiracies about almost anything you can imagine. During the Covid crisis, conspiracies were rampant about mind control, changing our DNA so we were no longer human, and hundreds of other baseless claims. When John Kennedy was assassinated, the conspiracies began to fly and still do. Was it a CIA plot, the mafia, or the Cubans? Was Lee Harvey Oswald set up? No conclusive evidence has ever come forth.

One conspiracy is true, and that was the conspiracy to kill Jesus. "Then the chief priests and the elders of the people gathered in the palace of the high priest, whose name was Caiaphas, and plotted together in order to arrest Jesus by stealth and kill him" (Matt. 26:3-4). Men who were supposed to be spiritual leaders of the Jews were evil. After raising Lazarus, John writes "So from that day on they made plans to put him to death" (John 11:53). What was the reason for this determination to kill Jesus? Envy (Matt. 27:18). It is little wonder that Jesus "had compassion for them, because they were like sheep without a shepherd" (Mark 6:34). Despite their authority, they were petty, jealous, and filled with murderous intent.

It was sin that took Jesus to the cross. The sin of the leadership of Israel, the sin of the crowd who cried "Crucify Him!," and our sin. Wendell Winkler once preached about the cross and said, "To continue to sin is like holding up the knife that killed your parents and proclaiming how beautiful it is." satan "conspired" with all of us to kill Jesus, but Jesus had other plans. His death saves us. His death erases the sins of our lives and washes away the stains.

Today, I will... meditate about the depth of forgiveness. Jesus said, "Father, forgive them, for they know not what they do" (Luke 23:34). If He can forgive these conspirators, He can forgive me too. We should take these thoughts to worship with us!

"When Jesus Had Finished All These Sayings"
Today's Scripture: Matthew 26:1-16

As a child, my mom would read Aesop's Fables to me. These "wise stories" taught me about decision-making. Solomon was instructed by God to write the book of Proverbs that we might have wisdom in our decision-making as God's people.

Jesus spends time in the days before His death teaching important lessons in Matthew 25. He warns about being careless—the parable of the foolish virgins. He taught about wasting our resources—the parable of the talents. He forecasts our judgment concerning good things we did or did not do for our fellow man.

The institution of the Lord's Supper on the night before His death indicates the solemnity of this memorial feast. It is the final major thing Jesus does before He goes up to the Mount of Olives, prays, and is arrested.

Do we live our lives carelessly like the five foolish virgins? Do we rush to get ready for worship with little thought about the price he paid that we might have this privilege? Like the one talent man, do we squander the resources God gives us by never using them in His service? We may not think these "sayings" have much to do with the table of the Lord while they have much to do with it.

The Lord's Supper is about the sacrifice of Jesus. It is a reminder of the body and blood given in our place. It is a reminder that He is coming again and that we cannot know when (also a part of His sayings, Matthew 24).

Today, I will… examine my life to see if I am diligently seeking God's kingdom and His righteousness, and using my talents wisely (2 Cor. 13:5). I will consider these things every week in preparing to eat the supper of my Lord.

THURSDAY
A Dangerous Move
Today's Scripture: Matthew 26:1-16

Evil can quickly get by us. Government leaders make radical, immoral decisions and little is done about it. Sometimes these changes are made slowly, but other times very abruptly. Even if there is an uproar for a short time, it is quickly gone.

In the time of Christ, it was not much different. The leadership of Israel determined to kill Jesus stealthily. The term "stealth" or "dolos" in Greek means "deceit" or "cunning." This word emphasizes sinful motives. Israel's leadership was very corrupt. The High Priesthood was basically for sale. Annas had been deposed by Valerius Gratus, and his son-in-law Caiaphas was appointed in his place. The office was merely political as the Jews no longer appointed the heir of Aaron. Once a breach in divine revelation of this magnitude happens, it is not a great leap to kill Jesus.

The chief priests and elders knew they had to do this quietly to avoid accusations about killing Jesus during the feast. Jerusalem would swell to several hundred thousand during Passover. They tried Him at night —illegally—and took Him to Pilate very early in the morning. The crowd still gathered, but it would have been larger had Jesus been crucified later in the day.

It was a risky move to kill Jesus. This reveals the brazen nature of satan. He thought that by killing Jesus, he would win the battle over good. However, from the beginning, God knew this would not happen, "he shall bruise your head, and you shall bruise his heel" (Gen. 3:15). Jesus chose to die and through His resurrection dealt satan a death blow. Sin can be completely and thoroughly forgiven. When we take the Lord's Supper, there is more than the somber recognition of Jesus' death. There is also the celebration of life beyond this one through Him.

Today, I will… take stock of the cost of sin and how it perverts our motives.

FRIDAY
Would We Have Done the Same?
Today's Scripture: Matthew 26:1-16

It is hard to know what we would do until we face the same circumstances as others. Caiaphas said, "Nor do you understand that it is better for you that one man should die for the people, not that the whole nation should perish" (John 11:50). Perhaps we too would have condemned Jesus thinking we were saving our nation. Living under Roman rule was hard. Titus would come down in 70 A.D. and destroy Jerusalem. Jesus made it clear "Render to Caesar that which is Caesar's" (John 11:50), but the Jews were determined to kill Him. Jesus was not anti-Roman, anti-government, and was not a political Zealot.

The Jews thought they were doing the nation a favor. They could get rid of a troublemaker and get back to the business of appeasing their Roman despots. Killing Jesus was not at the top of the Roman agenda. Pontius Pilate tried to release Jesus multiple times during his examination. He could not find anything wrong with Him. He offered Barabas to the people, but they kept crying for the blood of Jesus.

I am sure we do not see ourselves as one who would have called for the death of Jesus. Yet, we sin, the very thing that took Jesus to the cross. With this being the case, are we any better than they were? No! Paul says, "For our sake he made him to be sin who knew no sin, so that in him we might become the righteousness of God" (2 Cor. 5:21). He took our sin so that we do not have to die.

The Lord's Supper ought to humble us. We recognize that we are guilty of sin and He is not. We recognize that our sins caused the cross. We acknowledge that our sins took Jesus to the cross just as if we were crying out, "His blood be on us and on our children" (Matt. 27:25). Unfortunately, we would have crucified Jesus.

Today, I will… acknowledge my sins in prayer and ask to be humble to partake of the Lord's Supper in a worthy manner.

HIS FINAL WEEK
THURSDAY

THE LAST SUPPER

Table Meditation
Scripture: 2 Corinthians 13:5; 1 John 1:7

The unleavened bread (symbolizing holiness—being set apart from the world's permeating yeast of vanity; His very body made flesh and dwelt among us in holiness—a purposeful life) and the fruit of the vine (symbolizing the blood from the sacrificed unblemished obedient—Hebrews 5:8-9—Lamb of God as described from the Exodus 12) are the emblems we take each first day of the week when we assemble as disciples.

Scripture states (2 Corinthians 13:5) that we should examine ourselves as to whether we are in the faith—a hint back to the pursuit of holiness represented by the unleavened bread and the value of the blood that keeps on cleansing us from all sin (1 John 1:7), when we walk in the light.

While eating the supper commanded in the Law of Moses on the 14th day of Nissan, Christ taught us about the new supper. We no longer live under that old law but under the new covenant, the new testament, and the new law of Christ. The supper we eat shows the world that we have been humbled by his obedience to the Father. We deny ourselves daily and take up our crosses to follow Him. Because He laid down His life for us, He makes us to be at peace with God and man.

God be praised for raising Christ the Son to overcome death and for glorifying Jesus, our Lord and our Redeemer.

MONDAY
Christ's Institutes the Lord's Supper
Today's Scripture: Matthew 26:26-30

The Bible says, "Now as they were eating, Jesus took bread, and after blessing it broke it and gave it to the disciples, and said, "Take, eat; this is my body." And he took a cup, and when he had given thanks he gave it to them, saying, "Drink of it, all of you, for this is my blood of the covenant, which is poured out for many for the forgiveness of sins. I tell you I will not drink again of this fruit of the vine until that day when I drink it new with you in my Father's kingdom." And when they had sung a hymn, they went out to the Mount of Olives" (Matthew 26:26-30, ESV).

Every Lord's Day, Christians the world over assemble to partake of the Lord's Supper. The goal is to remember the death, burial, and resurrection of Jesus Christ. The purpose is to bring to the mind of the one who is partaking in what our Lord did in giving Himself for us. It is not just something in which we participate so that we may check it off the list.

The bread represents his body. Jesus said, "Take, eat; this is my body." It is reminiscent of the Old Testament instruction. When the Israelites left Egypt, they look unleavened bread (Exodus 12:8). To the children of Israel, the unleavened bread symbolized God's deliverance from Egyptian captivity. To Christians today, it represents what Jesus did to deliver us from darkness. The Holy Bible says, "He has delivered us from the domain of darkness and transferred us to the kingdom of his beloved Son, in whom we have redemption, the forgiveness of sins" (Colossians 1:13-14, ESV).

"For as often as you eat this bread and drink the cup, you proclaim the Lord's death until he comes" (1 Corinthians 11:26, ESV).

Today, I will…pray that as I eat the bread on the first day of the week, I will remember what my Lord has done for me.

A Picture of the Cross
Today's Scripture: Galatians 6:14

When a person eats the bread during the Lord's Supper, does the mind go back to the cross of Christ? When our Lord was crucified, his body was pierced. The Bible records, "But one of the soldiers pierced his side with a spear, and at once there came out blood and water" (John 19:34, ESV). Matthew records Jesus' words when He instituted the Lord's Supper, "Now as they were eating, Jesus took bread, and after blessing it broke it and gave it to the disciples, and said, "Take, eat; this is my body" (Matthew 26:26, ESV).

When one partakes of the bread during the Lord's Supper, that person goes back to the cross. In one sense, it draws a picture of the cross in the mind. Bread represents the body. This recalls the words of Luke in the book of Acts where Luke records, "On the first day of the week, when we were gathered together to break bread, Paul talked with them, intending to depart on the next day, and he prolonged his speech until midnight" (Acts 20:7, ESV). Paul's words in the Galatian letter also bring this to mind. He wrote, "I have been crucified with Christ. It is no longer I who live, but Christ who lives in me. And the life I now live in the flesh I live by faith in the Son of God, who loved me and gave himself for me" (Galatians 2:20, ESV).

When a person partakes of the bread, it does exactly what God intended for it to do—reminds that person of the body of Jesus Christ and the suffering he experienced for mankind. It is a picture of the cross of Christ. Paul further explains this when he wrote, "For as often as you eat this bread and drink the cup, you proclaim the Lord's death until he comes" (1 Corinthians 11:26, ESV). So, when we eat this bread, it brings to mind the cross of the Lord Jesus.

Today, I will…pray that as I contemplate the death of Christ I will remember the precious cross of Christ.

The Memorial of His Death
Today's Scripture: Mark 14:22-25

The Bible says, "For as often as you eat this bread and drink the cup, you proclaim the Lord's death until he comes" (1 Corinthians 11:26, ESV). "As of January 2021, there are 130 National Monuments that are managed by various federal agencies. From New York's Statue of Liberty to California's Muir Woods, these monuments are as diverse as they are beautiful."[1] As we have those memorials to remember the fallen, we have the Lord's Supper on the Lord's Day to bring to memory the death of Christ.

The Lord's Supper is a memorial. We eat the bread as a memorial to Christ Jesus who gave his life for us. Jesus said, "Take eat this is my body" (Matthew 26:26, ESV). "Memorial Day is an American holiday, observed on the last Monday of May, honoring the men and women who died while serving in the U.S. military."[2] Once each year, we honor those military men who gave their lives for us. Once each week, we honor our Lord Jesus Christ, who gave his life so that we can be saved. Every Lord's Day, we assemble and "eat the bread" as a memorial to what Christ has done for us.

Life is hectic. Working, raising families, and engaging in various activities saturate the mind with the world. However, every Lord's Day, we have the opportunity to put all of that in the background and remember what Jesus Christ did for us, and we do that when the communion bread is passed. We let our minds go to the cross, the pain, and the suffering of our Lord. In our families, we display pictures, and we celebrate birthdays and anniversaries. We do that at various times of the year, but every first day of the week, we come together and worship. Part of that worship is remembering that Christ gave his body for us.

Today, I will…pray that as I partake of the bread on the Lord's Day, I will remember and be thankful for Jesus Christ, who died for me.

---

[1] https://geojango.com/pages/list-of-national-monuments

[2] https://www.history.com/topics/holidays/memorial-day-history

Our Relationship with Christ
Today's Scripture: 1 Corinthians 10:16

"The cup of blessing that we bless, is it not a participation in the blood of Christ? The bread that we break, is it not a participation in the body of Christ" (1 Corinthians 10:16, ESV)? Today's scripture says much about our present relationship with Christ. Notice that the scriptures say, "The bread that we break, is it not a participation in the body of Christ?"

"Is it not a participation?" When the Christian partakes of the bread, he reveals a present ongoing relationship with Christ. The Bible says, "For as often as you eat this bread and drink the cup, you proclaim the Lord's death until he comes" (1 Corinthians 11:26, ESV).

It is a time to focus! We focus on the suffering of our Lord. We focus on who He is. We focus on our relationship with Him. We have a relationship with Christ because he died for us. The scriptures record, "But God shows his love for us in that while we were still sinners, Christ died for us" (Romans 5:8, ESV).

We often say the bread is emblematic of Christ's suffering. It is. Therefore, we focus on our relationship with Him. That relationship with Him comes through our obedience to the gospel (1 Corinthians 15:1-4). When we are baptized into Christ, we put Him on (Galatians 3:27), we are freed from sin (Romans 6:17-18), and our sins are washed away (Acts 22:16). We die to the world, buried with Christ, and raised to walk in newness of Christ. Therefore, when I eat that bread, I remember not only what Christ did for me but also what I did in obedience to Him.

Today, I will…pray that my life may be an example of the life of Jesus Christ and that the world may see Christ in me.

FRIDAY
A Reminder of His Return
Today's Scripture: 1 Corinthians 11:26

The Bible records, "For as often as you eat this bread and drink the cup, you proclaim the Lord's death until he comes" (1 Corinthians 11:26, ESV). Every Lord's Day, we partake of the bread, which represents the body of our Lord Jesus Christ. In addition to remembering His suffering and His cross, we remember that He will return. The Bible says, "until he comes." Also, we read, "For the Lord himself will descend from heaven with a cry of command, with the voice of an archangel, and with the sound of the trumpet of God. And the dead in Christ will rise first" (1 Thessalonians 4:16, ESV).

Many years ago, my wife and I went to visit our son, his wife, and their three sons. Our son's wife told us when we arrived that one of the boys would go all day to the window to see if we had arrived. He anticipated our arrival. She said, "He was so anxious for you to come." Have you ever anxiously waited for someone to come? With the excitement and the thrill, the adrenalin flows. When Jesus ascended after His resurrection, we read, "And said, "Men of Galilee, why do you stand looking into heaven? This Jesus, who was taken up from you into heaven, will come in the same way as you saw him go into heaven" (Acts 1:11, ESV). Christ will return! We are reminded, "But concerning that day and hour no one knows, not even the angels of heaven, nor the Son, but the Father only. For as were the days of Noah, so will be the coming of the Son of Man" (Matthew 24:36-37, ESV).

Every Lord's Day, when one partakes of the bread, that person remembers the return of our Lord Jesus Christ. What a thrill! The Lord is returning, and He has left us a reminder in the bread every first day of the week.

Today, I will…pray that as I look for the Lord's return, my life may reflect His life, "until he comes."

Table Meditation
Scripture: 1 Peter 2:24

Is repetition acceptable with the Lord's Supper? Absolutely. It relates to the recurrence of an action or event. The example of the first-century church is recorded in Acts 20:7, "On the first day of the week, when we were gathered together to break bread" (ESV).

Repetition is dangerous when the act is taken for granted and it becomes redundant or routine. This is a hindrance that opens the door for satan to render our participation in the Lord's Supper inadequate.

How many times have we struggled with this on a Sunday morning?

My prayer to God is to help us understand the significant meaning of the suffering, death, and resurrection of His Son and our Savior, Jesus Christ. These are the most significant events in the history of mankind. Without them, we have no hope. 1 Peter 2:24, "He himself bore our sins in his body on the tree, that we might die to sin and live to righteousness" (ESV).

My prayer to God is to help us understand the love, compassion, and willpower of Christ to allow these events to happen.

My prayer to God is to help us understand His love and willingness to allow these to happen to His perfect and only begotten Son for sinners like me.

MONDAY
An Ordinary Cup
Today's Scripture: Matthew 26:27

Have you seen the movie *Indiana Jones And The Last Crusade*? It depicts archaeologist Indiana Jones searching for the "Holy Grail." This grail was supposedly the cup Jesus used at His last supper with His disciples. Jones was trying to find it, and so were others because the cup was said to have supernatural powers and grant immortality to those who drank from it.

Even if you haven't seen the movie, I am sure you have observed that people try to place special meaning on the cup used in the Lord's Supper. We need to remember that the movie is a work of fiction. There is no "Holy Grail" or a special cup. Instead, a humble, ordinary cup is used at Jesus' Last Supper. As Matthew 26:27 tells us, "And He took a cup, and when He had given thanks He gave it to them, saying, 'Drink of it all of you'" (ESV).

Did Jesus take the Holy Grail? Did Jesus take the special cup? Pay close attention to what Matthew says. He notes that Jesus took "a" cup. That one-letter word has a powerful message for us: There is no power in this ordinary cup. Rather, the power lies in the meaning.

The Lord's Supper cup or cups are just ordinary vessel(s) that contain ordinary contents, the fruit of the vine. Those two ordinary things have an extraordinary meaning. The cup may be an ordinary vessel, but it's a vessel that gives an extraordinary message to all of us. The message that the blood of Jesus would be spilled so that the New Covenant could begin (Hebrews 9:16). Understand that the value should not be placed on this ordinary cup but rather on the meaning of the contents in the cup.

Today, I will…praise God that He can take an ordinary vessel and have it contain an extraordinary message.

TUESDAY
A Cup of Anguish
Today's Scripture: Matthew 20:22-23; 26:39

Do you ever use the word "anguish" in your everyday conversations? It is a powerful word. The Oxford English Dictionary defines "anguish" as "physical pain or suffering, especially intense bodily pain; agony, torment" or "severe mental suffering or distress; intense grief or sorrow." Physical and mental torture is a simpler way to define it. Luke's account of Jesus' in the garden captures what it means to be in agony. "And being in agony he prayed more earnestly; and his sweat became like great drops of blood falling down to the ground" (Luke 22:44, ESV).

Does anguish come to mind when you drink the cup during the Lord's Supper on Sunday? Do you think about the anguish that Jesus went through? Do you focus on the blood that was spilled? Not only the blood that spilled while He was flogged and while He hung from a cross, but also while He was praying to the Father that this cup could pass from Him. Jesus used the "cup" synonymously with the intense suffering He would go through so that His blood could be spilled. Jesus was approached by James and John's mom in Matthew 20:20-21 asking if her two boys could sit on His right and left in His Kingdom. Jesus responds, "You do not know what you are asking. Are you able to drink the cup that I am to drink?" (Matthew 20:22, ESV). What cup was Jesus about to drink? Earlier in the text, Jesus explains to His disciples the anguish He would face. That was the same cup He prayed three times to pass from Him in Matthew 26:39. What is fascinating about that prayer is the ending, "Nevertheless, not as I will, but as you will" (Matthew 26:39, ESV). What an example of submission and selflessness!

How much anguish would be too much for you to endure? Could you face the flogging? Could you carry the cross? Could you listen to nails being driven through your hands and ankles? I know I wouldn't be able to go through much, but I am truly thankful Jesus did.

Today, I will…be thankful for the anguish Jesus was willing to go through on my behalf.

A Cup of Redemption
Today's Scripture: Exodus 6:6-7

It is morning time, and you are about to leave the house. What is your go-to cup for your coffee as you head out the door? Are there a few options that you can choose from? Or maybe you use a cup that your spouse wishes they could get their hands on to wash it. You have used it over and over, and the inside is stained from the coffee. Cups are a popular commodity. There are big ones, small ones, and colorful ones. We have particular cups for particular things. During the days of Jesus, the Jews also were particular about cups.

Traditionally, during the Passover meal, each person would have four cups to drink from. Each cup was to be drank during a certain part of the meal (Mishnah Pesahim 10:1-7). Before each cup was drunk, the Jews would recite a portion of Exodus 6:6-7. "Say therefore to the people of Israel, 'I am the Lord, and I will bring you out from under the burdens of the Egyptians, and I will deliver you from slavery to them, and I will redeem you with an outstretched arm and with great acts of judgment. I will take you to be my people, and I will be your God, and you shall know that I am the Lord your God, who has brought you out from under the burdens of the Egyptians" (Exodus 6:6-7, ESV).

In Matthew 26:27, we read about Jesus taking the cup and blessing it. Which cup did He use? Luke 22:20 tells us that after the completion of the meal, Jesus took the cup and blessed it. Matthew and Mark both record that this was during the meal. They were not as detailed as Luke. The International Standard Bible Encyclopedia says that this was the third cup that had been drunk. If true, this cup would have coincided with "I will redeem you" from Exodus 6:6, giving this cup the title of "the cup of redemption."

How appropriately titled! Jesus came to redeem us from our sins. The payment was His blood. The emblem that represented this was the fruit of the vine contained in the cup. Paul tells us, "We have redemption through his blood" (Ephesians 1:7, ESV). Praise be to God for the redeeming blood of His Son.

Today, I will...write out Exodus 6:6-7 four times and praise God for the redeeming blood of His Son.

A Cup Worth Blessing
Today's Scripture: 1 Corinthians 10:16

Are you familiar with the famous chef Emeril Lagasse? He is the TV chef who screamed "BAM" when he added seasoning to the dish he was cooking. When you look up why Emeril would shout "BAM," it was initially just a way to keep the production crew awake during filming.

When we say the blessing for the food we are about to eat, what do you imagine God doing to your food? I imagine God screaming "BAM" and tossing a little blessing on the food. I wonder if that same thought process has filtered into the Lord's Supper prayers. Sometimes, it seems that we think God is sprinkling a little "something extra" in the fruit of the vine when we say the blessing during the Lord's supper. We ask God to please bless the cup which contains the fruit of the vine. What do we expect God to do when we ask God to bless the cup? Are we expecting Him to sprinkle a little special dust in the cup? What should be our expectation?

Matthew 26:27 reads, "And he took a cup, and when he had given thanks he gave it to them" (ESV). I want you to notice that Jesus "had given thanks" for the cup. In 1 Corinthians 10:16, Paul writes, "The cup of blessing that we bless, is it not a participation in the blood of Christ?" (ESV). We bless the cup, and we give thanks for the cup. Paul and Jesus help us see fully what the blessing of the cup is all about. We are giving thanks to God for the redeeming blood of Christ. We are not asking God to put a little extra "BAM" in the grape juice. We recognize what has been offered for the payment of our sins, and because of that, we spend time in prayer and reverence as we say a blessing or a thanksgiving praise to God.

Today, I will…give thanks to God at each meal and snack that I eat.

A Cup for All
Today's Scripture: Matthew 26:27

I was not built to play basketball. I am 6'3", but I have what some may call an adverse relationship with gravity. Gravity does not allow me to jump very high. I was built to push people, and that helped me excel on the offensive line in football. All people are not meant to be involved in all sports, but God invites all people to come into His Kingdom (1 Timothy 2:4; 2 Peter 3:9).

God does not exclude anyone from coming to His table in the Kingdom. Take a close look at what Jesus says in Matthew 26:27 concerning the cup. "Drink of it, all of you" (ESV). Notice two very important observations from Jesus' words.

The first important observation is that Jesus commanded everyone at the table to drink. Matthew is the only account that uses this command. We imply from this observation that drinking the cup is not optional. We have been commanded to drink, so we drink. I grew up in a popular denomination that partook of the Lord's Supper every Sunday. When I observed and participated in this memorial, I noticed that some people did not partake in the fruit of the vine. I even joined them some days. Why? Why would they do that? Why would I do that? Why would I not want to partake of the fruit of the vine? It represents the blood shed for me. Also, we have been commanded. Drinking the cup is not optional.

The second important observation is that Jesus said for all to drink. Once we have obeyed the Gospel, we are qualified to partake of the Lord's Supper. No matter who we are. God is not a respecter of persons (Romans 2:11). He does not care if you are tall, big, small, rich, poor, or even gravitationally challenged. Jesus does not exclude anyone from drinking the cup. He even includes the man who will betray Him in this last supper. It is an incredible feeling to know that Jesus invites me to drink the cup.

Today, I will…be thankful that God invites all to drink of the cup.

Table Meditation
Scripture: Genesis 31:51-55

There is an old Bedouin tradition that is still practiced today where two parties may settle a conflict by participating in negotiations, which culminate in a meal known as sulha in the Arabic language. It is a meal of reconciliation. Biblically, this seems to be the meal that the former shepherd boy, David, references in Psalm 23:5. Perhaps its earliest origins are reflected in Genesis 31:51-55, where Jacob and his family flee home to the Promised Land. On the 10th day of this journey, Laban overtakes their caravan, but God has intervened in a dream and they have a final meal together in peace. Traditionally, once the sulha meal is eaten, the offended parties are never allowed to bring up the incident again. Relations were to continue as if the offense never happened.

As we partake of the Lord's Supper, we participate in a relatively simple meal that is steeped in layers of meaning and rooted in the Passover feast. On a basic, but profound, level it is a memorial meal that honors the reconciliation of man to God. This restoration is what the Father accomplished through the obedient work of Christ the Son.

Participation in this meal is both personal and corporate. I take the bread representing his body, knowing full well it should have been me on that cross, not him. I have done nothing and could do nothing to deserve this gift. While brothers and sisters around the world also partake of the fruit of the vine, I am struck with the blessed idea that he did not just take my place on the cross. His worthy blood cleanses us and redeems us for life everlasting in heaven.

Because of my obedience to His Will, I am justified. The scroll recording my sins has been cleaned by the blood of the Lamb. I am reconciled!

MONDAY
The Blood of the New Covenant
Today's Scripture: Hebrews 8-9

If you watch television long enough, you will see a commercial advertising something as "new and improved." Whether it is a product you are familiar with or not, when you hear words like "new" or "improved," you understand the company is marketing its product as being greater than the previous or older model.

Not long before He would be betrayed and crucified, Jesus sat in an upper room with His disciples and instituted the Lord's Supper (Matthew 26:26-30). Jesus used the bread and the fruit of the vine as a symbol for His body and His blood. After He had given them the bread, Jesus took a cup and told His disciples to drink it. Then He said, "For this is my blood of the covenant, which is poured out for many for the forgiveness of sins" (Matthew 26:28, ESV).

Notice the phrase "blood of the covenant." A covenant was a binding agreement between two groups that was often sealed by blood. Both Luke and Paul refer to the blood of the covenant as the "new" covenant (Luke 22:20; 1 Corinthians 11:25) in contrast to the previous covenant God made with Israel at Mount Sinai, which used the blood of bulls (Exodus 19 & 24; Deuteronomy 5:1-5).

The sacrifice of Jesus created a new relationship, or covenant, with God (Jeremiah 31:31-34), one dependent upon the blood of the perfect lamb. The death of Jesus would bring an end to the old covenant (Colossians 2:14) and introduce a new, even better covenant between man and God (Hebrews 8:5-13; 9:11-17).

As we participate in the Lord's Supper each week and focus on the fruit of the vine, may we never forget the wonderful covenant we are now a part of because of the blood Jesus shed. Jesus' death brought us into a new and much better covenant with God.

Today, I will…give thanks to God for the new covenant I am a part of because of the blood that Jesus shed.

TUESDAY
My Blood
Today's Scripture: Philippians 2:1-11

Reconciling the deity of Jesus with the humanity of Jesus is challenging. Sometimes, we spend so much time thinking about the divinity of Jesus that we overlook His human characteristics. Was Jesus divine? Of course He was. He was with God from the very beginning (John 1:1-3). Was Jesus human? Absolutely! The apostle John said, "And the Word became flesh and dwelt among us, and we have seen his glory, glory as the only Son from the Father, full of grace and truth" (John 1:14, ESV). Although Jesus was fully God, while He was walking on this earth, He was just as much a human as the rest of us. Jesus experienced many of the same human feelings, temptations, and pains as the rest of us (Hebrews 4:14-16).

As Jesus instituted the Lord's Supper, He told His disciples that the contents of the cup, the fruit of the vine, represented something very special. Jesus said, "For this is my blood of the covenant, which is poured out for many for the forgiveness of sins" (Matthew 26:28, ESV). We need to see how personal this was for Jesus. Jesus wanted His disciples to understand the blood that created this new covenant was His very own blood. The blood of sacrificial animals was not sufficient. Jesus willingly experienced intense pain and suffering and shed His blood for each of us.

When we gather around the table each Lord's Day and remember the sacrifice Jesus made on Calvary's cross, may we never forget that He was very much human when He was enduring all that pain (Philippians 2:5-8). Jesus could have called twelve legions of angels, but He didn't (Matthew 26:53). Instead, He bravely and sacrificially shed His blood as the perfect and spotless lamb of God (1 Peter 1:19).

Today, I will…think about the blood Jesus shed and the pain He experienced and say a prayer of thanksgiving that He suffered and died for me.

WEDNESDAY
He Chose the Blood
Today's Scripture: John 10:1-18

At some point in your life, you have done something to cause your body to bleed. You may have fallen and scraped a knee. You may have cut yourself or caused a gash in your skin. While I wasn't there to see how you responded, I guess that you cleaned yourself up and worked to stop the bleeding. Our response to bleeding is to try and stop the flow of blood. But that was not the case with Jesus. While He could have prevented himself from bleeding by escaping death on the cross, instead, He chose the blood.

We make sacrifices for those we love. As a friend, you make sacrifices for those friendships. And certainly, if you are married or if you are a parent, sacrifices are an integral part of those relationships. But here's the truth: most of us are only willing to make great sacrifices for people we love and are close with.

I would be willing to give my life to save the lives of my wife and children. I'm sure many of us feel the same way. As much as I love people, I do not think I would be willing to suffer and die a cruel death for just anyone. But that is exactly what Jesus did.

Jesus told His disciples that His blood for the new covenant was being poured out for many (Matthew 26:28). When Jesus suffered and died on the cross, it was not just for those closest to Him. Jesus did not allow His blood to be poured out for a select few, but for "many," for all people (Hebrews 2:9; I John 2:2).

Jesus chose the blood not just for His closest friends and apostles, He chose the blood for all mankind. He chose the blood for you and for me. When we partake of the Lord's Supper, let's remember that Jesus chose to sacrifice His life so that we can live.

Today, I will…meditate on the choice Jesus made to shed His blood for me.

THURSDAY
There Is Power in the Blood
Today's Scripture: Ephesians 2

In 1899, Lewis E. Jones wrote the words to a hymn that has been performed by Dolly Parton, Marty Robbins, Alan Jackson, and Bill Gaither. Many of us are very familiar with this song:

> "Would you be free from the burden of sin?
>
> There's power in the blood, power in the blood.
>
> Would you o'er evil a victory win?
>
> There's wonderful power in the blood."

"There's Power in the Blood" is a great song to sing, but the message behind those words is even greater. When Jesus instituted the Lord's Supper, He told His disciples that His blood was going to be poured out for many for the forgiveness of sins (Matthew 26:28). Jesus' blood had to be poured out so that you and I could have our sins forgiven.

At one time, we were dead in our trespasses and sins, separated from Christ, and without hope because we were without God (Ephesians 2:1, 12). Because of Jesus and His sacrifice on the cross, we who were once far off have been brought near by the blood of Christ (Ephesians 2:13).

The sacrifice of blood has always been an essential means of atonement. Every year, the Israelites offered blood sacrifices to atone for their sins (Leviticus 16). However, the blood from those animal sacrifices could never truly take away sin (Hebrews 10:1-4). Instead, Jesus came to earth and shed His blood so we might have forgiveness of our sins (Hebrews 9:11-28).

The wages of sin is death (Romans 6:23), and death is exactly what you and I deserve. But because of the blood of Jesus, we have hope. His blood is powerful enough to cleanse us from all our sins (1 John 1:5-10). Every time we gather around the table of our Lord, may we reflect on the precious blood that was shed and the wonder-working power of that blood.

Today, I will…remember the wonder-working power of the blood of Jesus.

FRIDAY
Accessing the Blood
Today's Scripture: Romans 6:1-14

Today, we still feel the impact of the words Jesus spoke to introduce the Lord's Supper to His disciples. Jesus shed His precious blood on Calvary's cross for all mankind so that we could have forgiveness for our sins. But as we bring this week's thoughts to a close, we cannot meditate on the blood of Jesus without talking about how we access the blood for the forgiveness of sins.

All of us need God's forgiveness for our sins (Isaiah 1:16). And the only thing that will forgive us of those sins is the blood of Jesus. In Romans 6:3-4, Paul tells us that baptism represents the death, burial, and resurrection of Jesus. In Acts 22:16, we see that Ananias told Paul, "And now why do you wait? Rise and be baptized and wash away your sins, calling on his name" (ESV). Notice the phrase "wash away your sins." The only way for our sins to be washed away is by being baptized into the blood of Jesus Christ. When we do that, we receive the forgiveness of our sins (Acts 2:38).

Every week, we participate in the sacred memorial feast of our Lord. Taking the cup reminds us that Jesus poured out His precious blood for each one of us so we can have the forgiveness of our sins and the hope of eternal life (Romans 6:23). When we partake of the Lord's Supper, we can't only go through the motions as if what we are doing is not important. What we do each week is of great importance because it is a reminder of what Jesus did for us. He bled and died so that you and I did not have to. Praise be to God for His marvelous love in sending His Son to be the sacrifice for us.

Today, I will…reflect on the significance of baptism and the access it provides to the cleansing blood of Jesus Christ.

Table Meditation
Scripture: Revelation 5:1-14

In Revelation 5, God had a scroll in His hand. A strong angel then asked, "Who is worthy to open the scroll?" No one was able to open it. Someone then said, in essence, "I know one who can open the scroll!" Then, in the midst of the throne, a lamb appeared and took the scroll. Some in heaven erupted in song, "Worthy are you to take the scroll and to open its seals, for you were slain, and by your blood you ransomed people for God" (Revelation 5:9, ESV). The rest of heaven joined in saying, "Worthy is the Lamb who was slain, to receive power and wealth and wisdom and might and honor and glory and blessing!" (Revelation 5:12, ESV).

Before you eat this bread representing the body of Christ, whisper, "You are worthy!" Do the same as you drink the cup. For Jesus IS worthy of this memorial that we Christians will partake of until time is no more.

MONDAY
Something to Remember
Today's Scripture: Matthew 26:29

"I tell you I will not drink again of this fruit of the vine until that day when I drink it new with you in my Father's kingdom" (Matthew 26:29). The institution of the Lord's Supper was Jesus reminder to his disciples to remember and not forget. We look back and remember what Christ did for us, and face sobering the reality of the price of our salvation.

On a recent Memorial Day weekend my father and I drove several hundred miles to decorate the graves of our family members. We did it to pay respect to those whose impact on our lives cannot be overstated. We remember because we must not forget. My new grandson is named Thomas Monan, who was named for my great-grandfather who died in 1941. As I grow older, the words of Rudyard Kipling ring true: "Lord God of Hosts, be with us yet, lest we forget —lest we forget!"

When Christians gather around the table each week, we remember the one who died so that we might live. We remember that "for our sake He made Him to be sin who knew no sin, so that in him we might become the righteousness of God" (2 Corinthians 5:21).

Martin Luther describes the power found in this remembrance: "The operative cause of the Supper is the Word and institution of Christ, who ordained it. The substance is bread and wine, prefiguring the true body and blood of Christ, which is spiritually received by faith. The final cause of instituting this is the benefit and the fruit, the strengthening of our faith, not doubting that Christ's body and blood were given and shed for us, and that our sins by Christ's death certainly are forgiven."[1]

Today, I will… remember the love of Jesus that led him to walk the path to the cross.

---

[1] Luther, Martin. *Table Talk.* https://ccel.org/ccel/luther/tabletalk/tabletalk.

TUESDAY
Something to Practice
Today's Scripture: Matthew 26:29

Jesus instituted the Lord's Supper while he was at the table with his apostles. For two millennia, Christians have continued to follow His example. Dr. Everett Ferguson, one of the world's pre-eminent scholars on the subject of early Christianity, writes: "The Lord's Supper is our primary reason, but not our only reason, for coming together as a church. The Lord's Supper is the church's act of thanksgiving for and remembrance of the death and resurrection of Jesus. It is our communion with the Lord and with one another (1 Corinthians 10:16)."

It is mystifying that most of the Protestant world does everything it can to downplay, ignore, and reject the weekly observance of communion. In 1825 Alexander Campbell noted, "Much darkness and superstition are found in the minds and exhibited in the practice of the devout annual, semi-annual, and quarterly observers of the breaking of bread. They generally make a Jewish Passover of it…"

When churches make space in their services for everything except the Lord's Supper, the question is, "Why? Jesus specifically commands His followers "Do this in remembrance of me" (Luke 22:19). How anyone could reject this for a musical selection is baffling. When seeker-sensitive churches started springing up, they quickly decided that potential attendees preferred a concert over an ancient ritual mentioning blood, suffering, and death.

No matter. We are to practice what Jesus commands, not what focus groups prefer.

Today, I will… commit myself to a weekly appointment with the Lord at His table.

Something to Examine
Today's Scripture: Matthew 26:29

The Lord's Supper provides the rare and powerful opportunity for self-introspection: "Whoever, therefore, eats the bread or drinks the cup of the Lord in an unworthy manner will be guilty concerning the body and blood of the Lord. Let a person examine himself, then, and so eat of the bread and drink of the cup. For anyone who eats and drinks without discerning the body eats and drinks judgment on himself. That is why many of you are weak and ill, and some have died" (1 Corinthians 11:27-30).

Several questions come to mind: Are we fully present in taking the Supper? Are we thinking of other things? Are we just going through the motions? And, finally—Are we truly following the Lord or just pretending?

There is a haunting line in the Gospels we dare not miss: "While he was still speaking, Judas came, one of the twelve..." (Matthew 26:47). The betrayal by a friend still stings as we read of it today. Dietrich Bonhoeffer writes:

> *Judas, one of the twelve.* Do we feel anything of the horror with which the evangelist wrote this little phrase? Judas, one of the twelve—what else was there to say? Judas, one of the twelve—this says that it was impossible that this happened. And yet happen it did.

As we contemplate the change that happened with Judas, we need to look deeply within our own hearts. Do we love Jesus? Is he worthy of our allegiance? Will we follow him into the dark? Let the Lord's table be the place where we examine ourselves.

Today, I will... engage in a fearless, searching examination of my commitment to Christ.

THURSDAY
Something to Proclaim
Today's Scripture: Matthew 26:29

The act of eating the bread and drinking the cup on the first day of the week is the most important function of the Christian assembly. The apostle Paul declares, "For as often as you eat this bread and drink the cup, you proclaim the Lord's death until he comes" (1 Corinthians 11:26).

This means that every Christian is preaching a sermon every time the Supper is observed. The Gospel is comprised of the death, burial and resurrection of Christ. The taking of the bread and cup is the proclamation of God's plan of salvation (1 Corinthians 15:3-4). Everett Ferguson writes,

> The church gathers on the first day of the week to take the Lord's Supper. We neither invite to the table nor exclude from it. We do not invite—the Lord has already issued the invitation. We exclude in a formal way only our own members who are under the discipline of the church.

The Lord's Supper is a church act. It is not, biblically speaking, a sacrament according to the accepted definition of sacrament, whether viewed as the outward sign of an inward grace or as an act that itself conveys grace simply by its performance. Nor is it a general religious act of devotion that can be engaged in at any time. In this respect, it is unlike prayer or song.

The Lord's Supper belongs in the setting of the gathered church. When Jesus instituted the Lord's Supper, He was meeting at the table with His apostles (Luke 22:14). The apostles represented the soon-to-be-established church, of which they were the beginning group.

When Paul gave instructions to the Corinthian Christians for the proper observance of the Lord's Supper, he did so for the occasions "when you come together as a church" or in church (1 Corinthians 11:18-20). The Lord's Supper is a communion of the saved (10:16-17,21), not a means of grace to the unsaved. It is out of place in contexts other than the gathered church.

The appointed day of observance for the Lord's Supper is the first day of the week, the day of the resurrection. It has no special relevance on another day. Although the Lord's Supper was instituted on (probably) a Thursday night, only after the crucifixion could it be a remembrance of Jesus' death and only after the resurrection could it be a proclamation of the resurrection (1 Corinthians 11:23-26).

Today, I will... proclaim that Jesus is the only name under heaven given among men by which we must be saved.

FRIDAY
Something to Celebrate
Today's Scripture: Matthew 26:29

Most who take the Lord's Supper do so with a sense of sadness and reverence. Alexander Campbell noted the infrequent occasions on which the Supper was observed in the Protestant world with "a morose piety and an awful affliction of soul and body, expressed in fasting, long prayers, and sad countenances on sundry days of humiliation, fasting, and preparation. And the only joy exhibited on the occasion is that it is all over..."

By contrast, Campbell describes the way the intelligent Christian views this sacred institution in a different light:

It is to him as sacred and solemn as prayer to God, and as joyful as the hope of immortality and eternal life. His hope before God, springing from the death of his Son, is gratefully exhibited and expressed by him in the observance of this institution. While he participates of the symbolic loaf, he shews his faith in...the Bread of life. While he tastes the emblematic cup, he remembers the new covenant confirmed by the blood of the Lord. With sacred joy and blissful hope he hears the Saviour says, "This is my body broken — this is my blood shed for you." When he reaches forth those lively emblems of his Saviour's love to his Christian brethren, the philanthropy of God fills his heart, and excites correspondent feelings to those sharing with him the salvation of the Lord. Here he knows no man after the flesh. Ties that spring from eternal love, revealed in blood and addressed to his senses in symbols adapted to the whole man, draw forth all that is within him of complacent affection and feeling to those joint heirs with him of the grace of eternal life.

We need to understand the celebratory aspect of the Lord's Supper. It is not comparable to a pep rally; it is the solemn satisfaction of knowing that Christ has conquered every enemy, with death as the final foe. That is something to celebrate.

Today, I will... celebrate the Good News of Jesus.

Table Meditation
Scripture: 1 Corinthians 10:16

We call it "The Lord's Supper," "The Breaking of Bread," "The Lord's Table," and "Communion." My favorite is "Communion!" When we think of the word in general terms, we think of the sharing of a feeling and a thought. For the Christian, Paul says in 1 Corinthians 10:16, "The cup of blessing which we bless, is it not the communion of the blood of Christ? The bread which we break, is it not the communion of the body of Christ?" (NKJV). The ESV uses the word "participation" instead of "communion." The Lord's Supper is a participation with Christ concerning His death.

Something else happens that is a very beautiful thing. This participation is not only with Christ but with each other as Christians. Before changes brought about by COVID-19 occurred, I can remember times when I thought about asking the church to wait until we all received the bread, then we could take it together. However, I never did that. Then came COVID-19, and we began using the disposable containers. There was nothing wrong with the way it had been done in the past. But for me, it is a sweeter kind of communion when we all partake of the bread at the same time, and then the fruit of the vine at the same time, and while Christ meets us there!

In 1922, Tillit S. Teddlie wrote these words: "When we meet in sweet communion where the feast divine is spread; hearts are brought in closer union while partaking of the bread. Precious feast all else surpassing, wondrous love for you and me, while we feast Christ gently whispers; 'Do this in my memory.'"

Dining with Christ
Today's Scripture: Mark 14:18-21

Meals were an important part of the ministry of Jesus. He sat at many tables and shared food with many people. Jesus ate with friends, enemies, Pharisees, and tax collectors. He dined during His ministry and after His resurrection. He promises to eat and drink with us anew in the kingdom of God! To Jesus, the meal matters.

As His life draws near to its purposeful end, He desires to have one last meal (Mark 14:18). This meal is with His twelve disciples, His friends. This meal is memorable, meaningful, and beautiful, but also somber and tragic. This final supper will be remembered and reenacted by His followers for thousands of years and throughout the globe. Yet this meal is shrouded with imagery of betrayal, abandonment, suffering, and death.

In this meal, Jesus redefines the significance of various Passover foods. The cup that was shared is the blood of His covenant. The bread that was consumed is His body. The blood of the covenant is no longer the blood of some animal but of the perfect Son of God Himself, who willingly offered Himself for us. As the meal begins, Jesus declares that one of His disciples will betray Him (Mark 14:18). Right after the meal, Jesus tells His disciples that they will all fall away. Soon, He is betrayed, arrested, denied, and abandoned. Humanity's failures are present before, during, and after the meal.

Yet, Jesus still shared this meal. And He still promises to share it again (Mark 14:25). Why? Because to Jesus, the meal matters. It matters during this age and in the age to come. The meal brings people together. The meal is a symbol of the kingdom. Of all the possible ways Jesus could have provided for us to gather and remember Him every week, He chose the Lord's Supper; that is, He chose His meal.

Today, I will…contemplate the significance of shared meals. I will dine with my brothers and sisters and follow the example of Jesus.

TUESDAY
Failure at the Table
Today's Scripture: Mark 14:18-21

Jesus says something that surely makes everyone uncomfortable. Mark introduces this meal with these words: "And as they were reclining at table and eating, Jesus said, 'Truly, I say to you, one of you will betray Me, one who is eating with Me'" (Mark 14:18, ESV). Notice the structure of this verse. It begins with them reclining together around a table. The table forms a sacred bond among followers of Jesus. We continue to gather around the Lord's table (1 Corinthians 10:21). Next, the word "eating" is used twice. Once to introduce the words of Jesus and a second time near the conclusion of His words. Eating is an act of fellowship and unity. It was practiced regularly by the early church in imitation of the Lord (Acts 2:42, 46). Right in the middle is the pivotal word "betray."

Even in His final meal, surrounded by friends and disciples, reclining at the table and eating, He is with His betrayer. He is with a denier. He is with those who will abandon Him. Saying "goodbye" is hard enough. But when the farewell is marred by failures, pains, and regrets, it becomes excruciating. The disciples feel "grieved" as they eat with Jesus (Mark 14:19).

The table can never be about the perfection of those sitting around it. Jesus ate with tax collectors and sinners regularly. Jesus ate with the Pharisees. And even when He ate with His disciples, He was still eating with sinners. When we take the Lord's Supper, we will never be surrounded by perfect people. The meal is a reminder of the perfection of our Lord, who invites us to it. The meal celebrates His perfect sacrifice. It is a thanksgiving for His perfect forgiveness.

Today, I will…commit to being present at the table as one of many imperfect participants welcomed by the Lord.

WEDNESDAY
Affirming Our Commitment
Today's Scripture: Mark 14:18-21

A paragraph in Psalm 41 is especially relevant to our text. Note these words, "They say, 'A deadly thing is poured out on him; he will not rise again from where he lies.' Even my close friend whom I trusted, who ate my bread, has lifted his heel against me. But you, O Lord, be gracious to me, and raise me up, that I may repay them" (Psalm 41:8-10, ESV). The phrase, "who ate my bread" is likely alluded to by Jesus when He says, "one who is eating with Me" (Mark 14:18). The connection is clearer when comparing the Greek of Mark 14:18 to the Septuagint translation of the Psalm.

Both in Psalm 41 and during the Last Supper, a meal—which often symbolizes friendship and unity—has become a setting for betrayal. After Jesus told His disciples that one of them would betray Him, "They began to be grieved and to say to Him one by one, 'Surely not I?'" (Mark 14:19, NASB 2020). The disciples began to ask, grammatically construed to indicate a negative answer, "Certainly I am not the betrayer, right?" That's an important question to ask ourselves.

We eat the Lord's Meal (Supper) weekly. We eat as honored guests at the Lord's Table. Are we unified with Him? Do we live in a way that honors Him? Do we betray Him when we are with our friends or facing temptation? We like to think that we would never be the betrayer. We like to think, like Peter, that we would never betray Him and that we will never fall (Mark 14:19, 29). Sometimes, the spirit is willing, but the flesh is weak.

Today, I will… reaffirm my commitment to be faithful to Jesus. I will choose Him and follow Him daily. I will stand and even suffer with Him if that is what I am called to do. I will never betray my Lord.

THURSDAY
All Signs Point to Judas
Today's Scripture: Mark 14:18-21

Jesus has predicted His betrayal. This whole paragraph centers on that betrayal. The words "betray" and "betrayed" are used in verses 18 and 21 to bookend the scene. We know that the betrayer is Judas. Mark told us that back in Mark 3:19. Mark 14:1-11 offers a contrast between a woman who gave her most expensive gift to honor Jesus and Judas who greedily betrayed Him for money. Judas will not only share a meal with Jesus but will also kiss Him (Mark 14:44). Both of these signs of loyalty and friendship are insincerely offered in cruel betrayal. His true loyalty is to wealth.

Rather than bluntly stating that Judas was the betrayer, Jesus instead offers several clues about who the betrayer will be. Verses 18 and 20 mirror each other. Verse 18 says, "one of you," while verse 20 says, "one of the twelve." Verse 18 says, "one who is eating with Me," while verse 20 says, "one who dips with Me in the bowl." It seems that these clues did not demonstratively point to Judas specifically, as the disciples all defend themselves, and there is no major reaction against Judas.

Our scene does not directly identify Judas as the betrayer, but it does pronounce a "Woe to that man by whom the Son of Man is betrayed!" (Mark 14:21, ESV). A better translation would be "through whom" instead of "by whom." This suggests that Judas is the agent through whom Jesus is betrayed, but Judas is perhaps serving another. The Gospel of John says that satan put the betrayal into Judas' heart (John 13:1) and then entered His heart (John 13:27).

Judas, however, is personally responsible for working with satan to betray the Lord. Judas, through greed, opened up the door to evil in his life. He became the agent through whom the greatest evil took place.

Today, I will…close the door to satan in my life. I will offer my kiss (love) to the Lord and eat at His table with sincerity and truth.

Consequences
Today's Scripture: Mark 14:18-21

What you do matters. Our actions have consequences. While reclining around the table, Jesus discusses the consequences of Judas' betrayal. Jesus says, "For the Son of Man goes as it is written of Him, but woe to that man by whom the Son of Man is betrayed! It would have been better for that man if he had not been born" (Mark 14:21, ESV).

This passage suggests that one consequence of the betrayal is that "the Son of Man goes..." To "go" is the language of leaving one place for another. This is a metaphor for death. The "Son of Man," described in Daniel 7, is given a kingdom and glory and praise from all the nations (Daniel 7:13-14). That unexpectedly happens through His death and resurrection.

Another consequence of Judas' betrayal is that the Lord pronounced "Woe" upon Him. Then, Jesus says it would have been "good" or "better" for Judas to have never been born. His life and existence became a net negative. There will be eternal consequences for his actions. John describes Him as the one lost "son of destruction" (John 17:12). Judas loses his life and soul.

There are some tragic stories in the Bible. The life of Judas is one of them. We do not know much about him, but we know he had one of the greatest opportunities the world has ever seen. He could have done great things in the kingdom. He could have reclined at the table with Abraham, Isaac, and Jacob. He could have been a ruler in the age to come (Matthew 19:28). He could have lived in the presence of God for eternity. But he traded it for some extra change in his pocket. Yet, God can often turn tragedy into opportunity. God used the betrayal of Joseph by his brothers to save the lives of many (Genesis 50:20). Likewise, God used Judas' betrayal to bring about His kingdom and the salvation of mankind.

Today, I will...rejoice in the salvation offered through the Lord as I prepare for the Lord's Supper.

Table Meditation
Scripture: Isaiah 53:4-6

Our time at the Lord's table is certainly "collective." It is a sharing with each other; it is a communion (common union). We should certainly be mindful that partaking of these emblems is something we do as a group, together on the first day of each week.

But it is also individual. What WE proclaim at the table, the Lord's death—1 Corinthians 11:26—should be deeply personal and, in many ways, individual. For example, consider the powerful statements of Isaiah 53. This text describes what Jesus endured for ALL of us. But do we sometimes get lost in the collective WE of these statements? Do we fail to remember the part each one of us has played in all of this? As we read this passage, notice how much more personal this passage becomes when WE becomes ME. Replace WE with I and OUR with MY.

> Isaiah 53:4–6 (NASB 1995)
>
> Surely ~~our~~ MY griefs He Himself bore, And ~~our~~ MY sorrows He carried; Yet ~~we ourselves~~ I MYSELF esteemed Him stricken, Smitten of God, and afflicted.
>
> But He was pierced through for ~~our~~ MY transgressions, He was crushed for ~~our~~ MY iniquities; The chastening for ~~our~~ MY well-being fell upon Him, And by His scourging ~~we are~~ I AM healed.
>
> ~~All of us~~ I like a sheep have gone astray, ~~Each of us has~~ I HAVE turned to ~~his~~ MY own way; But the Lord has caused the iniquity of ~~us all~~ ME to fall on Him.

As we share these emblems TOGETHER may we never get lost in the collective WE, but always be mindful of what it means to ME.

Remember
Today's Scripture: Luke 22:1-19

I remember when my father died early on December 26, 2008, at 3:15 AM. A few years later, my mother died on October 28, 2017. Then, most recently, my baby sister died on June 18, 2021. As you can imagine, each time, I had a rush of memories that poured over me. Then came a flood of tears. I simply wanted to scream, "Will somebody please remember my dad, mother, and sister, please do not forget them!"

We are almost programmed to remember dates. New Year's Day—January 1, Independence Day—July 4, November 11—Veterans Day, Memorial Day—the last Monday of May, Pearl Harbor Day—December 7, 1941, and many other significant days in our lives. They call us to remember.

In the Old Testament, there were many memorials and days of remembrance. There are at least three cases of biblical characters laying memorial stones, and these become significant locations throughout biblical history. Bethel is where Jacob memorialized his vision. Gilgal is where Joshua commemorated the Israelites' miraculous entrance into the Promised Land. Samuel erects an Ebenezer stone after God thwarts the Philistine's attack. The Ebenezer stone is so memorialized we have it mentioned in one of our well-known hymns, "Come Thou Fount of Every Blessing." 1 Samuel 7:7-12 depicts the Israelites under imminent attack from the Philistines. God leads them to victory, so Samuel erects a large stone and names it "Ebenezer," meaning "the stone of help." Samuel recognized the source of their victory and publicly declared it. By permanently commemorating God's goodness, it ensured that the Israelites would not forget God's grace. The memorial stones made sure that all glory went to God.

Should we as Christians not pause and remember each Lord's Day remembering Jesus Christ in His death burial and resurrection? The Lord's Supper calls us to remember. Plan now to partake of the holy feast on each Sunday this year and remember our Lord and Savior.

Today, I will…begin preparing for the sacred feast on Sunday. Oh, what a Savior!

Remember to Remember

Today's Scripture: 1 Corinthians 11:23-26

When we are called to remember, our deepest thoughts fly to the forefront of our minds. These are usually strong thoughts, oftentimes bringing with them a great deal of emotion. Maybe there is great joy after seeing a picture of your grandchildren's first day at school, all dressed and anxious about what the new year will bring. Perhaps you saw a scene in a movie that just grabbed your heart, and it took your breath away. Maybe you saw a television commercial during holiday time, and you were swept away to a simpler time around a warm fire, sipping a cup of hot cocoa and surrounded by family and friends.

Psychologists tell us that nothing stirs a memory more than smell. I can recall going to my parents' house after my dad died. Just walking into that old house—the memory of certain smells washed over me like a huge wave of emotion. I made a quick trip to the bathroom, where my dad shaved with an old shaving brush in a shaver's mug and some Old Spice shave crème. I still have a bottle of his Old Spice liquid soap. Each time I smell it, it takes me back to "good times" when he was alive. It is remarkable that a small memory can have such an impression on us, isn't it?

When I was a child and did not know the true meaning of the Lord's Supper, I recall smelling the homemade communion bread as it was passed. Then came the tray with those small glass cups filled with grape juice. Oh, how I loved that church building being permeated with the fragrant smell of grape juice as the tray was passed one to one another.

When Jesus instituted the Lord's Supper in that Upper Room, He was no doubt thinking of me and you and having a rush of memories when we would partake of the Lord's Supper each Sunday!

I have often wondered at the Passover if Jesus witnessed the lambs being slain, the blood poured out on the ground, and the pungent odor of blood in the air. Jesus is our Passover Lamb.

Let us prepare now for The Lord's Day and look forward to the blessed opportunity of communing with Jesus.

Today, I will… pray for God to help me prepare my mind, heart, and soul for Sunday's great feast.

WEDNESDAY
From Heart to Heart
Today's Scripture: 1 Corinthians 11:27-29

The Lord's Supper is a command to be part of our worship service. When we come together, we sing, pray, give back to God, feast on His Word, and commune around the Lord's Table. All these commands come together when we worship as a Body of Christians.

Some would argue that the Lord's Supper is the most important part of worship. I certainly agree, but would we want to leave out any of the other acts of worship? I seriously doubt it. Which one? Giving? Praying? Maybe another? All acts of worship are important.

When I was a teenager, I remember two very special people in our congregation. Their last name was Womack. His name was Ralph, and his wife was Holly. I loved them. He was about as country as country could be, and when Ralph presided at the Lord's Table, I always loved it. There were a few things you could count on in the worship service to always be the same. Ralph's prayers were two of those constants. Ralph would pray this prayer: "Dear God, as this bread is passed from hand to hand, may love flow from heart to heart!" WOW! That was it! Then, when the fruit of the vine was passed, he would pray: "Dear God, as this fruit of the vine is passed from hand to hand, may love flow from heart to heart!" Ralph knew it better than all of us. He had an old deep south drawl; his voice was deep, slow, and weathered, but our brother Ralph had it spot on in his preparation for the prayers around the Lord's Table. Let love flow from heart to heart. He had it right, didn't he?

Sunday when you partake of the emblems of the Lord's Supper, will you plan on letting "your love flow from heart to heart!" If you plan now to be in the right frame of mind and prepare your heart before you go to the church building to worship, prepare to offer your love and thanks to Jesus for His matchless gift of His Body and His blood. His love truly flowed with love to your heart and mine. Let's prepare our hearts.

Today, I will… begin preparing my heart for Sunday worship.

THURSDAY
Prepare Yourself
Today's Scripture: Isaiah 53

If you have flown commercially in the last several years, you know the protocol for takeoff and landing. Usually, the flight crew makes an announcement over the intercom something like this: "Prepare yourself for takeoff." That means buckle up, sit back, and be ready to begin your flight.

On Saturday afternoon it would be good thinking for all Christians to "prepare themselves" for the partaking of the Lord's Supper on Sunday. We should all give more thought in preparation for the communion service than just one song before the supper is served in the worship assembly.

When I see the bread being passed in the Lord's Supper each Sunday, as that tray is being passed from one to another, I have several thoughts:

Did you know for thousands of years the matzo loaf has gone unchanged? The bread is a thin cracker-like loaf made with absolutely zero amount of leavening (leavening allows the bread to rise) making it impossible to rise like regular bread. That is why the loaf is flat.

The traditional matzo is flour combined with water, which is then kneaded, rolled, and baked within 18 minutes. Any later, and it will begin to rise. It must be baked at 500-600 degrees for just under three minutes to ensure no rising takes place.

When I prepare myself for eating the bread I see the brown colored stripes on the bread. Those stripes remind me of Isaiah 53:4-5, "Surely our griefs He Himself bore, And our sorrows He carried; Yet we ourselves esteemed Him stricken, Smitten of God, and afflicted. But He was pierced through for our transgressions, He was crushed for our iniquities; The chastening for our well-being fell upon Him, And by His scourging we are healed" (NASB 1995).

Surely you see those stripes in the bread and it takes you to the beaten and flogged body of our Savior. Prepare yourself for the Lord's Supper, beginning today. It will mean so much more to you.

Today, I will…prepare myself for partaking the Lord's Supper on Sunday.

FRIDAY
Remember and Reflect
Today's Scripture: Luke 22:14-20

Every child who has attended a worship service has seen and smelled the communion tray filled with little cups of grape juice as the tray is passed. In each cup, the grape juice represents the blood of Christ that was shed for us in His suffering on Calvary.

In the 1800's churches that did not use alcoholic wine in the communion service faced a problem. The problem was keeping raw grape juice at room temperature was not easy. There was no refrigeration. The common use of a refrigerator was not popular till 1913. A man named Thomas B. Welch developed a process of pasteurizing grape juice to keep it from fermenting.

Sunday, when the communion tray is passed from one to another, and you see and drink the contents of the cup, those contents remind each person that Jesus poured out His blood on the cross. His side was riven by a soldier's spear. The Bible teaches us that "blood and water" came forth. In John 19:31-34, we read, "Then the Jews, because it was the day of preparation, so that the bodies would not remain on the cross on the Sabbath (for that Sabbath was a high day), asked Pilate that their legs might be broken, and that they might be taken away. So the soldiers came, and broke the legs of the first man and of the other who was crucified with Him; but coming to Jesus, when they saw that He was already dead, they did not break His legs. But one of the soldiers pierced His side with a spear, and immediately blood and water came out" (NASB 1995).

As you read, please reflect on what Jesus did for you. He gave His life blood that you might live. The Lord's Supper should never cause you to yawn or be distracted as you partake. Preparing your mind each day of the week in preparation for the sacred feast will help ensure you focus as the bread and the fruit of the vine are served.

May the Lord's Supper never grow old to you like a ritual. May it truly be a highlight of the worship service as you remember Jesus and His death, burial, and resurrection.

Today, I will…prepare myself to partake of The Lord's Supper in a worthy manner. I will begin today.

HIS FINAL WEEK
THURSDAY
10:30 PM-1:00 AM

Table Meditation
Scripture: Matthew 26:53-54

There have been numerous times in my life, especially my young life, when I did stupid things that I wasn't proud of. In Kindergarten, I got a paddling for being a magician. It just so happened that I'd seen one on TV who pulled a tablecloth off of a table, and all of the dishes stayed on the table! When I tried it on the paint table at school, it didn't quite work out like it did on TV.

I don't know what happened at your house when you came home from getting in trouble at school, but I always worried way more about what was going to happen to me when there weren't teachers and principals around to ensure my safety when I got home to Mom and Dad. They used all means available to impress upon my hiney that they were in charge and meant business when I crossed the line.

But it isn't those times of observing my parents' power that have stuck strongest in my memory when I think about their discipline. Far more embedded in my memory are a few times in later adolescence when I really messed up and really crossed lines and brought embarrassment and shame upon Mom and Dad. Something very different sticks in my memory: Mom and Dad, with tears in their eyes, looked at me, fighting back their anger and sadness, and told me how disappointed they were in what I did but that they wanted me to know that they loved me, that they cared about me, and that they were

there for me, and that it was up to me whether or not my situation was going to get better or worse.

It has been said, "Of all manifestations of power, restraint impresses men the most." I'm reminded that one of the most astonishing things about the greatness of God's power is that in his dealings with us, his greatest power is his restraint.

This is no more apparent than in what God did when He sent His Son and ultimately held back as Jesus was hanging on a cross for you and me. We've all sung the song "Ten Thousand Angels," where the chorus says, "He could have called 10,000 angels,"[1] which reminds us of this very fact. Indeed, when Peter tries to use the sword to defend Jesus during his arrest, Jesus looks at him and says, "Or do you think that I cannot appeal to My Father, and He will at once put at My disposal more than twelve legions of angels? How then will the Scriptures be fulfilled, which say that it must happen this way?" (Matthew 26:53-54, NASB 1995). Indeed, he could have.

But maybe, just maybe, the greatest demonstration of God's sovereignty for us is the gentle reminder that he loved us so much that he chose not to intervene. It is this restraint that makes the Supper we share possible.

---

[1] Overholt, Ray. "Ten Thousand Angels." Lillenas Publishing Company, 1959 & 1987.

A Place of Prayer for Our Lord
Today's Scripture: Luke 22:39-44

Even today, in and around Jerusalem, there are many beautiful gardens where one can get away to rest, meditate, and pray. The Garden of Gethsemane is only mentioned by name twice in Scripture. Matthew and Mark describe the scene in this garden where Jesus prayed to His Father, was betrayed, and arrested. Luke and John parallel what the other writers of the Gospel tell us, but they do not name the garden.

The word Gethsemane means, "oil press." The name itself suggests that it is a cluster of olive trees where an oil press could be found. Since at least the fourth century it has been accepted that the garden is across from the Kidron Valley, east of Jerusalem, on the western slope of the Mount of Olives.

Our Lord was deeply grieved in this garden, "to the point of death" (Mark 14:34, NASB 2020). It was in Gethsemane where He asked His Father over and over again, "Father, if You are willing, remove this cup from Me, yet not My will, but Yours be done." (Luke 22:42, NASB 2020). It was here where, "His sweat became like drops of blood, falling down upon the ground." (Luke 22:44, NASB 2020)

It has been suggested that Jesus did not just pray this prayer three times, as it is recorded in our modern translations. Rather, He asked it over and over and over again. Our Lord was human, and like most of us, He did not want to die. We sometimes forget that He was only thirty-three years of age. In our day we would say, that's way too young.

However, His ultimate desire was to do the will of His Father. We see it throughout His life, but we see it most in His hour of suffering. The question for us as we strive to live a life of faith and one that glorifies our Father is, can we make our ultimate desire become a heart that wants to please Him?

Today, I will…seek to make every desire of my heart one that seeks to do the will of my Father.

TUESDAY
Walking with Jesus
Today's Scripture: John 18:1-2

Through the years, millions of people have made the walk down the winding road from the Mt. of Olives to the Garden of Gethsemane. No doubt, our Lord made this walk numerous times during His three-year ministry. John tells us that Jesus often met there with His disciples (John 18:2). It is possible that He met them there with them to discuss the work they were doing, or perhaps to teach them about how they could live in such a way to glorify God. Yet, it is most probable that He met them there to pray.

On the night of betrayal, Jesus did not come from the Mount of Olives. He took a different path, one that He probably had taken on previous trips to the Garden. John tells us, "When Jesus had spoken these words, He went away with His disciples across the ravine of the Kidron, where there was a garden which He entered with His disciples" (John 18:1, NASB 2020).

On other occasions, Jesus would take his disciples up to the mountain to pray or in the wilderness to pray. Once the disciples decided to follow Christ, they were with Him continually. They ate meals together, they prayed together, they taught others together, and they were with him as he healed the sick, gave sight to the blind, and caused the deaf to hear. They would spend nights with Him on a boat, in the wilderness, and making journeys from place to place.

When they ate the Passover with Him He told them that He would eat the Supper with them again in the Kingdom. Every time we gather as disciples of our Lord around the table He is with us. It is a rich blessing knowing that when we eat the bread and drink the cup, Jesus is with us.

He wants us to spend time with Him every day, not just one day a week. Are we willing to walk with Him in every part of our lives?

Today, I will…walk with Jesus in every decision and choice I make.

Praying with Jesus
Today's Scripture: Mark 13:32-42

There have been many discussions among men of God concerning whether or not we can pray to Jesus, or must we only pray through Jesus. The question I would like to discuss today is, are we willing to take the time to pray WITH Jesus? We know beyond any shadow of a doubt that He is our mediator (1 Timothy 2:5). It seems to me that in His role as mediator, we are actually praying with our Lord.

Our brother Mark tells us that in this place, "called Gethsemane," Jesus invited His three closest followers to pray. He found them sleeping three times and asked them why they were sleeping. Mark says that He said to Peter, "Could you not keep watch for one hour?" (Mark 13:37). Our Lord's words to His disciples then, continue to ring true in our hearts to this day. "Keep watching and praying, so that you will not come into temptation; the spirit is willing, but the flesh is weak" (Mark 13:38, NASB 2020).

In John 17, Jesus prayed a comprehensive prayer to His Father. This prayer came after the conversation he had with the disciples about leaving to prepare for us a home in Heaven and that the Comforter would come to guide them into all truth. In this prayer, Jesus asked our Father not to help us live in the world, but not be like the world. He further prayed that all of His followers would be one as He and the Father are one.

As we gather around the table of our Lord, we are reminded that we are to be united. We are also reminded that throughout the week we should be Christlike examples for the people of the world, but we must not live like the world.

The question we must ask ourselves is can we remain awake and alert? Can we pray with our Lord without losing focus? This kind of focus on prayer will keep us from being overcome by temptation. This will help us have a spirit that is stronger than the evil one.

Today, I will…remain focused on Jesus, I will pray with Him, and I will not be overcome by the evil one.

THURSDAY
A Place of Betrayal
Today's Scripture: Matthew 26:46-50

That night in the Garden of Gethsemane is a stark reminder that even when we have been close to Jesus, it is still possible for us to betray Him. Judas had been with Jesus to hear Him teach, to hear Him pray, to see Him perform miracles, to watch how He cared for people, to eat the Passover with Him, and to have his feet washed by Jesus.

Matthew describes the intent of the heart of Judas. They had been at the house of Simon in Bethany when the woman poured expensive alabaster on His head. All of the disciples became indignant, thinking that it was a waste of money. "Then one of the twelve, named Judas Iscariot, went to the chief priests and said, 'What are you willing to give me to betray Him to you?' And they set out for him thirty pieces of silver. And from then on he looked for a good opportunity to betray Jesus" (Matthew 26:14, NASB 2020).

One thing we can learn from what happened with Judas is that betrayal is not something that happens suddenly. Judas had made up his mind some time before what happened in the Garden of Gethsemane. Another follower of Jesus explains how sin progresses. "Each one is tempted when he is carried away and enticed by his own lust. Then when lust has conceived, it gives birth to sin; and sin, when it has run its course, brings forth death" (James 1:14-15, NASB 2020).

The Word of God reminds us of the necessity of keeping a watch on our hearts. "Test yourselves to see if you are in the faith; examine yourselves! Or do you not recognize this about yourselves, that Jesus Christ is in you—unless indeed you fail the test" (2 Corinthians 13:5, NASB 2020). Each time we gather with God's people around the Lord's table we remember how our Lord passed the greatest test in His life.

Today, I will…examine my heart and seek to pass the tests that come my way.

FRIDAY
A Garden of Commitment
Today's Scripture: Philippians 2:8-9

Many lessons from the Garden of Gethsemane are forever implanted in our hearts. Think of lines spoken that night that are still used in our language today. Words such as, "he who lives by the sword, will die by the sword." How many times have you said, or heard someone say, "The spirit is willing, but the flesh is weak." The statements and others remind us of what our Lord did for us that night in the garden.

The greatest lesson we learn from that night is that Jesus remained committed to His purpose regardless of what He endured. He was mocked, ridiculed, arrested, and betrayed. Despite all that, our Lord did not quit, He did not give up, and He did what He came to do. Luke tells us that Jesus came to seek and save the lost (Luke 19:10). Philippians 2:8-9 explains that "...He humbled Himself by becoming obedient to the point of death: death on a cross. For this reason also God highly exalted Him..." (NASB, 2020).

On that night in the garden, Jesus showed His commitment to purchasing the Church with His own blood. He taught us to remain faithful and committed to our God no matter what happens. Every Sunday when we eat the bread and drink the fruit of the vine, we remember our Lord's commitment to us.

"For I received from the Lord that which I also delivered to you, that the Lord Jesus, on the night when He was betrayed, took bread; and when He had given thanks, He broke it and said, 'This is My body, which is for you; do this in remembrance of Me.' In the same way He also took the cup after supper, saying, 'This cup is the new covenant in My blood; do this, as often as you drink it, in remembrance of Me.' For as often as you eat this bread and drink the cup, you proclaim the Lord's death until He comes" (1 Corinthians 11:23-26, NASB 2020).

Today, I will...do my best to imitate my Lord's commitment in everything I do.

HIS FINAL WEEK
FRIDAY MORNING

Table Meditation
Scripture: Mark 14:22-26

That We Remember

A prominent and important action in our Sunday worship involves the partaking of the communion sacraments. Baptized believers are participants in remembering what our Lord and Savior did for us. His sacrifice on the cross has redeemed us from our sins, and we actively proclaim His death on the cross as we participate in this memorial Supper each week.

On the night of his betrayal, Jesus called his apostles together for the last time to tell them what was about to happen. He knew it would be difficult for his followers to understand and remember. So, the inspired words of Scripture provide us with guidance for reference and reflection. Each week, as we come together as a church body for the Lord's Supper, we turn to the Word that helps us focus our thoughts on what Jesus commanded in remembrance of Him.

Jesus' Words

> Mark 14:22-26, "While they were eating, Jesus took bread, and when he had given thanks, he broke it and gave it to his disciples, saying, 'Take it; this is my body.' Then he took a cup, and when he had given thanks, he gave it to them, and they all drank from it. 'This is my blood of the covenant, which is poured out for many,' he said to them, 'Truly I tell you; I will not drink again from the fruit of the vine until that day when I drink it new in the kingdom of God'" (NIV).

1 Corinthians 11:26 urges us to proclaim the Lord's death until He returns!

That He is Relevant Today

Today, we place priority over daily practices that we feel have relevance in our lives. Is Jesus relevant in my life? Do I have a personal relationship with Jesus? Consider this question, am I a fan of Jesus or am I a player on His team? Brothers and sisters, Jesus wants us to be players on His team. As we observe these emblems, let us not be distracted by the daily routine of life. Let us be active participants in the Kingdom, seeking a personal relationship with Jesus.

As we consider Christian living in the 21st century, is Christianity relevant? Let us be mindful that we need his loving grace (unmerited favor) just as much today as when He walked on this earth. We need to grow in our relationship with Jesus daily.

MONDAY
The Suffering
Today's Scripture: Matthew 26:47–50; John 18:2–6

Crucifixion was a nasty business because it was the execution of a human being. The Roman Empire had it down to a science. "All crucifixion involved the victim being beaten with a leather whip containing shreds of metal or bone, which tore the flesh, which weakened the victim and caused great loss of blood. The victim was forced to carry the crossbar, which was tied to them, where the victim was led to the place of execution."

Hebrews 12:2 reminds us that Jesus "endured the cross, despising the shame."

But in our reading today from Matthew 26:47–50 and John 18:2–6, we are reminded of another aspect of suffering Jesus endured: the suffering of betrayal.

Judas sold out to the religious leaders for thirty pieces of silver (Matthew 26:14–16). Then he led them to Jesus' place of private prayer. Once there, he tried to disguise his betrayal with a common kiss, as if nothing was wrong.

Jesus called Judas "friend" in Matthew 26:50 while knowing what Judas was doing. He reminded him of their relationship even as his acts of betrayal took place.

I am sure we have all at one time been betrayed. A date said, "Yes," but stood you up. A parent turned away from you when you needed him or her most. A child said they were coming, but never showed up because they were out with friends. A spouse promised, "Til death do us part," but ended up in the arms of another.

Betrayal hurts. It is painful. Jesus experienced that suffering, too. When we come to the Lord's table, we remember Christ's death on the cross. Remember that it was not only physical pain but emotional pain as well.

Today I will... be strengthened in my faith. Christ endured the suffering of the cross so I can be healed, even if I have been betrayed.

Today, I will... be strengthened in my faith. Christ endured the suffering of the cross so I can be healed, even if I have been betrayed.

TUESDAY
Something Spiritual
Today's Scripture: Matthew 26:51-54

The Lord's Supper is not just another "act." It is not merely something we do. It is not only a tradition. It is not mystical. It is scriptural. It is spiritual. It points to the spiritual and scriptural crucifixion of Jesus.

Jesus says He could have called twelve legions of angels (Matthew 26:53). He does not. He explains why: "But how then should the Scriptures be fulfilled, that it must be so" (Matthew 26:54)?

Jesus was bound by inspired scripture (2 Timothy 3:16), even when things seemed bleak. Had he called the twelve legions of angels, the Old Testament Scriptures would not have been fulfilled and we would not be saved. Jesus deliberately decided to obey God and to submit to His will as foretold in the Old Testament. This was more important to Him than saving His life by defeating the mob who came to Him with swords and clubs.

In this act of obedience, Jesus shows how to follow and obey God.

What a great lesson for us: in Jesus' darkest hour He continued to obey God's word.

We can often forget why we come to the Lord's Table, sometimes we might think it is about us. We can be like the Christians at Corinth in 1 Corinthians 11 and make the Lord's Supper about what we like or dislike. For example, some may like this communion container or that communion container; another dislikes the taste, or how it is served. But it is not about us. It is not what I like or dislike. The Lord's Supper (as well as all of our worship) is not about us. It is about doing God's will. It is about Christ and obeying scripture.

Today, I will… obey the scriptures and strive to put God's will over my likes and dislikes.

Whom Do You Seek?
Today's Scripture: John 18:4-8

Washington D.C. has over one hundred memorials dedicated to presidents, national heroes and heroines, wars, and major events in our nation's history. I have stood at the base of the Washington Monument, walked the steps of the Lincoln Memorial, and toured Thomas Jefferson's Memorial. I have never gone to these memorials expecting to meet Washington, to talk to Lincoln, or walk with Jefferson. I was there to honor, to learn about, and to be reminded of our nation's history.

How different it is when we come to the Lord's memorial, the Lord's supper? Yes, there are similarities; we do come to the Lord's Table to honor, learn about, and to be reminded of Jesus's sacrifice. Unlike the memorials in Washington, we come proclaiming His return (1 Corinthians 11:26) and we come to meet Him, the living Lord (Revelation 1:10).

In John 18:4-8 the mob with swords and clubs came to carry Jesus away to crucify Him. They sought Jesus for evil purposes.

As followers of Christ, we seek Him today to have fellowship with Him (1 John 1:7). One way we do this is by meeting Him around His Table. We seek His presence, and we expect to meet Him. Although we do not physically see Christ at the Table, He is there. As we eat the bread and drink the cup, we do this in remembrance of His body and His blood. Unlike those memorials to the men and women in Washington D.C., Christ is present.

In Matthew 28:20, Jesus concludes the great commission with this promise, "and behold, I am with you always, to the end of the age."

Today, I will... pray that the Lord will help me to be aware of His presence as I remember His sacrifice for my sins, even when I cannot see Him with my physical eyes.

THURSDAY
We Are In This Together
Today's Scripture: John 18:12

Near my house, there is an outdoor drama of the life of Christ. I have only gone to this event once but like any other live dramas there are actors and props, and there are even real horses. Today's reading reminds us that his arrest was no drama, show, or skit. These were real soldiers, real pain, real betrayal, and real blood.

John 18:12 reveals that it was a group effort that took Jesus to the cross, "So the band of soldiers and their captain and the officers of the Jews arrested Jesus and bound him" (ESV). Later in Acts 2:36, we are taught that everyone's sin helped crucify Jesus.

As we surround the Lord's table to remember the sacrifice of Jesus for our sins, may we remember we are involved in this together. All of us have sinned (Romans 3:23). All of us were involved in Christ's crucifixion (Acts 2:36). All of us who have been baptized into Christ participate in this memorial meal (1 Corinthians 11:24-25).

Jesus's death was not a pageant that only a few skilled actors performed in. Neither is the Lord's Supper. Jesus was crucified by all who sin. All who sin may benefit from the salvation He offers. Those who have obeyed the gospel can come to His table.

All of us are participants and partakers of the unleavened bread and the cup. All of us come to the table to partake. We do not come to a stage or even an altar. All of us come to eat and drink. All social classes, languages, ethnicities, employed/not employed, elderly/young, male/female, married/widowed/single are there. We are in this together!

Today, I will… make it a point to gather with other Christians on the Lord's Day and declare the Lord's death for our sins. I will be reminded of the unity we have with each other in Christ.

Spiritual Standards
Today's Scripture: Matthew 26:55-56

The telephone operator in a Cape Cod town received a call every morning asking for the correct time. Finally, overcome with curiosity, she asked the inquirer, "Would you mind telling me why you call about this time every day and ask for the correct time?"

"Sure, I'll tell you," the man said. "I want to get the exact time because I'm the man who blows the whistle at noon."

"Well, that's funny," said the operator, "because every day at the stroke of noon I set our clock by your whistle."

How often do we set spiritual standards for ourselves based on what others are doing?

Jesus based His spiritual standards on scripture. He was committed to fulfilling what the scriptures foretold about His life, ministry, death, burial, and resurrection.

No human being can look into the future and tell what is going to happen tomorrow. Only knowledge from God could predict the future. The prophets knew Jesus was coming because God told them. The inspired words they spoke are scripture. Jesus devoted His life and mission to fulfilling the scriptures.

In Matthew 26:56, Jesus stated, "But all this has taken place that the Scriptures of the prophets might be fulfilled" (ESV).

Then in Galatians 4:4, we read, "But when the fullness of time had come, God sent forth his Son" (ESV).

Jesus' spiritual standards were based on the Scriptures. He came at the right time, just as God had planned.

When we come around the Lord's table to remember Jesus' crucifixion, we remember that it was no accident. It was fulfilled according to the Scriptures.

Today, I will… live my life according to the standards of Scripture and not on the standards of others.

Table Meditation
Scripture: John 12:31-33

Today, we remember. We create in our minds the image of a body on a cross. Not just anyone's body—rather the Son of Man, the Son of God, the sacrificial Lamb, the Savior of mankind. Not just any cross—but one glistening with sinless blood willingly offered. Jesus identified that depiction of Calvary as the motivation that would draw us to him (John 12:31-33).

Today, we affirm. We repeat our allegiance to the new covenant that His blood ratified (Matthew 26:28; Hebrews 12:24). When we put on Christ in baptism, we accepted God's gracious offer of His covenant. Each week, we have the opportunity and obligation to examine ourselves, determining if our devotion remains vibrant (1 Corinthians 11:27-28).

Today, we commune. We participate jointly because we share the same Savior (1 Corinthians 10:16-17; Matthew 26:29). Togetherness in the Lord is critical to His plans for the church. The Corinthians neglected that obligation, but Paul demanded it (1 Corinthians 11:17-22, 33).

Today, we proclaim. We announce that while His death is the low point of man's history, through His resurrection, humanity's greatest victory is won (1 Corinthians 11:26). Our declaration is one of death but then life, of sadness but then joy, of momentary loss but then eternal victory. We confess that the price He paid was beyond any reasonable expectation, but we rejoice that He loved us enough to become poor so that we might be rich (2 Corinthians 8:9).

Let us pray.

Why Annas?
Today's Scripture: John 18:13-24

As the darkness turned into light from the torches coming down the hall, I am sure Annas grew nervous. He knew what they were doing was wrong. It was illegal to conduct this trial. However, in his mind, desperate times call for desperate measures. As the features of Jesus' face became recognizable, Annas wanted to ensure he got the first crack at Him.

As we read through the events of John 18:13-24, the question may come to mind: why Annas? He had served as the High Priest years before yet relinquished his job to his son-in-law Caiaphas. Annas might have influence but no longer any real authority. Again, why Annas? If we omitted the encounter with Annas, the story doesn't change. So why did our Lord insist on this part of the story being recorded for us to read two thousand years later? It might be that if we look close enough, we see ourselves in Annas. Annas may have had a hard time letting go of the power he used to have. He must have thought, "How dare this carpenter's son come into my world and think that he has more authority than me, doesn't he know who I am?" Annas wanted to hold on to his old self and wasn't about to stand by and have someone take it away from him. He was way too important to submit to the will of an untrained carpenter's boy.

Although we may not be bold enough to make those statements, don't our thoughts and actions often imitate his? As Christians, don't we have a hard time letting go of our old selves? When it comes to our wants and desires, don't they usually win out over the one He wants us to have? Maybe our Lord wanted us to see what trying to hold onto the old self can do to us.

Today, I will…do more to let go of my old self and submit my will to the Master.

TUESDAY
Make a Defense
Today's Scripture: 1 Peter 3:15

In an attempt to allow Jesus to incriminate himself, Annas questioned Jesus' teaching and about his disciples (John 18:19). I'm sure he assumed that their harsh treatment of Jesus might cause him to criticize them. Or He might try to assert His claim as the Son of God more forcefully. If Jesus did, it would speed up getting rid of Him. Yet rather than criticize or judge, Jesus takes a very different approach. "I have spoken openly to the world. I have always taught in synagogues and in the temple, where all Jews come together. I have said nothing in secret. Why do you ask me? Ask those who have heard me what I said to them; they know what I said." (John 18:20-21, ESV).

Jesus knew that those who had heard His teaching would support Him because they knew what He taught. The question for us to consider as we commune together is: What if someone were to ask us about the teaching of Jesus? Today, at this very moment, if placed on the spot, would we be able to provide an answer that would show that we are His disciples?

Peter tells us we should always be prepared to "make a defense to anyone who asks you for a reason for the hope that is in you" (1 Peter 3:15, ESV).

Today, I will…because of what Christ did for me, be more diligent to give a defense for what Christ means to me.

WEDNESDAY
Take Heed, Lest We Fall
Today's Scripture: 1 Corinthians 10:12

What happened to Peter? Just hours before Jesus was arrested, we find him being insistent about the strength of his faith (John 13:37-38). Then, we see him putting his life on the line for Jesus in the garden by pulling his sword on Malchus. Now, when confronted by a servant girl, he denies that he even knew Jesus. What happened? As one person put it, Peter the Brave became Peter the Shamed. Peter fell into the same trap many of us do: we overestimate our own abilities.

Two Texans were trying to impress each other with the size of their ranches. One asked the other, "What's the name of your ranch?" He replied, "The Rocking R, ABC, Flying W Circle C, Bar U, Staple Four, Box D, Rolling M, Rainbow's End, Silver Spur Ranch." The one who asked the question was very impressed and exclaimed, "Whew! That's some name! How many cattle do you run?" The rancher answered, "Not many. Very few survive the branding."[1] That is exactly what happened to Peter, isn't it? He branded himself as someone who was a spiritual giant with a whole lot of faith. Aren't we all guilty of the same trap? When there is a difference between what we think we can do and what we actually do, the stress is typically too great, and we fall. We must be careful to heed the words of Paul, "Let anyone who thinks that he stands take heed lest he fall." (1 Corinthians 10:12, ESV). How do we not fall into the same trap? Steve Magness, who is a performance coach for professional athletes, once wrote, "Admitting our weaknesses can actually increase our resilience."[2]

Today, I will...be just as aware of my weaknesses as I am of my strengths.

---

[1] Hewett, James S., *Illustrations Unlimited*. Tyndale House, 1988. 438

[2] Magness, Steve. *Do Hard Things: Why We Get Resilience Wrong and the Surprising Science of Real Toughness*. HarperOne, 2022.

THURSDAY
The Condemned Heart
Today's Scripture: Romans 12:1-2

One evening, while waiting for a bus, a young man was standing with a crowd of people looking in the widow of a taxidermist shop. In the center of the window was a large owl that attracted the attention of all who passed by. The self-appointed expert began to criticize the job done on it. "If I couldn't do better than that," he said pompously, "I'd find another business. Just look at it. The head is out of proportion, the pose of the body is unnatural, and the feet are pointed in the wrong direction." Just then, the owl turned its head and gave the fellow a broad wink. The crowd laughed as the critic slinked away.[3]

Many times, we criticize because our version of reality does not align with the truth. In the trial of Jesus, we also have a "self-appointed expert" who believes his version of reality is the truth. John makes sure that we understand that it was Annas who had thought it would be better that one man die for the people (John 18:14). Annas had allowed his power, his culture, and his traditions to go to his head and cloud his vision from seeing the truth of who Jesus was. If we are not careful, the same thing will happen to us. We allow ourselves to "conform to this world" and not be "transformed" (Romans 12:1-2, ESV). We allow our culture and traditions to paint a false view of reality for us. We begin to see things that just are not true. For instance, we begin to see things once viewed as evil now accepted as good. We justify ourselves by our good deeds and misuse grace as a license for sin. In reality, it is Annas who is on trial here, and he has allowed his heart to be condemned.

Today, I will…make every effort to not allow my vision of truth to become clouded by the world, my traditions, or my expectations.

---

[3] Bible Illustrator #662, 1/1998.8

FRIDAY
The Greatest of Regrets
Today's Scripture: John 18:24

With a quick Google search, we can find that the most common regrets people have about their lives are that they did not take enough risks or that they were not as assertive as they should have been. That surprised me because when I think of my greatest regrets, they usually have to do with me putting my foot in my mouth, losing my temper, or doing something I should not have done. I believe the officer of the High Priest in John 18:24 would agree with me.

Even though we do not have any record of this man's past or future, I would venture to say that striking the Savior of the world would have been one of his greatest regrets. I'm sure that it felt like the right thing to do at the moment. After all, it was his job to protect the integrity of the High Priest's office. Yet, when the tomb was found empty, I'm sure the reality of his actions set in. He must have thought, "If I could do it all over again, things would be different." However, we must not be too critical of this officer because our situation is not much different. I would venture to say that the sins we commit today hurt Jesus much more than the actions of the High Priest's officer. At least he could have the excuse that He didn't know Jesus was the Son of God, whereas we not only know but accept it, and we continue to hurt Him with our sin. Realizing that everyone at the table of Jesus has hurt Him in some capacity, we can find comfort in knowing that His love for us is unchanged.

Today, I will...because of what Christ did for me, look forward to spending time around His table with Him. Who knows, if that officer got an opportunity to make his amends with Jesus, he is welcome to sit with me.

Table Meditation
Scripture: 1 John 4:9

I can't help but think that when John was writing his gospel, he was smiling as he recounted the events of chapter 20. John tells us Mary Magdalene went to the tomb first and saw that the stone sealing the entrance had been removed. Frightened, Mary ran to tell Peter and "the other disciple"—the one Jesus loved—John. John says "both went running," but he outran Peter and reached the tomb first. This was the first, and I believe only, athletic taunting found in the Bible! John had to smile when he recalled outrunning his friend Peter not once, but twice in chapter 20.

But what ultimately brought a smile to John was what they found when they went inside—just linens used to wrap the body of Jesus. John said he "saw and believed." From that point on, everything changed! The world changed. It affects us today. What tremendous power on display by God. Paul describes it in Ephesians 1—the incomparable great power of God he exerted when raising Christ from the dead. God placed all things under him and appointed Jesus Christ head over everything for the church. John describes it like this in 1 John 4:9, "This is how God showed His love among us: He sent his one and only Son into the world that we might live through him" (NIV). The Lord's Supper represents the power and love that God gives us in Jesus Christ.

MONDAY
Part of the Plan
Today's Scripture: Matthew 26:29

The blessing to weekly commune with Jesus and fellow disciples at His Table offers an amazing introspection as we dine with the King of Kings (1 Timothy 6:15). While being referred to as the Lord's Supper (1 Corinthians 11:20), it is a spiritual meal that impacts a variety of emotions. It was and is a part of God's master plan for his people.

The trial before Caiaphas, the Jewish high priest at the time, was a legal fiasco that led to Jesus' death on the cross. The table of the Lord had been in the mind and plan of God for a long time. Jesus used the Passover to transition into the institution of His memorial (Matthew 26:17-29). The Passover reminded them that death could be avoided by proper use of the blood of a lamb (Exodus 12:11-13).

After Jesus' death, the Passover would cease to be observed, and Jesus' new memorial would be celebrated by all his followers, not just the Jews (Galatians 3:26-28). Jesus instituted this spiritual feast before his death but explained that He would not participate in this event again until after His death. It would be observed in the church—the Father's kingdom (Matthew 26:29).

After Jesus died and was resurrected, His promise and prophecy were fulfilled when disciples came together to "break bread" (Acts 20:7). This looked backward to the cross but with a present and forward promise. His Table became a weekly reminder of the great price paid for the opportunity to be reconciled with God.

The final communion will be heaven, when the redeemed of all ages will gather in a common union with our God and his Son. We will forever dine and dwell together. There will be no need for a weekly reminder, as we will be in His presence forever.

If only the Jews and Caiaphas had known that they were not stopping Jesus but enabling Him to accomplish his mission!

Today, I will...be grateful for the Divine plan that reaches from the Passover to eternity.

Rejection to Reconciliation to Reflection
Today's Scripture: John 1:29

Of all people, the Jews should have recognized Jesus as the Messiah (John 1:41). The prophecies were clear and concise. Jesus' life—filled with unparalleled teaching (Matthew 7:29) and undeniable miracles (John 20:30)—provided more than ample evidence of His divinity. The trial before Caiaphas was one of many examples of Jews rejecting the only true hope.

One can only imagine their delight when they convinced the high priest to see Jesus through their eyes. It seemed like the ultimate victory to see their rejection of Jesus culminate in His removal.

The rejection of Jesus by these people was motivated by envy (Matthew 27:18). It was perpetrated by spiritual blindness. It was so biased and prejudiced that they sought false witnesses with false testimony when no evil could be found in Jesus (Matthew 26:59-60).

This mockery of a trial that contributed to the crucifixion of Jesus was a piece of the process that led to something much different than rejection. The death of the sinless Lamb of God afforded all accountable people the opportunity of reconciliation (John 1:29). How ironic!

The rejection by these misguided religious people became part of God's plan to use rejection as a pathway to redemption. Through different eyes, we now reflect upon Jesus' death—the result of rejection. We are able regularly to examine our lives to see if we are rejecting or embracing Jesus. The words of Paul invite and challenge us to not only reflect upon Jesus' death but also to examine and reflect upon our lives as we eat the bread and drink the cup (1 Corinthians 11:28). What a powerful weekly mirror!

Today, I will…reflect upon my blessing of reconciliation with God through the sacrifice of Jesus.

WEDNESDAY
He Deserves Death
Today's Scripture: 2 Corinthians 5:21

Caiphas the high priest listened to the false witnesses who spoke against Jesus (Matthew 26:61). Caiphas asked Jesus why he did not defend himself against these accusations (Matthew 26:62). Caiphas became incensed when Jesus spoke of power and "coming on the clouds" (Matthew 26:64).

Interestingly, Caiphas asked this misguided crowd what their judgment was (Matthew 26:66). Nothing could have pleased them more than to answer this question. "He deserves death" was their biased and ignorant recommendation (Matthew 26:66). The legal system does not always get it right, especially when truth supported by the evidence is not on the agenda.

Death was and is deserved! Scripture clearly identifies that death is the penalty for sin (Romans 6:23). The problem with this sentence is that Jesus had no sin (1 Peter 2:22). Just like those Jews, we can become blinded by the misguided judgment as to who is guilty and who can save.

When we spend time together weekly at His Table, it centers around death. It is worthwhile to meditate on who died and who should have died. It was for us and our guilt that God made Jesus who did not sin to be that sin for us so that we might become the righteousness of God (2 Corinthians 5:21).

The Lord's Supper reminds us that death is what we, not Jesus, deserve. We are overwhelmed by Jesus' death, which gives us life and takes away our sentence of death. Weekly, we are impressed by Jesus taking our place. The need for us to die to sin and live in the newness of life is one of many takeaways from our weekly communion (Romans 6:4).

How could the Jews get it so wrong, and God get it so right? Amazing grace!

Today, I will...be assured that death was deserved, but I was guilty—not Jesus.

THURSDAY
So Close and Yet So Far Away
Today's Scripture: Matthew 26:57-67

The trial that brought Jesus before Caiphas in Matthew 26 resembles a kangaroo court more than an ethical legal procedure. It was not the first nor last travesty of justice that has left decreasing confidence in a system whose pillars should be honesty and integrity. It leaves a greater sense of disappointment in the people involved.

A man is seized, falsely accused, spit upon, slapped, struck, and mocked. Innocent until proven guilty would ring hollow in this circumstance. While this type of activity would not be uncommon in many lawless and God-abandoned venues, the cast of characters in this legal setting is both surprising and disappointing.

Judas, one of the twelve chosen by Jesus, led a mob to take him and scream for his death. Who were these people? An apostle, scribes, elders, chief priests, Sanhedrin Council, and the high priest of the Jews. If you could handpick the most religious and God-fearing people of that day, this would seem to be that group. This would appear to be the group closest to God and ready to receive God's son.

Of all the people Jesus should have been able to depend on, you think this would be this group, but it was not. Of all the people you would imagine who would be close to God, it would be these—but they were not. They could not have been further away. Even Peter followed at a distance (Matthew 26:58).

Judas sat at the table with Jesus in the upper room, but he was only close in physical distance. His heart was a long way off.

This is a wonderful opportunity to look within and see how close I am to Jesus. The weekly memorial we enjoin together presents a time of reflection to see if we are close to God only in name, title, religious affiliation, physical location (church building), or truly in heart and soul.

Today, I will…look and see how close I am to Jesus.

FRIDAY
Missions Accomplished
Today's Scripture: Philippians 1:12-18

The Jews had a mission that they were determined to see to completion —get rid of Jesus. God had a mission He was even more determined to accomplish—allow Jesus to die once for all mankind (1 Peter 3:18). Though these missions seemed to be in opposite directions, they each had a role in the wonderful memorial we are blessed to fellowship together each Sunday.

The mission of the Jews reflected blindness, ignorance, prejudice, and envy. Religious activity is not always approved by God nor always in harmony with His will or mission (Matthew 15:8). This trial in Matthew 26 is evidence of hearts grown dull, ears that can barely hear, and closed eyes (Matthew 13:15).

It is not unusual for God to turn the "mission" of His enemies into the furtherance of the gospel as evidenced by Paul (Philippians 1:12-18). The early Christians used the mission of some who persecuted them to motivate them to accomplish God's mission by spreading the gospel (Acts 8:4).

While the misguided mission of the Jews was to have Jesus killed, Jesus used the cross to accomplish His mission by making the ultimate sacrifice for sins and offering forgiveness to those who were carrying out this mission (Luke 23:34).

Jesus was determined to die on the cross. The message of that death and the hope it brings was shared on Pentecost in Jerusalem (Acts 2). It was there that Peter addressed those whom he declared had crucified Jesus and called on them to repent and be baptized (Acts 2:36, 38).

I wonder if any of those involved in that trial before Caiphas heard the message on Pentecost or sometime later and responded to Jesus' invitation (Matthew 26:57-68)? If they did, a change of heart and mind would have enabled them to dine each first day of the week at His Table.

The Jews and Jesus both had a mission, and both were accomplished to the glory of God.

Today, I will…rejoice in the mission Jesus accomplished on the cross.

Table Meditation
Scripture: 1 Corinthians 1:18

Paramount in our Christian faith is communing together each first day of the week to remember the life-altering gift of our Savior, Jesus Christ. In these moments, when appropriately focused, we reflect on the body of our Lord as He hung on our behalf; and we reflect on His blood, which flowed to save us from the only destiny we could know as weak and sinful individuals—an eternity separated from God and everything good and righteous.

Our faith in Jesus centers around the cross, as does our hope, along with the confidence He embodied in His perfect life, death, and resurrection.

Without appropriate worship and discernment, it is easy to spend these cherished moments in vain, without realizing the blessings and assurances that come from communing together in remembrance. Forgetting causes us to further drift from our faith and our Lord. 1 Corinthians 1:18 reads, "For the word of the cross is foolishness to those who are perishing, but to us who are being saved it is the power of God" (NASB 1995).

When we reflect on His gift, partake of the bread, and drink the fruit of the vine, we boldly proclaim His death while He sustains and builds our faith, along with that of our fellow Christians.

In quietly centering our thoughts on the cruel yet beautiful cross, we see now the very gift we hope to see for all of eternity—Jesus Christ Himself.

Table Interruptions: A Life Out Of Focus

Today's Scripture: Matthew 26:69-75

Can you imagine Peter's embarrassment if he had access to Matthew's account of the life of Jesus? Seemingly without reservation, Matthew shared some of Peter's biggest blunders. Matthew recorded Peter's moment of doubt as he attempted to walk to Jesus on the water (Matthew 14). He preserved Peter's misstep regarding the temple tax (Matthew 17). But he also, along with the other Gospel writers, highlights Peter's most notorious moment—when he verbally denied Jesus despite his promise to stand with Jesus through any adversity.

This week's devotionals focus on this story and what this memorable event teaches us about our relationship and daily communion with God.

The remainder of the week will emphasize individual reasons that our fellowship and connection to God get interrupted. But the emphasis for today is the overall picture presented in the text. Namely, Peter's life was profoundly out of focus on the night he denied his relationship with Jesus, his Lord and Master.

No matter the reasons, any man whose life lacks spiritual focus will also lack an abiding connection to God and Christ. The result will be distance, disconnect, and discontent. Despite God's longing for closeness, a lack of focus will rob us of that blessing.

Do you ever feel disconnected from God? Do you ever feel the distance growing between you and the One who created you? Do you ever feel that despite your best efforts, you cannot close the gap? Friend, you are not alone. You need to refocus. Like Peter, you must stop looking at the crowd around you. You must stop simply reacting to the questions of the world. All of this will take your focus off of Jesus and the commitment you've made to Him.

Today, I will…simplify my thoughts and focus on Jesus. He will be at the forefront of every decision. I will not listen to the world nor be distracted by their questions. He will be in all of my thoughts.

TUESDAY
Table Interruptions: Forgetfulness
Today's Scripture: Matthew 26:69-75

My paternal grandfather lost his physical batter with cancer when I was nine years old. My memories of him are faint and scarce. It is difficult to remember what his voice sounded like and to recall his mannerisms and the particulars of his personality. Due to my inability to remember, I don't feel as close to him as I do to my maternal grandfather who is still alive today. The difference is not a depth of love, but rather an ability to remember experiences, circumstances, and situations of our relationship.

Communion and connection are fueled by both the future and the past. We look to the future hoping and longing to keep our relationships strong. We are also motivated by the memories of yesterday and how our relationships have developed over time. If we forget either one of these aspects of daily fellowship, we can also lose sight of how important fellowship truly is.

Peter's forgetfulness—of both the past moments of intimacy with Jesus and His future promises of an even closer connection—led to the disastrous events described in our text. Jesus warned of that very night and of those very actions just hours before Peter engaged in them (Luke 22:31-34). Also, on that same night, Jesus promised to come again and take Peter with him to His father's house (John 14:1-5). But somehow, even for a brief moment, Peter forgot.

When we let the distractions of the world interrupt our remembrance of all that Jesus has done for us and all that He has promised to do for us, our relationship with Him is bound to suffer. Peter forgot, and so can we.

Today, I will...talk to someone (my spouse, my children, my coworkers, my preacher, etc.) about my relationship with Jesus. That conversation will include my journey to becoming His disciple and the greatest blessings He has given me.

WEDNESDAY
Table Interruptions: Fear
Today's Scripture: Matthew 26:69-75

The gospels are abundantly clear. Jesus wants us to live a life without fear. His ministry, His teaching, and His presence were all aimed at removing the fears that cripple our daily lives and replacing those fears with faith in a better hope, a better system, and a better future.

This desire to alleviate our fears was not merely so that we could have peace of mind. Jesus realized the hindrance that fear would be to a vibrant and fulfilling relationship with Him. Do you recall the night that Jesus slept in the boat, and the disciples thought they were going to die in the storm? Their fear for physical safety caused them to question both the power of Jesus and also his pity toward them (Mark 4:38). Remember, Peter was a part of the group that let fear interrupt his trust that night.

Now, fast-forward a couple of years, and you will come to the scene from our reading. Again, this is another time when Peter looked at the storm raging around him. Again, on this occasion, Peter let fear lead him to distrust and an interruption to his walk with the Lord. He had drawn a sword to defend Jesus just hours before, and now he repeatedly denied that he had ever been with Him.

I am confident that fear is still an interruption for all of us. We are not immune. Whether we are overwhelmed by the world around us with all of its wickedness, or frightened by the intimidation tactics of worldly influences, fear plays a real part in our daily lives.

Today, I will…remember to pause in moments of fear and remember my faith. I will not let the world intimidate me into silence or shame. Today, my faith will be stronger than my fear.

Table Interruptions: Shame

Today's Scripture: Matthew 26:69-75

One of the lesser-emphasized blessings of Christianity is the sense of belonging—having a seat at the table. When Jesus is your Lord, He is also your friend. He told the disciples, "No longer do I call you servants, for the servant does not know what his master is doing; but I have called you friends" (John 15:15, ESV). When you walk with Him, you also feast with Him. Never forget this great promise: "Behold, I stand at the door and knock. If anyone hears My voice and opens the door, I will come in to him and eat with him, and he with Me" (Revelation 3:20, ESV).

Have you ever struggled with the reality of this idea? That you belong at the table with Jesus? That you are worthy to sit with Him? That He enjoys your presence and fellowship? If you have, guilt or shame might be the reason.

The story of Peter's denial ends on a sad, desperate note. After Peter had repeatedly and aggressively denied Jesus, the text woefully reads, "And immediately the rooster crowed. And Peter remembered the saying of Jesus, 'Before the rooster crows, you will deny me three times.' And he went out and wept bitterly" (Matthew 26:74-75, ESV).

Shame is a byproduct of sin and a major interruption to our daily communion with God. Even though we feel unworthy and, because of our sin, are unworthy, Christ does not see us this way. He moves closer to us and longs with a deep, abiding love to forgive, restore, and renew that relationship. If shame disturbs my connection to God, it will only be because I let it. Remember, "There is therefore now no condemnation for those who are in Christ Jesus" (Romans 8:1, ESV).

Today, I will...rejoice in my forgiveness. I will celebrate my place at His table. I will not focus on shame but rather on victory. I will not dwell on my past but on what He has presently made me and the future that awaits me in heaven.

Table Interruptions: Disappointment
Today's Scripture: Matthew 26:69-75

One of the greatest hindrances to healthy relationships is unrealistic and unfulfilled expectations. This is true in marriage relationships, church life, school choices, earthly friendships, and vocational pursuits. If we believe we are getting one thing only to receive something else, disappointment will follow. Due to the disappointment, the relationship will be strained, and at times, it will be impacted forever.

On the night that Peter denied Jesus three times and his regret manifested itself in bitter tears, Peter was suffering from extreme disappointment.

Peter's journey of discipleship, while often marred by his mistakes, was one of great faith and sacrifice. Looking back at the beginning of that journey, Peter rightly told Jesus, "See, we have left everything and followed you" (Matthew 19:27, ESV). Granted, this choice gave Peter no reason to brag, but it did highlight his faith. As a result, Peter expected something in return. The passage above ends with these words of Peter, "What then will we have?"

I have often wondered, as Peter watched the events of that night unfold if Peter felt disappointed by what transpired. Did he really leave all to follow a man who was just going to die? Did he really forsake his occupation and religion to join a cause that would end in disgrace and shame? Is this really what he signed up for?

You see, our inability to see the fullness of God's plans can lead to disappointment with certain stops along the way. The events of that night led to the defeat of satan on the cross and significant victory over death in the resurrection. Peter would later say that his renewal of hope was due to the resurrection of Jesus (1 Peter 1:3).

When you feel discontent with God's plan or when you feel disappointed with where you are in your discipleship journey, remember Peter.

Today, I will…measure my disappointment against my hope. I will temper my discontent with His promises. I will focus on what lies ahead, not simply on where I stand right now.

Table Meditation
Scripture: Romans 5:8

"To keep the feast, Lord, we have met, And to remember Thee, Help each redeemed one to repeat, 'For me, He died, for me.'"[1]

Does this memorial demand reverence to God and His Son? We MUST focus our minds with purpose for this occasion, for "whosoever shall eat this bread and drink this cup of the Lord in an unworthy manner, shall be guilty of the body and blood of the Lord" and "eateth and drinketh damnation to himself, not discerning the Lord's body" (1 Corinthians 11:27, 29, KJV). Think about the "Lamb of God." The worthy dying for me, the unworthy! The just for the unjust! The righteous for the unrighteous! "But God commendeth (demonstrates) His love toward us, in that, while we were still yet sinners, Christ died for us" (Romans 5:8, KJV).

"Greater love hath no man than this, that a man lay down his life for his friends" (John 15:13, KJV).

Why did God's Son have to suffer so? Because of our sin! Sin demands justice. Justice demands penalty or payment for sin. Jesus took our place on the cross. Our sin is so bad and destructive in God's sight that Jesus was the only true, perfect, and sinless sacrifice that could cleanse us (Hebrews 10:4; Colossians 1:14).

The blood of Christ. The only agent that can cleanse our souls. Isn't it wonderful that this same soul-cleansing blood of the Son of God still avails itself today to the penitent sinner—even me? He died for me.

---

[1] Hart, Joseph. "That Dreadful Night," 1759.

MONDAY
The Number of Trials Jesus Endured
Today's Scripture: Luke 22:66-71

I struggle to patiently endure temptation. Jesus shows me perfect patience and endurance.

How many trials did Jesus go through? No, not how many temptations or struggles did He face. But, how many times did He stand before a religious or national authority figure facing accusations of law-breaking? Six! That may not be as shocking to you as it is to me, but wow, six.

Jesus' first three trials were with a Jewish leader or group. The first trial was with Annas (John 18:12-13). The second was with Caiaphas (John 18:24). The third was in front of the assembly of the elders of the people, both chief priests and scribes. This group is called the Sanhedrin (Luke 22:66ff). After these Jewish "court" trials, Jesus faced three Roman trials. The fourth trial was with Pilate (Luke 23:1-5). After Pilate, Jesus was sent to Herod—that's five (Luke 23:6-7). After Herod's trial of mockery and contempt, Herod returned Jesus to Pilate. This was Jesus' sixth and final trial (Luke 23:11, 13-25).

Why point out the number of trials Jesus faced? Well, think about it for a moment…have multiple people made false claims against you back-to-back-to-back-to-back-to-back-to-back? No? What do you think that was like for Jesus? How do you think that tested Him? Sometimes I read Hebrews 4:15, which says, "For we do not have a high priest who is unable to sympathize with our weaknesses, but one who in every respect has been tempted as we are, yet without sin" (ESV), and think, yes, He understands! As I consider the number of trials Jesus had to endure, I read Hebrews 4:15 and think: He may understand perfectly what I have had to endure, but I have NO IDEA what He had to endure.

Today, I will…face every temptation with the patient endurance of Jesus on trial, six times over.

TUESDAY
The Nature of the Trials Jesus Endured
Today's Scripture: Luke 22:66-71

The Jewish Law was not followed in Jesus' trial. It has been said, "Two of the enlightened systems of law that ever existed were prostituted to bring about the destruction of the most innocent man who ever lived."[1] Per Jewish law, there could be no conviction without two witnesses. Jesus did not contest. He could not testify against Himself. "Jesus only deviated from [H]is subsequent posture of silence before the juridical powers of [H]is day to address [H]is stature as Christ and [H]is unique relationship with God."[2] A capital case must be tried in public, never at night, on a Friday, Sabbath, or a feast day with the verdict being unable to be announced anytime less than on the third day post determination.[3]

Combine these chilling rejections of Jewish law with the fact that Jesus had a leading Jewish family conspiring against Him (Annas, father-in-law of Caiaphas, was either the former or current High Priest, making Caiaphas either the current or incumbent High Priest). Jesus was illegally taken under the cloak of darkness to Annas, then to the house of Caiaphas, and pushed inside, which broke Passover law. Notice how the soldiers themselves, the ones transporting Jesus, would not enter because to do so would defile them at Passover (John 18:28).

These "trials" were fraudulent, deceptive, and sinful. God knew all along. You see, it was before the foundation of the world that God had a plan to redeem mankind, and it required a sacrificial lamb to be fraudulently charged and found guilty (Luke 22:22; Ephesians 1:3-14). God used the sinful work of man to bring about salvation for all mankind!

Today, I will…pause to pray when I see or experience the sinful work of man. I will thank God for His work and ask Him to help me see how He is still working through the sin around/in me.

---

[1] William A. Herin, *The Trial of Jesus*, 7 Fla. L. Rev. 47 [1954]: p. 57

[2] Melvin Otey, "Jesus's Objections During His Preliminary Examination and Modern Notions of Due Process," 35 Reg. Univ. L. Rev. 91 [2022]: p. 96

[3] Herin, *Trial of Jesus*, 47-48

WEDNESDAY
The Neutrality of Pilate
Today's Scripture: Luke 22:66-71; Luke 23:1-25

Pilate had an opportunity to be moved by the sacrificial silence of Jesus while on trial, yet remained neutral.

The Sanhedrin, acting as the supreme court of ancient Israel (Deuteronomy 16:18-20), came to Pilate with accusations so egregious that they thought Pilate would place the verdict of death upon Jesus without hesitation or evidence! What led them to this conclusion? Luke 22:69, when Jesus said, "But from now on the Son of man shall be seated at the right hand of the power of God" (ESV). They thought this "blasphemy" deserved execution. They pitched it as a revolt against Caesar and, thus, a potentially fatal blow to the tenuous relationship between Jews and Rome.

The Sanhedrin came to Pilate practically foaming from their mouths, hoping to elicit an equally emotional rage from Pilate. But no. He remained neutral. Pilate spoke to Jesus and found no guilt. The Sanhedrin was "urgent" (Luke 23:5) in their attempts to move Pilate. But, Pilate sent Jesus away just to receive back again from Herod hours later. He then appeased the crowd and cast Jesus off to be killed. Pilate was influenced from all around, yet remained nauseatingly neutral.

Are you hindered by neutrality when you consider the sacrifice of Jesus on the cross? satan wants us to be that way. Anytime something becomes a routine, even something good such as worship through gathering around His Table, it is liable to become a mindless activity.

How do we fight against this? We engage the heart and mind. Proverbs 4:20-27 explains that the heart is the source of the springs of life. Philippians 2:5 leads us to have "this mind among yourselves, which is yours in Christ Jesus," a mind of love-motivated action, sacrifice, and submission to the will of God (Philippians 2:1-11).

Today, I will...examine the crucifixion of Jesus from a new perspective, to fight against being neutral towards the sacrifice of Jesus. Use the five basic human senses and imagine what it must have been like to be hung on the cross.

Jesus Knew the Sanhedrin Would Not Believe

Today's Scripture: Luke 22:66-71

Early in Jesus' ministry, John 2:23-25 says, "Now when he was in Jerusalem at the Passover Feast, many believed in his name when they saw the signs that he was doing. But Jesus on his part did not entrust himself to them, because he knew all people and needed no one to bear witness about man, for he himself knew what was in man" (ESV). Jesus knew what was in mankind. He knew their intentions, beliefs, and misgivings. Jesus also knew He was being led to the cross (John 17). John 12:23 says, "The hour has come for the Son of Man to be glorified" (ESV). Jesus here turned His eyes to the cross of Calvary, knowing what the outcome would be.

Since Jesus knew these things, it should be no surprise that as Jesus stood before the council of the Sanhedrin, He knew exactly what was in them! In Luke 22:67-68 the Sanhedrin engaged Jesus, saying, "'If you are Christ, tell us.' But he said to them, 'If I tell you, you will not believe, and if I ask you, you will not answer'" (ESV). Jesus knew. He had to take false accusations and public shame while *knowing* they would not believe Him!

God is perfectly aware of what is in each of us today, too. What does He see? Does our Lord see neutrality, immaturity, laziness, or idolatry? Does He see humility, honesty, integrity, or faithfulness? What does He see? While we cannot have the "mind of Christ" that can know what is in each person, we are commanded to pursue the mind of Christ through the work of the Holy Spirit in us (Philippians 2:5-11; Galatians 5:16-26).

Today, I will...imagine Jesus in holy silence before the Sanhedrin, *knowing* their disbelief. I will envision how Jesus was surely thinking about accomplishing the will of His Father and emulate that mentality throughout the day.

FRIDAY
The Cost of Sin Is Always More Than You Think
Today's Scripture: Matthew 27:3-10

Sin always costs something. At the moment when we choose sin, whether it is premeditated or reactionary, we believe the cost is worth it because of what we gain. Whether it is reactionary satisfaction, unholy physical pleasure, or greedy gain, the "gain" is always a shame upon the holy nature of God when we sin. We must realize that whatever the cost of sin seems to be, as we are involving ourselves in it, it always costs more than we initially thought.

Judas received thirty pieces of silver to betray Jesus. Biblically, thirty pieces of silver could be an allusion to Zechariah 11 when Zechariah was given thirty pieces of silver from Israel in payment for his prophecy. The Lord told Zechariah to take the pieces of silver and throw them back to them. Why? It was given in contempt. Thirty pieces of silver is the payment given in Exodus 21:32 when an ox killed a slave. The owner of the ox was to pay the slave's master 30 pieces of silver for their life. So, giving a prophet of God the wages of a dead slave is a direct shot at the prophet and the Lord Himself! But is that all it cost Judas? No.

Matthew 27:3 says, "When Judas…saw that Jesus was condemned, he changed his mind" and brought back the money. Judas did not realize that his sin would cost him much more. Judas had guilt, shame, remorse, sorrow, anger, frustration, grief, and much more. Why? Judas *saw* the conviction of Jesus. He betrayed his friend, mentor, or, at the very least, an innocent person. He knew the sin was not worth it.

Today, I will…change my mind about sin and realize it will *always* cost me more than I think. I will read 2 Corinthians 7:10 and be sure that my sin leads me to godly sorrow, repentance, and salvation!

Table Meditation
Scripture: John 3:16

"For God so loved the world, that he gave his only Son, that whoever believes in him should not perish but have eternal life" (John 3:16, ESV).

In Paul's letter to the Romans, he concisely spells out our world's tragedy! "We all have sinned and fallen short of the glory of God" (Romans 3:23, ESV), and "the wages of sin is death" (Romans 6:23, ESV).

It is eye-opening when we apply "perishing" to our spiritual well-being, as stated in the opening verse. When we stray from God, disobedience fills our lives and souls. The world tries to persuade us to be like one of them. Without divine intervention, we "perish."

But that doesn't have to be how our story ends. The Scriptures say, "God so loved the world, that he gave his only Son, that whoever believes in him should not perish but have eternal life." Elsewhere, Jesus says: "The thief comes only to steal and kill and destroy. I came that they may have life and have it abundantly" (John 10:10, ESV).

God's Son died on that cruel cross so that we might not perish. While we are commanded to remember this occasion, we should also have the desire in our hearts to show thanksgiving that Christ gave his life for you and me.

MONDAY
See the Irony?
Today's Scripture: John 18:28

The Jewish leaders who had arrested Jesus under the cover of darkness led Him to the high priest's residence for an illegal trial. (NOTE: Sanhedrin regulations provided for capital cases to be decided only in the daylight. "In cases of capital law, the court judges during the daytime, and concludes the deliberations and issues the ruling only in the daytime."[1]) When they were finished with their accusations, they led Him away to the headquarters of the Roman governor, Pilate.

Once they arrived, they would not enter, reasoning that entering the realm of the pagan governor would make them ceremonially unclean. They would thus be prohibited from eating the impending Passover meal. All the while they were sinfully leading the sinless Passover Lamb, Jesus, to His death. Can you see the irony?

When we come to the table of the Lord's Supper, we come having been defiled by sin but cleansed by the blood of that perfect Passover Lamb. We, who are so weak and sinful, commemorate the sacrifice of this sinless One. Our defilement is the very reason He had to endure the lawless mob, the farcical trials, the humiliation, pain, and suffering so that we could stand undefiled before a Holy God. Can you see the irony?

The writer of Hebrews admonishes us to "draw near with a true heart in full assurance of faith, with our hearts sprinkled clean from an evil conscience and our bodies washed with pure water" (Hebrews 10:22, ESV). Let us gather around His table with the sincere desire to remember Him with a pure heart.

Today, I will…take time to reflect on my motives for remembering Christ—not to justify my own sinful actions but to acknowledge His sinless sacrifice.

---

[1] https://www.sefaria.org/Mishnah_Sanhedrin.4.1

TUESDAY
Answer the Question!
Today's Scripture: John 18:29-30

Some of us will do almost anything to avoid answering a direct question. We look for loopholes, for ways out, to avoid confronting the truth that honest answers will bring. We might even be deceptive to distract from a truthful response.

Such was the case when the Roman governor, Pilate, went outside to question the Jewish leaders who had brought Jesus, bound, to his headquarters. Quite logically, Pilate wanted to know what charges they were bringing against Jesus. Notice their evasive answer, to paraphrase, "Of course He is evil. Why else would we have dragged Him here?" They didn't answer the question, did they? Instead of specifying charges against Jesus, they gave a vague response that He was "doing evil."

Jesus often stumped many of the religious leaders who questioned Him (For examples, see Matthew 21:23-27; 22:41-45; Mark 2:6-12; 12:13-17; Luke 20:27-40). On this occasion, he has stumped them with His sinless life! They could not find Mosaic laws that He had broken, nor Roman rules that He had violated, so they resorted to unspecified "evil" that they claimed He had done.

If our lives were examined carefully, something could be discovered that we had done wrong. Maybe we exceeded the posted speed limit, made an illegal turn, left information out of our tax return, or committed some other lawless deed, even if done unintentionally. Our accusers would not have to depend on a vague accusation to "convict" us of wrongdoing.

Instead of honestly answering the question posed by Pilate, Jesus' accusers misled him with unspecified "evil" accusations to carry out their murderous intentions. It is appropriate to ask, "Are you a sinner in need of the Savior?" Answer the question!

Today, I will…deal honestly with my own sinfulness as I remember the One who knew no sin—Jesus the Christ!

Convenient Obedience
Today's Scripture: John 18:31-32

satan once tempted Jesus with Scripture. "Then the devil took him to the holy city and set him on the pinnacle of the temple and said to him, 'If you are the Son of God, throw yourself down, for it is written, "He will command his angels concerning you," and "On their hands they will bear you up, lest you strike your foot against a stone"'" (Matthew 4:5-6, ESV). Jesus could have conveniently used this passage to give in to satan's desires, but He refused. Jesus never took the easy way out.

When the Jewish leaders brought Jesus to Pilate, it was expedient for them to assert that they could not "lawfully" put someone to death. The Law of Moses, which they claimed to strictly adhere to, provided for multiple occasions of capital punishment (see Exodus 21:12, 14-17; Leviticus 20:2, 9-16; 24:15-16; Deuteronomy 17:2-5; 22:25), but they were conveniently submitting to Roman rule to ensure Jesus' crucifixion. John declared that this was done to fulfill Jesus' own prediction about His death (see John 3:14-15; 12:32-33; Deuteronomy 21:22-23; Galatians 3:13-14).

When we commemorate Jesus' sacrifice on our behalf in the Lord's Supper, Paul tells us we "proclaim the Lord's death until He comes" (1 Corinthians 11:26, ESV). The Jewish leaders conveniently obeyed Roman law about their right to put Jesus to death, perhaps to exonerate themselves of guilt and to put Him to a shameful death by crucifixion. When we partake of the Lord's Supper with discernment, we are telling the truth about why Jesus died and rose again.

Today, I will…proclaim around His table the truth about the death, burial, and resurrection of Jesus by the words that I speak and the way that I serve Him.

THURSDAY
Are You the King?
Today's Scripture: John 18:33-36

Pilate seemed baffled by the Jewish leaders' accusations against Jesus. In this interview, Pilate asked Jesus if he was "the king of the Jews." Jesus' response indicated that the Jewish leaders may have informed Pilate of their plan to bring Jesus before him. Pilate seems perplexed by the hatred these Jews had for such a "king" as Him.

Instead of answering Pilate's question directly, Jesus educated him about the nature of His kingdom. His kingdom was to become a "not of this world" kingdom. Soldiers would be defending Jesus against these Jews if His kingdom was like the kingdoms of this world. Surely Pilate understood what Jesus was saying about the importance of military might in worldly kingdoms. Pilate was likely guarded by soldiers as he interviewed Jesus!

Each of us must decide for ourselves if we are willing to submit to King Jesus. We must acknowledge the spiritual nature of His kingdom and the spiritual battles we must fight as servant-soldiers in His kingdom. When we gather around His table, we understand that we are not participating in a meal that sustains us physically, but one that recalls the spiritual battle that Jesus won for us by His death and resurrection.

Today, I will…acknowledge Jesus as King of my life and see the spiritual nature of the feast at His table.

What Is Truth?
Today's Scripture: John 18:37-38

After talking with Jesus, Pilate declared to the Jewish leaders that Jesus was not guilty. He said there is "no guilt" in Him at all! Peter, who had denied any connection with Jesus (John 18:15-18, 25-27), later acknowledged Jesus' sinlessness with these words: "He committed no sin, neither was deceit found in his mouth. When he was reviled, he did not revile in return; when he suffered, he did not threaten, but continued entrusting himself to him who judges justly" (1 Peter 2:22-23, ESV).

In this interview, Jesus affirmed His kingship. His kingdom was based on truth and would be populated by those who listen (adhere) to the truth He proclaimed. Jesus had claimed that He was "the Way, the Truth, and the Life" (John 14:6, ESV). He said His followers would hold to the truth and would be liberated by it (John 8:31-32). He also claimed that the truth of the Word of God was how His followers would be "sanctified" or set apart from the world (John 17:16-17).

This talk about truth was not well-received by Pilate, for the Roman governor asked, "What is truth?" By questioning whether truth could be known, Pilate was rejecting the voice of Jesus. Refusing to acknowledge the truth about Jesus is still the ultimate rejection of His kingship and kingdom (see Matthew 10:32-33; John 3:16-18; 8:24).

Today, I will…acknowledge the life-giving nature of the embodiment of truth—Jesus the Christ. At His Table, I will remember the price He paid so that I could be set free!

Table Meditation
Scripture: 1 Corinthians 10:17; 11:26

We remember Jesus' sacrifice on the cross every Sunday around this memorial Table. We take this opportunity to remember and reflect upon the death of our Lord and Savior.

We look *backward* upon his pain and suffering: the scourging, the nails, the struggling for breath, and the separation from the Father.

We also look *inward* to God's grace in the death of His Son when we contemplate our guilt and His wonderful grace. We enjoy the forgiveness of grace against the contrast of our guilt. Because Jesus died for all, all were under a death sentence. The love and grace of the God who saved us should make us resolve to live up to the clothing we put on at baptism.

We also look *upward* and *outward* as we commune with our Lord and Savior and with our brethren. "Because there is one bread, we who are many are one body, for we all partake of the one bread" (1 Corinthians 10:17, ESV). Jesus freely gave his life in our place so we could receive salvation and enjoy a new relationship in looking up to the Lord and out to our brethren.

We look *forward* to our Lord's return. "For as often as you eat this bread and drink the cup, you proclaim the Lord's death until He comes" (1 Corinthians 11:26, ESV). We proclaim Jesus' sacrifice and that he is still alive and will return in the future.

MONDAY
The Table Setting
Today's Scripture: Psalm 23:5

"You prepare a table before me in the presence of my enemies…" (Psalm 23:5, ESV)

When he stood before Herod, do you suppose Jesus thought, "How many more times will I do this?" He had already appeared once before Annas (the former high priest), Caiaphas (the current high priest), and twice the Sanhedrin. The Jews hid behind Roman law, which stated Rome must carry out capital punishment. The Jews wanted Jesus pronounced guilty and for Rome to move swiftly. Three times, Pilate (Rome's governor in Jerusalem) rendered the verdict on Jesus: "Not guilty!" (Luke 23:4, 13, 22). The people didn't care.

The Jews alleged, "He stirs up the people, teaching throughout all Judea, from Galilee even to this place" (Luke 23:5). Pilate thought, "Galilee? Herod! A different jurisdiction. That's my way out!"(Luke 23:6-7). This would be Pilate's first attempt to wash his hands of Jesus and have Him seated at a different table.

Herod was the ignoble overseer of the Galilee region. The city itself was disdained by the Jews because, during reconstruction, graves were unearthed. Dwelling there would have made a Jew unclean. Herod built the city, anyway. The entire Herodian family was morally bankrupt. John the Baptist pointed it out and, by the scorn of Herod's wife, was beheaded (Matthew 14:1-12). Until now, Herod had only heard of Jesus, and that was enough for Herod to fear Him (Matthew 14, Mark 6, Luke 9). At one point, Jesus was warned to flee the region because Herod wanted Him dead (Luke 13:31-33). Luke 23 records the final encounter with Herod.

Whose table was this, anyway? Jesus did not need Pilate's pardon. The innocent never do. Jesus could endure Herod's humiliation. The genuinely humble always can. It may have been Pilate's hall and Herod's jurisdiction, but it was Jesus' table. God had appointed this time, the moment, this setting. Pilate, the representative of authority, and Herod, the representative of apathy, were no match for the Sovereignty of Jesus.

Today, I will…read Psalm 23 and be mindful of my circumstances, especially the unwanted ones, and remember God prepares a table for me in the presence of even those things that would do me harm, just as He did with His Son.

TUESDAY
The Table Seeking
Today's Scripture: John 12:21

Over the previous three years, Herod had heard about a stranger from Galilee. Herod was familiar with all the renown that accompanied Jesus. When Herod first heard of Jesus, he feared that "Jesus" was the name given to John the Baptist, whom he had beheaded. The murderous Herod was convinced that John the Baptist had risen from the dead, and this Jesus was him (Mark 6:14). No wonder Jesus was warned, "Herod wants to kill you" (Luke 13:31). Herod was terrified.

For whatever reason, be it the passage of time or the hardening of Herod's conscience, Herod's fearful concern toward Jesus dissipated into frivolous curiosity. When Jesus arrives to Herod from Pilate, Herod is delighted because he has been eager to see Jesus perform a miracle like some carnival sideshow (Luke 23:8). Herod's singular interest in Jesus is for amusement alone. Devastating.

Herod questioned Jesus "at some length" (Luke 23:9, ESV). Aren't you the least bit curious about what he asked? Herod strikes me as many things, but an intellectual is not one of them. "How's your revolution coming?" "Could your army not make it?" "If we bring you a lame man, will you heal him?"

The faithful ponder many things throughout their journey with the Master. In some manner, the followers of Jesus say, "I just want to ask Jesus _____." Still, some of the saddest people today are "Herods." They still seek Jesus from a place of intrigue but not investment. They still drift from fearing His name to mocking the name above all names.

"Sir, we wish to see Jesus" (John 12:21, ESV) should be the heart's cry of every seeker. We must not seek the Jesus we want but the Jesus we need. Let curiosity surrender to conviction. We must not seek Him for amusement or appeasement of our desires. We look to Him in awe of all the majesty that is His.

Today, I will…write a list of questions (one or one hundred) and consider all that I would ask Jesus if I could question Him "at some length." Then I will ask myself, "How has He already answered me?"

The Table Sounds
Today's Scripture: John 1:19-20

Growing up, at our dinner table (Dad would insist it's called "supper"), my late brother and I heard the prayers of Dad every evening before sharing what our Mom had prepared. Dad gave thanks for our lives and our family. He was filled with gratitude. He gave thanks for our Mother without fail. He thanked God for his sons. Then he would ask God to supply what we needed with the words, "Thou knowest our needs, more so than we do." It was the sound of his prayer; I can still hear it today. He was so right.

Most courtroom movie scenes depict some moment of chaos, where the courtroom is filled with murmuring and mayhem. But the scene always includes the judge banging the gavel and demanding: "Order in the court!" He threatens the disruptors with charges of contempt. What happens, though, when the judge is the one leading the way with the sound of contempt? Where do you look for order when all you can hear is chaos from judge to jury?

Herod's trial of Jesus was anything but orderly. The chief priests were "vehemently accusing" Jesus (Luke 23:10, ESV). Herod's questioning was anything but thoughtful or reserved. Luke records Herod's scornful interaction with our Lord when he says, "Herod with his soldiers treated Him with contempt and mocked Him" (Luke 23:11, ESV). While appearing before Herod, Jesus would be mocked with words and wardrobe. Once Herod had offered his own personal humiliation of Jesus, he sent Him back to Pilate.

Don't you wonder what Jesus heard? At the table of Herod, we hear mocking and contempt; they are voices of animosity and outrage. Jesus could hear all of these words, but His silence may have been the most piercing sound of all, "He made no answer" (Luke 23:9, ESV). Earlier, when His hair was not matted with spit and blood and before His body was brutally battered, he had prayed, "Not My will, but Yours, be done" (Luke 22:42, ESV). Now before Herod, with all the commotion around Him, perhaps these words still echoed in his heart.

Today, I will…listen beyond the noise and chaos of life around me and listen thoughtfully to the voice of the Sovereign of heaven above. I will be "swift to hear" what the Master says to me.

THURSDAY
The Table Silence
Today's Scripture: Isaiah 53:7

Can you imagine if you were a builder, perhaps a woodworker, and something you crafted by your own imagination and skill suddenly began mocking you? Stop and think about it for a moment. What would be your response? Consider (although impossible) you are the "Alpha and Omega" (Revelation 1:8, ESV); the one who "is before all things, and in him all things hold together" (Colossians 1:17, ESV); the one whom "without him was not any thing made that was made" (John 1:3, ESV); the one who, "upholds the universe by the word of His power" (Hebrews 1:3, ESV). We know what the One who is all these things did: He took it.

Wrapping our heads around this scenario is impossible. Standing before Herod, having the interrogation and questioning turn to mocking and deriding, the Son of God, the creator of all things seen, took it.

History does not hide how reprehensible the Herodian family was. But history also gives some indication that at least Herod Antipas was not entirely provocative to the Jews. The Jewish people struggled with the Roman custom of putting images of living rulers on currency. They viewed these coins as idols. Herod did not make an issue of this, but make no mistake about it, taunting Jews was a sport.

Herod was still in charge, regardless of how we view him. He's the judge of this farce of a court. But the defendant, the One on trial, King Jesus, never answers a single question of Herod's. Outrageous. Herod believed he was the superior one in this duel, but Jesus was the one who demonstrated true power. "He opened not his mouth" (Isaiah 53:7, ESV). The silence of Jesus was deafening.

How often have we "stood" before Jesus, and our own constructed curiosities have prompted us to question Him, accuse Him, and even ridicule Him as though He owed us something? How often have we been met with silence? How often did we listen for the answer in His silence?

Today, I will...consider where I need to be silent in my life so that my faithfulness in deed (what I choose to do and choose not to do) reflects my loyalty to my Lord and Savior.

FRIDAY
The Table Service
Today's Scripture: Luke 22:27

Hours before Jesus would appear before Herod to be mocked and humiliated, our Lord demonstrated His divine purpose when He laid aside His outer garment, girded Himself with a towel, and washed the disciples' feet (John 13:1-20). His entire ministry centered on the act and art of service. He said "service" was why He came (Mark 10:45). He pointed to "service" as the pathway to greatness (Matthew 20:26). He told parables about "faithful" servants (Matthew 25:21) as opposed to "slothful" and "wicked" servants (Matthew 25:26; 18:32).

From these declarations come His ultimate demonstration of service. Through His silence and His endurance, Jesus serves in conditions we can hardly grasp. Jesus served Herod, the chief priests, Pilate, the mob of accusers, and so on.

From the table, after supper, He rose and served the apostles, washing their feet and showing a humility they could not grasp. Let us not forget that Judas would leave the table that night to betray His Savior, walking on clean feet.

Jesus served those who, after three years, still frequently misunderstood His words and message to them (John 12:16). Perhaps what is most significant is that Jesus allowed none of these shortcomings to keep Him from serving with His all. This, more than anything else, was missed by Herod. Imagine the twisted mind of Herod, thinking that mutual hate for Jesus served to bring friendship between him and Pilate.

Is it possible we could be guilty of the same broken thinking as Herod? Seeing Jesus accomplish things in our life, which, in truth, are not those things that truly bring us a better life, much less closer to Him? Is it possible I use Jesus to accomplish my will when I should be lost in doing His?

Today, I will…think of three things in my life and measure their place in my life against the will and life of Jesus. Have I come to the table to have Him serve my will or to surrender my will to His service?

Table Meditation
Scripture: 1 Corinthians 10:16-17

This past Summer, my five granddaughters were at Maywood Christian Camp outside of Hamilton, Alabama. The camp is five miles from Hamilton Church of Christ, where I serve as an elder. The campers spend a lot of time in Bible classes, devotionals, and evening worship. They learn about Jesus, his sacrifice for our sins, and what he expects from us to obtain the gift of eternal life. They see what the Christian life is and the love we have for one another from their camp staff, counselors, and fellow campers. Several campers are baptized into Christ at camp each year. Most of the young people in our congregation are baptized at camp. They are just beginning their Christian journey, committing themselves to Christ and the church. They partake of the Lord's Supper for the first of many times, being in the fellowship of fellow believers and drawing strength from that experience.

When we partake of the Lord's supper this morning, in addition to remembering Christ's death and resurrection, we must look inward and see if we are living up to the commitment that we made long ago and feel the excitement we felt when we were baptized.

1 Corinthians 10:16-17, ESV

"The cup of blessing that we bless, is it not a participation in the blood of Christ? The bread that we break, is it not a participation in the body of Christ? Because there is one bread, we who are many are one body, for we all partake of the one bread."

MONDAY
Barabbas or Jesus
Today's Scripture: Matthew 27:15-21; John 18:39, 40

At the feast of the Passover, it was customary that Pilate, the Roman governor, would release one prisoner of the people's choosing. Pilate, seeing Jesus as obviously innocent, asked the crowd if they wanted Him released. Matthew's account gives a glimpse into the deceptive inner workings of the Jewish authorities. He tells us the chief priest and elders persuaded the crowd to ask for Barabbas in order to destroy Jesus. The crowd roared, "Not this man, but Barabbas!" John 18:40 explains that Barabbas was a convicted criminal. Jesus was not. The Jewish authorities were so blinded by their envy and pride that they would rather see an innocent man murdered than a convicted criminal go free. Wow! What evil hearts. So, in an unjust turn of events and probably the greatest display of spiritual irony, guilty Barabbas (meaning "son of the father" in Aramaic) is set free, and Jesus, the innocent Son of the Father, is condemned to die as a criminal.

This unjust exchange, Barabbas for Jesus, is the entire gospel. Jesus, innocent on all counts, is sentenced to death and Barabbas, guilty on all counts, is set free. A simple reading of the text enrages us. Because it's not fair. It's unfair. As we read the text, we want to yell out over the crowd, "Let Jesus go and give Barabbas what he deserves!" Then we realize in the story of the gospel, I am Barabbas. I'm the guilty, condemned criminal, and Jesus, the Son of God, died so I can experience life and freedom. He took my place. The apostle Paul wrote, "For our sake He made Him to be sin who knew no sin, so that in Him we might become the righteousness of God" (2 Corinthians 5:21, ESV). Because Jesus died and was raised from the dead, all people have the opportunity to stand innocent before the God of heaven and earth.

Today, I will…live in gratitude to God, knowing Jesus took my place and my punishment.

TUESDAY
Jesus Is Scourged
Today's Scripture: Matthew 27:26; John 19:1

The Bible only briefly describes the torture the Roman soldiers inflicted upon Jesus. Matthew writes a single sentence: "Then he (Pilate) released for them Barabbas, and having scourged Jesus, delivered him to be crucified" (Matthew 27:26, ESV). John writes even more concisely, "Then Pilate took Jesus and flogged him" (John 19:1, ESV).

Crucifixion was a brutal, agonizing, and torturous death. But even before His crucifixion, Jesus endured another form of extremely painful torture. Jesus was scourged. Scourging was the worst kind of flogging. It wasn't a form of execution, but it could be brutal enough to be fatal. This torture consisted of being beaten with a whip that had at least three strands, each around three feet long, that were weighted with lead balls or pieces of bone. The weighted strands of the whip would strike the back of the individual so violently that the skin would break open. Jesus would have been fastened to a post, stripped of His clothes, and whipped from the shoulders down to His waist. The blood loss and pain would have left Jesus unimaginably weak. It's no surprise Simon of Cyrene was compelled to carry Jesus' cross (Mark 15:21).

Isaiah prophesied this torture approximately 700 years before it took place in Isaiah 53. The prophet wrote, "Surely He has borne our griefs and carried our sorrows; yet we esteemed him stricken, smitten by God, and afflicted. But He was pierced for our transgressions; He was crushed for our iniquities; upon Him was the chastisement that brought us peace, and with His wounds we are healed. All we like sheep have gone astray; we have turned—every one—to his own way; and the Lord has laid on Him the iniquity of us all" (Isaiah 53:4-6, ESV). Isaiah would go on to write, "It was the will of the LORD to crush Him" (Isaiah 53:10, ESV). By His wounds we are healed.

Today, I will…meditate on Isaiah 53 and Philippians 3:10, recognizing the pain and agony Jesus endured because of me.

WEDNESDAY
Behold the Man
Today's Scripture: John 19:2-5

After Jesus was scourged, the Roman soldiers dressed Him in a purple robe, fabricated a crown of thorns, and sarcastically crowned Jesus as "King of the Jews." They mocked Him, saying, "Hail, King of the Jews!" They slapped Jesus and humiliated Him. They did their best to make Him look foolish. Pilate brought the weakened and bloodied Jesus out before the Jews and said to them, "Behold the man!" It sounds strange, but we should listen to Pilate. We need to routinely stop, stare, and consider the man Jesus, the King of kings. From the perspective of a first-century Jew, the man Jesus didn't look like a king.

Isaiah wrote, "He had no form or majesty that we should look at Him, and no beauty that we should desire Him. He was despised and rejected by men; a man of sorrows and acquainted with grief" (Isaiah 53:2-3, ESV). In the moment, Jesus looked like a political criminal getting what He deserved. As Jesus stood next to Pilate, no one saw the will of God in action (Isaiah 53:10). When the people looked at Jesus, no one saw God's eternal plan unfolding before their very eyes. No one saw Jesus Christ the righteous as the propitiation (the atoning sacrifice for their sins, 1 John 2:1-2), but that's exactly what was happening. The eternal plan of God, put into motion after the actions of Adam and Eve millennia before, was about to be fulfilled.

Behold the Man! When the church gathers on Sunday to fellowship, sing, pray, and observe the Lord's Supper, our attention should be focused on Jesus. When we eat the bread and drink the cup, the words of Pilate should echo in our hearts and minds. Behold the Man! With his crown of thorns, bloody face, and dingy purple robe, the sight of Jesus would have been miserable to behold, but the glory of God was on display.

Today, I will…thank the LORD for the atoning sacrifice of Jesus and the forgiveness it alone provides.

THURSDAY
I Find No Guilt in Him
Today's Scripture: Matthew 27:24,25; John 19:6b

"I find no guilt in Him." Those are probably the most truthful words ever spoken by Pilate. Not once. Not twice. Three times, Pilate truthfully tells the Jews, "I find no guilt in Him" (John 18:38; 19:4,6). Pilate was ready to release Jesus, but the Jews had other plans and responded, "We have a law, and according to that law He ought to die because He has made Himself the Son of God" (John 19:7, ESV). Pilate's wife even warned him. "Have nothing to do with this righteous man, for I have suffered much because of Him today in a dream" (Matthew 27:19, ESV). One of Pilate's official duties was to keep the peace. When he saw the beginnings of a riot, he acquiesced to the Jews' demands and handed Jesus over to them to be crucified (Matthew 27:24).

The Bible testifies to the innocence of Jesus. "He himself bore our sins in His body on the tree, that we might die to sin and live to righteousness. By His wounds you have been healed" (1 Peter 2:24, ESV). "You know that He appeared in order to take away sins, and in Him there is no sin" (1 John 3:5, ESV). Jesus was tempted just like us, yet He was without sin (Hebrews 4:15). His innocence is what qualified Him to be our atoning sacrifice. "For our sake He made Him to be sin who knew no sin, so that in Him we might become the righteousness of God" (2 Corinthians 5:21, ESV). We will always struggle with temptation and sin, but we can look to the One without sin, a sympathetic Advocate who graciously offers us forgiveness.

Today, I will…know Jesus is sinless, righteous, and was crucified because of my guilt.

Let Him Be Crucified
Today's Scripture: Matthew 27:22, 23; John 19:6-7, 12-16

After releasing Barabbas, Pilate asked the Jews, "Then what shall I do with Jesus who is called Christ?"

Without hesitation, the crowd yelled, "Let Him be crucified!"

Pilate responded, "Why, what evil has He done?"

Again, without hesitation and with more enthusiasm, "Let Him be crucified!"

Pilate ordered Jesus to be scourged and brought Jesus out to the crowds again. When they saw the bloodied Jesus, they cried out yet again, "Crucify Him, crucify Him!"

Finally, to ensure Jesus' execution, the chief priests and officers goad Pilate with the potent accusation of opposing Caesar. About the sixth hour (noon) Pilate said to the Jews, "Behold your King!" The Jews cried out, "Away with Him, away with Him, crucify Him." Then Pilate asked, "Shall I crucify your King?" The chief priests answered, "We have no king but Caesar!" So, Pilate delivered Jesus over to be crucified.

The mob mentality is both ugly and terrifying. The Jewish officials had long wanted to get rid of Jesus. Finally, their chance appears, and they capitalize on it. The religious leadership got what it wanted. Why did they want Jesus dead? Matthew 27:18 says, "For he (Pilate) knew that it was out of envy that they had delivered Him up" (ESV). The answer is envy. The Jewish leaders were envious of Jesus. The success of Jesus' ministry was eroding these officials' power and influence. They were deeply envious of Jesus for doing good and being blessed by the Father (Acts 10:38). The religious leaders were so consumed with envy that when they saw the opportunity to destroy Jesus, they took it.

Today, I will…search my heart and motives for envy and jealousy, putting them to death because Jesus died for me.

Table Meditation
Scripture: 1 Corinthians 15:1-4

It can be easy for Christians to lose focus in an ever-changing world that continues to move further and further away from God. Since the establishment of the Lord's church in the first century, worldly influences have tempted Christians to lose their focus on things above. The church in Corinth is an example of this.

Paul received word that the church in Corinth was experiencing spiritual problems that led to division, strife, and a loss of focus. In his first letter to them, Paul took them back to the basics and reminded them of the good news they had originally believed and had taken their stand (1 Corinthians 15:1-4):

1. Christ died for our sins.
2. He was buried.
3. He was raised on the third day just as prophesied.

This is the foundation of everything we believe, what we stand for, and the basis of our salvation. When the world is closing in, and we feel ourselves begin to have spiritual struggles, we need to turn back to this basic truth. Jesus is who He said He was; He lived a perfect life as an example for us to follow; He died on the cross as a sacrifice for our sins; He conquered death and has gone to heaven to prepare a place for us.

When we take communion together every Sunday, we are taken back to the basics. We remember this great sacrifice made on the cross for us. We remember the importance of holding fast to the Gospel and striving to obey God's Word.

MONDAY
Say His Name
Today's Scripture: Luke 23:26

"Say his/her name!" is a phrase we hear a lot today. It is usually invoked to draw attention to the victim of a heinous crime or to show respect to someone who has gone unrecognized. Here, we use it because of the unusual fact that we are given the name of a man who was randomly picked out of the crowd. All of a sudden, this man, his name, his home, and even his family are front and center of the biggest drama in human history.

The man's name is Simon, a Jewish name like that of the man Jesus would call Peter. Simon is a Jew who lives in Cyrene, a region in North Africa, which today would be in Libya, close to the town of Tripoli. Cyrene was a center of the Jewish population. In Acts 2, we read of Jews and proselytes who came to Jerusalem from Cyrene for Pentecost and were there for the beginning of the church (Acts 2:10). Acts 6 speaks of the Synagogue of the Freedmen, which included both Cyrenians and Alexandrians. Simon was a devout man who came from a devout area for the Passover.

Additionally, Mark identifies Simon as the father of Alexander and Rufus (Mark 15:21). The Gospel of Mark was written somewhere between 50 and 60 A.D. The book of Romans about 56 A.D. Some members of the church were no doubt well-known to the recipients of these letters. In Romans 16:13, you read of "Rufus, a choice man in the Lord" and "his mother" who had become close to the Apostle Paul.

Here is a man plucked out of nowhere to help Jesus carry the cross. We know nothing about him. He was unfamiliar with Jesus. But he went all the way to the cross, and no one can do that without being impacted significantly. He becomes a believer. He went back to Cyrene and influenced others to believe in Jesus (cf. Acts 11:20). His wife became a believer, and his sons. Simon had a great impact on the church in northern Africa (cf. Acts 13:1).

The many rejected Jesus. But there were the few—the thief, the centurion, and the Cyrenian.

Today, I will…reflect on the good influence of men and women of faith who have gone before. "We stand on the shoulders of giants." I will not let their influence go to waste. I will influence someone for Jesus Christ.

TUESDAY

They Laid on Him the Cross

Today's Scripture: Luke 23:26

We are familiar with the concept of volunteering—freely giving of yourself and your time for a cause. Perhaps you have volunteered to help at church, with the PTA, or some civic activity or organization. Volunteering is noble and is universally applauded.

Have you ever been "voluntold?" They say that in the military one thing you never do is volunteer, but you will often be "voluntold." "Voluntold" is not so freely given and is not usually looked upon, particularly by the victim, as something quite so noble.

Matthew and Mark both use the word "compelled" concerning the seizing of Simon. Roman soldiers had absolute authority over all citizens. Do you remember Jesus' words to his disciples in the Sermon on the Mount (Matthew 5:41)? This is not the same idea that Jesus had in mind in Luke 9:23 and Luke 14:27 concerning taking up one's cross. Simon had come into town, presumably for Passover. We cannot assume that he knew anything about Jesus. He had no part in the previous proceedings. He is a stranger. But, he is "voluntold" to carry the cross.

We do not know why he did it. Perhaps it was a simple duty to obey a Roman command. Maybe it was some sense of sympathy for the bloodied and wearied Jesus. Whatever his motivation might have been, Simon becomes a sympathetic and revered character in the story of the cross because of his willingness to "take up the cross" and carry it to Calvary.

Simon meets Jesus in a most unique way. While it would appear to be a random choice from the vantage point of the soldiers, it could hardly have been random from the vantage point of God. His name is mentioned. His family is mentioned. This man for a moment becomes front and center in the story of Jesus' journey to the cross.

Today, I will…volunteer to serve Jesus. It just might change the course of your life.

WEDNESDAY
Out of the Crowd
Today's Scripture: Luke 23:27-30

Jesus was no stranger to crowds. Early in the book of Mark, the crowd was so great inside the house where he was teaching that four men had to let their paralyzed friend down through the roof (Mark 2:2-12). We are familiar with the feeding of the 5,000 (John 6:5-14) and the 4,000 (Mark 8:1-10). The crowds forced him into the mountain to present a sermon (Matthew 5-7), and to the seashore to share parables (Matthew 13).

On occasion, we see people singled out of the crowd: people like Andrew and John who left the crowd around John the Immerser to follow Jesus (John 1:37), people like the little boy with the five loaves and two fish (John 6:9); people like the twelve (Luke 6). In Luke 23:27-30, it is a group of women.

Women also appear prominently throughout the life of Jesus, from his mother Mary to his friends Mary and Martha. There was also Mary Magdalene and the woman with an issue of blood. The women were the last to leave the cross and the first to arrive at the tomb. It is not clear if the women mentioned here are those same women or some other group. Some have suggested they were professional mourners. Jesus, however, has a word of warning for them as He makes His way to the cross.

In a rather prophetic tone, Jesus addresses these women as representatives of the nation—"daughters of Jerusalem." He pointed out that they were weeping over the wrong thing: "Weep for yourselves and for your children" (His death versus the downfall of the nation). He then foretold the destruction of the nation due to their rejection of Him. The time of grace had faded away. Judgment was certain. The words of verse 30 are repeated in Revelation 6. There was no escape from this judgment.

Today, I will...step out of the crowd to see the true condition of society. Weep for the lost. And, proclaim Jesus' death as the only remedy to our sinful condition.

THURSDAY
A Final Word from the Storyteller
Today's Scripture: Luke 23:31

Jesus was a master storyteller. The gospels record approximately twenty-five parables. Some are recorded in all three synoptics. Matthew records five parables peculiar to his gospel, while Luke records ten. John is the only gospel writer who does not record any parables.

A distinctive feature of the parables is their vivid imagery. "A sower went out to sow." "A net that was thrown into the sea and gathered fish of every kind." A man having a hundred sheep lost one and left the ninety-nine to find the one. A woman loses a silver coin and sweeps the whole house to find it. A son requests his inheritance, wastes it, and returns to a forgiving father. The pictures leap off the page and burn into our imagination.

One writer calls the words of Luke 23:31, "parabolic." Another writer refers to them as a proverb. Either way, the imagery is vivid, and it tells a story. The basic meaning of Jesus' words is that if bad things happen when all is well, what will happen when it is not? The green tree symbolizes life and is therefore easy comparison to Jesus. But, who does the dry wood refer to?

One writer suggests that the word is an indirect reference to God's work of judgment. If God could judge His own Son for our forgiveness, what would his judgment be like on those who reject his offer of propitiation? Dry wood is that which is dead or cut down. If it is possible to consume live wood, how easy would it be to consume dry wood? If the Romans, as God's instrument, could do this to the green tree (Jesus), what are they going to do to the dry wood that has been cut off and is dead (Israel)? Jesus uses this vivid language to describe God's judgment on physical Israel.

Today, I will…cling to Jesus, the author and finisher of our faith, the propitiation for our sins, and our advocate with the Father. Without Jesus, I am cut off and dead, and ripe for destruction. Only in Jesus will I find life.

FRIDAY
Too Common Criminals
Today's Scripture: Luke 23:32-33

"Between two thieves
They crucified the Son of God"[1]

Matthew and Mark identify them as robbers or thieves. Luke, however, refers to them as criminals twice in our passage. Theirs was no petty theft. Their crimes incurred the death penalty of the Roman government.

It would be easy to assume we have nothing in common with such men. Most of us would never dream of stealing from someone else, or the other crimes they may have committed along with their theft. So, in one way, we might think of them as very uncommon thieves. They were the worst of the worst—men certainly deserving to die.

That, however, is exactly where we find commonality with these men. They deserved to be there and we do too. "All have sinned and come short of the glory of God" (Romans 3:23, ESV). 2 Corinthians 5:21 reads, "For our sake he made him to be sin who knew no sin so that in him we might become the righteousness of God" (ESV). Jesus' death is a reminder that we deserved to be there, but He did not. One of the robbers even took notice of this in verse 41: "And we indeed justly, for we are receiving the due reward of our deeds; but this man has done nothing wrong" (Luke 23:41, ESV).

That they were receiving their just punishment while Jesus had done nothing wrong creates another very uncommon circumstance. How did these two men find themselves in the company of Jesus? We ordinarily gravitate toward people of similar backgrounds and experiences. Although Jesus was known for dining with "publicans and sinners" (see Mark 2:15; 9:11; 11:19; Luke 15:1), these men were hardened criminals. At one point, one of them realizes their juxtaposed state and asks to join Jesus in paradise (Luke 23:42). Which is another very important reminder for us: those who deserve to die must draw near to one who did not deserve to die if we want to live. "We see him who for a little while was made lower than the angels, namely Jesus, crowned with glory and honor because of the suffering of death, so that by the grace of God he might taste death for everyone." (Hebrews 2:9, ESV).

Today, I will...reflect on my sinful condition before God. Realize that without the sacrifice of Jesus, I have no hope of living with Him. Resolve to remain in union with Him and not return to the crimes of my former life.

---

[1] J. R. Baxter, *He Bore It All*, 1926.

HIS CRUCIFIXION
FRIDAY
9:00 AM-12 NOON

Table Meditation
Scripture: Luke 22:44

The more we study the Word, the more we see Jesus. This may be seen in the words, "Do this in remembrance of Me." When we hold the unleavened bread and the cup in our hands, it means more than a piece of bread and a sip of juice. For the bread, we need to see the "big picture" of the Old Testament. The Old Testament is a path that moves from Creation to the Cross. It reveals God's providence for the salvation of all of us. Luke 24:44 says, "Then He said to them, "These are the words which I spoke to you while I was still with you, that all things must be fulfilled which were written in the Law of Moses and the Prophets and the Psalms concerning Me"(NKJV).

For the cup, it reveals the pain and ugliness of sin—the torture of beaten, torn flesh—this is the picture of our sin endured by Jesus. It is our death that Jesus experienced for us. And in the cup, we see the glory of God given to Jesus as our Savior. The blood He shed is our lifeline to eternity. In Jesus' resurrection, we have the surety of our living hope. A hope not of doubt, but a hope of promise for all of those who are in Christ Jesus.

Remembrance is having a greater love for God and His Son, the Messiah. It is because of His love that He left the majesty of Heaven and walked with us. His love taught us the Words of Life. His love suffered for us, paying the tremendous penalty of sin. His love has never wavered. I know He loves me because He died in my place. I happily sing, "Jesus loves me."

Remember His Agony
Today's Scripture: Matthew 27:32-34

A first century A.D. Roman crucifixion spike driven through the remains of a human ankle bone is on permanent display in the Israel Museum of Archaeology in Jerusalem. It was discovered inside the first century A.D. ossuary (stone carved bone box) of Jehohanan the son of Hagkol, in northeast Jerusalem. It is a gruesome reminder of the horrific and painful nature of crucifixion. When a man was crucified, he was affixed to the cross with nails driven through his wrists and feet; he most often died from either suffocation or asphyxia. During crucifixion, the weight of the body pulling down on the outstretched arms and shoulders would tend to paralyze the diaphragm and inhibit one's ability to eliminate air from their lungs. To avoid suffocation, a crucified man was forced to exact excruciating pain upon himself by pushing against the nails driven through the ankles. This enabled the diaphragm to properly exhale the air and carbon dioxide collecting in the lungs.

At Calvary, Jesus was bruised for our transgression and was stricken for our griefs (Isaiah 53). On the cross He suffered beyond measure and experienced the trauma of torture. While on earth, He hungered. He wept. He hurt. He labored. But especially at the cross, He suffered. So, when we come to the Table of the Lord to remember His death, let us never forget that He was in every way tempted like we are today (Hebrews 4:14-15). Jesus understands the pain of loneliness and isolation (Matthew 4:1; 13: 55-56; 26:36-40). He endured the emotional agony of separation (Matthew 27:46), and the torture of a bloody scourge and a tormenting cross. He tasted of death for all (Hebrews 2:9); He revealed Himself as a compassionate and loving God able to help those who are suffering (Hebrews 2:16-18); He is ready to save those who obey (John 3:16; Hebrews 5:8-9). Because of the agony of the cross, we can know that Jesus understands our pain and sorrow. It is one more reason that we should look forward to gathering at His Table: because it reminds that He both cares and understands.

Today, I will...remember the agony of the cross and what Jesus endured for me.

TUESDAY
Remember the Place
Today's Scripture: Matthew 27:32-35; John 19:16-18

Scripture tells us that Jesus was crucified at "a place called Golgotha (which means 'the place of the skull')", but we are never told why it has this meaning. Luke's account uses a Greek word known as *kranion* which is a general term for "skull." Did the place where Jesus was crucified resemble a skull? Or was this term used only because the site for crucifixion was connected to the death of criminals and malefactors? Some suggest that a place known as the Garden Tomb north of the Damascus gate in Jerusalem is the place where Jesus was crucified, because of natural skull like features formed on the face of a cliff near an ancient burial tomb. Others suggest that the Church of the Holy Sepulcher, west of the old city of Jerusalem, is the location for His burial. The Latin word for skull is *calva,* and thus the term "Calvary" became associated with the site of the crucifixion.

While we are never told why Golgotha meant "place of the skull," the imagery associated with this name calls to mind not only death, but also the need for death in God's plan of salvation. Because God is holy and cannot overlook the dictates of law, He must be just and punish wrong (Exodus 34:7b; Ezekiel 18:20). The penalty of death is required for injustice and sin (Romans 6:23). Someone who refuses to punish a criminal who is guilty of the law cannot be declared as just. So, for God to be just and yet also the one who justifies (or pardons) sinners, He must offer a substitute for punishment which satisfies the requirements of a penal code (Romans 3:23-27). This is exactly what Jesus did on our behalf. Sinners deserve to die, but Jesus died and atoned for our sins. We now have "at-one-ment" with God and come to His Table with rejoicing.

Today, I will...remember the place of His death while I sing the well-known hymn, "Lead Me to Calvary," written by Jenny Hussey: "Lest I forget his love for me" (1921).

Remember the Thief
Today's Scripture: John 19:17-19

Over the course of my ministry, I have been blessed to witness the baptism of several elderly individuals. One such lady was in her 90's and another was in the latter stages of congestive heart failure. Yet another was a man so old he could barely walk up the six steps to reach the baptistry. In each of those situations, I was reminded that it is never too late to join the vineyard of God's workers. Even those who appear at the eleventh hour are promised the same wages as though who arrive early (Matthew 20:1-15).

When Jesus was taken to the "place of the skull" to be put to death, He was crucified between two thieves. Scripture does not tell us what or how much they had stolen, only that they were thieves. At first, according to Matthew 27:44, both of them reviled Jesus. But as the day wore on one of them repented and asked that the Lord might remember him when He came again unto His kingdom (Luke 23:42-43). To this the Lord replied, "today you will be with me in paradise." The thief on the cross is a vivid reminder that as long as there is breath in your lungs and a will to be saved, it is never too late to accept the Lord's invitation to sit at His Table.

The beauty of the thief on the cross and his story can also be seen in the fact that God invites all to join Him at His Table. Whether they are sinners, tax-collectors, the outcast, or even penitent thieves, Jesus wants all to join Him (Mark 2:13-17; Luke 14:23). His Table communion with its emblems of His body and blood remind us that everyone needs salvation. There is none righteous, no—not one (Romans 3:11; 23). Truly, God doesn't want anyone to perish, for He desires that all should come to repentance (2 Peter 3:9).

Today, I will...let others know of the long-suffering of God who doesn't want anyone to perish.

Remember His Humiliation
Today's Scripture: Matthew 27:35-44

I'm not sure who authored the phrase, "words will never hurt me" from the familiar adage "sticks and stones may break my bones," but based on personal experience, I can confidently say that it is not accurate. The Bible tells us that words can cut like a sword (Proverbs 12:18) and break the spirit of a man (Proverbs 15:4). Words DO hurt, and they are meant not only to harm and disparage, but also to prejudice and discredit. Demeaning speech can often occur within a family, a religious debate, and of course most often in the arena of politics. The tongue is full of deadly poison and when it strikes it can sting and maim its intended target (James 2:5-9).

When we come to the table, it is important for us to remember how others were seeking to humiliate and disparage our Lord with their remarks. Not only did He endure hateful speech during His public ministry, but also while writhing in pain during His crucifixion. As His tortured body hung from the cross, the Bible says He was "derided," "mocked," and "reviled" (Matthew 27:35-44). These words in Greek were often associated with speaking harm, slander, profanity, abuse, disgrace and shame. I wonder how their words made Jesus feel. Both as God and as a man, our Lord possessed the capacity to mourn and weep. While the unimaginable physical pain of the cross is beyond our comprehension, the emotional pain He endured would have also been excruciating. Yet, despite His own physical and emotional pain, He bore OUR griefs and carried OUR sorrows (Isaiah 53:4).

Perhaps you have been hurt by what others have said and done to you. God wants you to know that the Lord had you in mind when He hung upon the cross. He made it His mission to feel what you feel and to hurt in the way you hurt. He understands and sought to take our hurt and shame upon Himself.

Today, I will...thank the Lord for bearing my humiliation and pain even while He was enduring His.

Remember His Love
Today's Scripture: John 19:25-27

It was a painful experience to see her die. She could only move her eyes, using them occasionally to look at who was talking or to discover who had entered her room. A massive stroke had ravaged her body and for over a week she lay lifeless on her bed in the home where her husband had died only months before. We watched and prayed, hoping that her body and mind could endure her pain. We were comforted in knowing she loved the Lord, and that she was surrounded by the children and family she had loved so much. Mom loved her family with great affection and desired to have them always nearby. As difficult as it was to watch her die, we wouldn't have been anywhere else. Her love for us was powerful, as was ours for her, and it chained us to that room until the very end. We didn't want her to suffer alone.

When Jesus was in agony on the cross, He likewise did not suffer alone. While the burden of a sinful world was only His to carry, He was nevertheless surrounded by His mother and friends until the end. The Bible tells us that His mother, along with Mary the wife of Cleopas, Mary Magdalene, and "many women" were present those hours He hung upon the cross (Matthew 27:55-56). I can't help but think that somehow it might have helped Him endure the pain.

Yet, what I think about the most when reflecting upon His death was not the love and respect shown to Jesus by His family and friends, but rather the love HE was showing to them. Undoubtedly, they were at His side because He had first loved them, and yet even in death His love was still evident. Though His body was writhing in pain, He remained focused on His singular mission to serve and save others (Matthew 20:28). Whether it was the thief who had earlier reviled Him, or the needs and concerns of His mother, Jesus "loved them to the end" (John 13:1, ESV).

Today, I will…follow the example of Jesus by loving others even to the end.

Table Meditation
Scripture: Romans 5:8

Paul says in Romans 5:8, "While we were still sinners, Christ died for us" (ESV). The psalmist explained in Psalms 107:14 that He brought us out of darkness and the shadow of death, and He broke away our chains. Today, without Jesus Christ, we are lost in our sins, and we are in darkness. However, through Jesus' humble obedience to God, He was victorious, and God has exalted his name above all names, Philippians 2:8-9.

When Christians examine and prepare to take the Lord's supper, we remember what Jesus endured. We remember the sacrifice, the life, the death, the burial, and His resurrection. We are called to do so each Lord's Day. But let's not forget that God, through His Son, was victorious over sin and death. God, through Jesus, made a way for us, and because our Lord was victorious, we are eternally blessed.   1 Peter 1:3-10 tells us that Christians have a living Hope through Jesus, an inheritance waiting for us in Heaven that is imperishable, undefiled, and unfading, and the salvation of our souls. Today, as we meditate on the sacrifice, let us also remember the victory of Jesus Christ.

MONDAY
The Why of the Gospel
Today's Scripture: Matthew 27:45-46

The time had come. The Lord had predicted, "I will make the sun go down at noon and darken the earth in broad daylight...I will make it like the mourning for an only son" (Amos 8:9-10, ESV). The sun should have been at its brightest. But from noon until three o'clock, darkness set the scene for the moment that would change history.

Imagine the heart of the Father. His wrath against sin was mixed with deep sorrow over His Son's death. Once, God had caused the very stars to declare His Son's birth. But now, in the end, the darkness of the skies declared the heaviness of His heart.

Jesus' prayer is both Scriptural and dramatic: "My God, my God, why have you forsaken me?" (Matthew 27:46, ESV). Jesus' prayer shows that He sympathizes with our struggles. Jesus asks, in a very personal moment, "Why me?"

Often, preachers will put a positive spin on this prayer. They rightly point out that Jesus quotes Psalm 22:1. The Psalm begins with doubts and ends with trust in God. That is true. But perhaps Jesus chooses these words because it is really how He feels. If Jesus wanted to communicate a positive thought, he could have quoted the very next Psalm (Psalm 23:1). Why choose this one? He feels abandoned and "forsaken." When Jesus says these words, maybe we should stand back in silence at the awful word "forsaken."

The question "Why?" is the toughest question to answer. When, what, where, and how can be answered by facts. Why requires a search for reasons. If we can answer why, we will understand the depths of the gospel.

This moment also teaches us the deepest meaning of faith. It is trusting God even when we feel forsaken. Here, in His last moments, Jesus reaches through the darkness, and, in agony and betrayal, grabs hold of God with all His might.

Today, I will...learn to trust God even in my darkest moments, even when I do not feel Him with me.

TUESDAY
The Mockers
Today's Scripture: Matthew 27:47-49

"And some of the bystanders, hearing it, said, 'This man is calling Elijah'" (Matthew 27:47, ESV).

The prophet Elijah was believed by the Jews of Jesus' day to be someone they could call on in times of trouble. He had not died but instead ascended to God in a chariot (2 Kings 2:11). Malachi 4:5 left Old Testament readers with the expectation that Elijah would return at the time of the Messiah.

Those hearing Jesus' call, "Eli, Eli," believed somehow that he was desperately trying to be proven right at the last moment of his life. They must have thought Jesus believed Elijah would show up and prove Him to be the Messiah, and maybe he would even save Him from death.

These bystanders are like so many who did not believe Jesus during His ministry. "He was in the world… yet the world did not know him" (John 1:10, ESV). They were energized by Jesus' defeat and by His agony. They did not actually wonder "whether Elijah will come to save him" (Matthew 27:49, ESV). They hoped for a show from a Messianic pretender.

But Jesus did not turn to spectacular events for rescue, though He could have. Instead, "Jesus cried out again with a loud voice and yielded up his spirit" (Matthew 27:50, ESV). The fact that Jesus cried out at all is strange, given that a crucified person usually died of suffocation. The reason He is able to do so is given in the text: He "yielded up his spirit." Jesus died by His own voluntary and active choice. This death, this moment, is the Gospel. God decreed that the penalty for sin is death (Genesis 2:17). Jesus, in this death, freed us from that penalty. He did so voluntarily. He did so "for the joy that was set before Him" (Hebrews 12:2, ESV). That joy is me. That joy is you.

Today, I will…strengthen my mind against becoming like the mockers and doubters. I will set my mind on forever being thankful He took God's wrath for me in my stead.

WEDNESDAY
God's Vindication
Today's Scripture: Matthew 27:51-54

"And behold, the curtain of the temple was torn in two, from top to bottom. And the earth shook, and the rocks were split" (Matthew 27:51, ESV).

The mockers and doubters had their moment. They enjoyed seeing Jesus' defeat as a Messianic pretender. But now, God replies dramatically to their mocking by vindicating His Son.

"Behold" grabs us by the shoulders and points us to the splitting of the temple veil. This scene visually explains the atonement and provides a profound understanding of Jesus' death. We could even say that the splitting of the veil is God's own interpretation of Jesus' work. The splitting of the temple veil says that the temple is now over (Matthew 23:38; 24:34), and access to God is now open. The Holy of Holies provided access to God's presence. The veil outside this room separated God's holy presence from sinful people. Jesus' work splits the veil and allows us to come right into God's presence.

"And the earth shook, and the rocks were split" (Matthew 27:51b, ESV) tempts us to think destructively, but the earth shaking and rocks splitting lead to something astonishing: "many bodies of the saints who had fallen asleep were raised" (Matthew 27:52, ESV). This moment is like the preview trailers that come on before the main movie. Matthew is telling us that in the death of Jesus, even death has died. Not only has Jesus opened the temple veil, but he has also opened the tombs and overcame death itself. Jesus conquers all.

The Greeks mocked Paul and the early church for teaching the resurrection of the body. Bodies are buried and they become dust. But the power of God makes empty tombs possible and not ridiculous. The split veil and the open tombs are God's answers to our biggest problems.

Today, I will...celebrate my complete and total access to God, and boldly "draw near to the throne of grace ... in time of need" (Hebrews 4:16, ESV).

THURSDAY
The Soldiers' Confession
Today's Scripture: Matthew 27:54-56

Those who mocked Jesus said, "If you are the Son of God, come down from the cross" (Matthew 27:40, ESV). Now, the centurions confess this very thing: "Truly this was the Son of God" (Matthew 27:54, ESV).

In Matthew, there were many questions and confessions about who Jesus truly was. God Himself had confessed Jesus as "beloved Son" twice (Matthew 3:17; 17:5). Peter confessed Jesus as Christ and Son of the living God (Matthew 16:16). The high priest asked if Jesus was the Christ (Matthew 26:63). Those who mocked said, in effect, "This can't be the Son of God." But the centurions answer, "Truly," He is (Matthew 27:54).

These centurions see what Jesus says and what Jesus does. To them, it is convincing. In fact, seeing and hearing Jesus is the only way anyone comes to faith. Proclaiming what Jesus says and does is the work of the church in general and every Christian in particular.

No sooner has Jesus died and the earth shaken, but people begin to come to faith. And the converts come from unexpected places. Who could have expected hardened Roman soldiers? Just as Jesus had earlier quoted Psalm 22:1, now we see the effects of His work in another of the Psalm's verses: "All the ends of the earth shall remember and turn to the LORD" (Psalm 22:27, ESV). These soldiers were "filled with awe," better translated as fear (Matthew 27:54). Fear can be a great motivator. All of Jesus' sermons in Matthew end with a fearful warning. Too many Christians experience churches that never call hearers to repentance. Many others focus on a harsh message that does not properly appreciate the mercies of the cross. The church should simply preach what Jesus says and does while maintaining proper reverence for God.

Today, I will…confidently confess Jesus as the Son of God, knowing that "everyone who acknowledges me before men, I also will acknowledge before my Father who is in heaven" (Matthew 10:32, ESV).

It Is Finished
Today's Scripture: John 19:28-30

Real love is substitutionary sacrifice. Think about it. Parents often sacrifice their comfort, time, and money for the betterment of their children. A good spouse sacrifices by putting their partner's needs and wants ahead of their selfish desires. Why? Because all real love involves substitutionary sacrifice.

Jesus gave all the love He could give through substitutionary sacrifice. To be sure, He accomplished many things on the cross. He defeated the forces of evil (1 Corinthians 2:8). He also demonstrated to the world the transformative power of love (John 13:35). But we also cannot miss the loving nature of His sacrifice. Isaiah 53:4–6 reminds us of the heart of the substitutionary Gospel: "Surely he has borne our griefs and carried our sorrows ... he was pierced for our transgressions; he was crushed for our iniquities; upon him was the chastisement that brought us peace, and with his wounds we are healed" (ESV).

In John 19:28–30, John uses the word "finished" twice. John is making an important point. The first time is found in verse 28, where it says Jesus knew "that all was now finished." What could this mean? I think Jesus knows He has done all that He set out to do. Jesus said He glorified God, "having accomplished the work that you gave me to do" (John 17:4, ESV).

The second time John records the word "finished" is found in verse 30, where Jesus says, "It is finished." Now He has finished His entire Messianic mission (John 1:18; 29), fulfilled all of Scripture concerning Himself, and filled to the fullest the will of His Father in Heaven (Matthew 26:39). Having done all, "he bowed his head and gave up his spirit" (John 19:30, ESV). Seeing all of His finished work, we too should bow our heads in awe at His greatness.

Today, I will...celebrate the "finished" work of Jesus by living out His finished work. And I will live out His work in my own life by sacrificially loving others.

Table Meditation
Scripture: John 1:29

Many of the feasts that are celebrated by the Jews during the Old Testament point to Christ. The Passover is an example. This feast remembers the last plague in Egypt when the death angel "passed over" the firstborn of each household. This parallels statements about Christ in the New Testament, in John 1:29, "Behold, the Lamb of God, who takes away the sin of the world!" (ESV). Every Sunday, we come together to remember the sacrifice that Christ made to shed his blood for our sins. It is that sacrifice that sets us free from sin's bondage (Romans 6:7).

One feast that is often overlooked is the Feast of Tabernacles (or Booths). This feast is a seven-day feast when Jews live in temporary structures or "tabernacles" to remind them of the 40 years in which the Israelites wandered in the wilderness. The feast is a humble reminder of life's frailty, that God is ultimately in control, and God is always with them.

As we come together on the first day of the week, let us not forget Christ. He is Emmanuel, "God is with us." He came down from heaven and put on a temporary tabernacle (a human body). He then bore the sins of the world as he hung on the cross in agony. He died for each one of us. He offered himself as a sacrifice, and that should humble us.

The Display
Today's Scripture: Luke 23:33

God wants his message to get out. He wants all men to see and hear his word. He told Habakkuk, "Write the vision; make it plain upon tablets, so he may run who reads it" (Habakkuk 2:2, ESV).

Write it down, and make it plain, so it won't be missed. Make the letters big, and the words clear so a man can read it while running. A billboard if you please. The hill of Golgotha was such a place. "And when they came to the place which is called The Skull, there they crucified him, and the criminals, one on the right and one on the left" (Luke 23:33, ESV).

The display there could not be missed. The location could not be forgotten. God's son was killed there. Friend and foe saw it. Paul called the event a matter of first importance. There were many things on public display that day.

From the first days of Jesus' public ministry, God connects Him to the Passover lamb. John the Baptist introduces Jesus with these words, "The next day he saw Jesus coming toward him, and said, "Behold the Lamb of God, who takes away the sin of the world!" (John 1:29, ESV). At the end of his preaching ministry, Jesus, while celebrating the Passover with his disciples, "And he took bread, and when he had given thanks he broke it and gave it to them saying, "This is my body which is given for you. Do this in remembrance of me." And likewise the cup after supper, saying, "This cup which is poured out for you in the new covenant in my blood" (Luke 22:19-20, ESV).

So God uses that day on the place of the skull. He displays the true meaning of the Passover. The bloodshed, the body, the sacrifice, the wrath of God, and His loving grace were on display for all to see. It cannot be ignored. Believe or doubt. Love or hate. Bow down or stand defiant. Write hymns or tell jokes. It is right here before your eyes. It is unavoidable. Jesus Christ, the son of God, died for you.

Today, I will… look with an unveiled face as I prepare to partake of the Lord's Supper. I will see, examine, and remember what happened on that hill far away.

TUESDAY
Sin
Today's Scripture: Luke 23:33

Golgotha was an ugly place. People died there. They died violently and in great pain. It was ugly. It smelled bad. It stuck in your memory. We can look away and refuse to see it, but it is still there.

Jesus talked about eyes that see not. We can avert our eyes, and edit our memories, but it is still there. When sin is on display it is really, really bad. Not that some people are bad but we are all sinners. Not that a few bad people killed Jesus but we killed Jesus. My sin and yours killed the only one who never sinned.

Jesus never told a lie, had a bad thought, or said a bad word. Jesus only did good. Everywhere he went, sick people were healed, hungry people were fed, and sad people were comforted. No wonder at the end of that day people went home beating their breast and crying.

We do what we can with sin. We deny it but it is still there. We call it something else but it's still there. We hold it back in one place but it breaks out in another. We stop but the stain is there. We—like the neighbors of the man with the legion of demons—finally realize that we can't control sin, regulate sin, or contain sin. Paul said it right, "As it is written: None is righteous, no, not one" (Romans 3:10, ESV). He said it even better here, "For all have sinned and fall short of the glory of God" (Romans 3:23, ESV).

Sin is embarrassing, corrupting, conflicting, convicting, and killing us. We know better and could do better, but we sin instead. Denying it just adds the sin of lying to our resume. Paul compares our situation to being chained to a dead man. "Wretched man that I am! Who will deliver me from this body of death?" (Romans 7:24, ESV).

There is no ignoring our problem. Sin is real. The cross is the greatest display of this truth and our dilemma. When the disciples heard Jesus say a camel could get through a needle's eye easier than a rich man entering heaven, their reaction was, "When the disciples heard this they were greatly astonished, saying, "Who then can be saved?" But Jesus looked at them and said to them, "With man this is impossible, but with God all things are possible" (Matthew 19:25-26, ESV). So we approach the cross with revulsion for sin and wonder for God, who turned such a bad day into eternal good.

Today, I will…examine myself. I will be ruthless in searching my life and my heart. I will praise God for giving his only son so that I may not perish but have eternal life.

God Is Sovereign
Today's Scripture: Luke 23:33

The qualities that identify God as sovereign are on public display at the place called the skull. To a casual observer that day, it looked like God lost. After all, His Son died.

But look again. God's sovereignty is shown in his omniscience. He knows everything. God is never surprised. He knew what was going to happen, when and where it was going to take place, and why it must happen. Peter tells us, "This Jesus, delivered up according to the definite plan and foreknowledge of God, you crucified and killed by the hands of lawless men" (Acts 2:23, ESV).

God not only knew about that day, he planned it. God always knew. When God told Eve of the consequences of sin, he also told her satan would bruise the heel of Jesus. He would never forsake this theme throughout the Old Testament. He said we would be healed by his stripes.

All through Jesus' ministry, he foretold this day. This foreknowledge is also proof of another quality of divinity. His eternal nature is displayed in his presence in the past. Peter tells us, "He was foreknown before the foundation of the world but was made manifest in the last times for the sake of you" (1 Peter 1:20, ESV).

Another quality of God that identifies Him as God is His power. God has all power. John records the words of Jesus, "For this reason the Father loves me, because I lay down my life that I may take it up again. 18 No one takes it from me, but I lay it down of my own accord. I have authority to lay it down, and I have authority to take it up again. This charge I have received from my Father." (John 10:17-18, ESV). Jesus did not lose his life. He gave his life. He did not die until he could say, "It is finished." Three days later, Jesus rose from the dead. No one but God could do this.

Many other signs happened that day that displayed his sovereign power. The sun quit shining. The dead were raised. An earthquake came on command. The veil in the temple was torn. And every single prophecy was fulfilled. For example, the Old Testament prophecies said Jesus would be betrayed for thirty pieces of silver, the money would be thrown into the temple and the money would be spent to buy a potter's field. How could anyone but God know such details? At the cross, we see the all-knowing, all-powerful God in charge.

Today, I will…submit to the sovereignty of God. There is none like Him.

THURSDAY

Love Displayed at the Skull

Today's Scripture: Luke 23:33

When I was a boy, every boy had a magnifying glass. It was a precious possession. The reason was not because it made a bug look bigger. No, it was the almost magical thing a magnifying glass did to sunlight. It took all the light that fell on it and focused the energy on one tiny spot. The effect was amazing.

What we see on the hill of the skull is focused sharply. At Calvary, we see all of satan's influence. All the lies, all the pride, all the greed, all the hatred, all the violence, all the blasphemy is brought into sharp focus. We see it in the shameful court proceedings. We see it in the beatings. We see it in the cursing. It would be hard to find a sin that was not displayed. But, there is something else shown to all.

At the cross, we also see all the power of God. All the grace, all the truth, and all the love of God displayed for all to see. We see Jesus praying for their forgiveness. We see Jesus' concern for His mother. We see Him showing love and forgiveness to a convicted thief dying next to Him. Yes, we see the wrath of God but it is directed toward sin, not the sinners. "For God so loved the world that he gave his only Son, that whoever believes in him should not perish but have eternal life" (John 3:16, ESV).

You see, God hates sin but loves sinners. God hates lies but loves liars. God hates murder but loves murderers. God hates immorality but loves the immoral. God hates divorce but loves the divorced. You get the idea. That's why Jesus said, "And I, when I am lifted up from the earth, will draw all me to myself" (John 12:32, ESV).

It is not God's wrath or power at Calvary that draws us to Him. It is His love. It is no accident that the verse everyone knows is John 3:16. It is no accident that the song everyone can sing is "Jesus Loves Me." Jesus said, "Greater love has no one than this, that someone lay down his life for his friends" (John 15:13, ESV). And it's the truth. No one loves you like God loves you.

Today, I will…cling to the love of God and return His love by my obedience to His commands and my imitation of His actions in my life toward others.

FRIDAY
The High Cost of a Free Gift
Today's Scripture: Luke 23:33

It is amazing that Saul, a leading Pharisee, became the Apostle Paul, the greatest proclaimer of grace—the gift of God. "For by grace you have been saved through faith; and this is not your own doing, it is the gift of God" (Ephesians 2:8, ESV).

Grace, by its very nature, cannot be bought or earned. But, knowing this, many people still think that if it is free, it must not be worth much. Being priceless, it cannot be bought, does not mean it is worthless. We own things we would never sell for any price, but that does not make them worthless. The idea of cheap grace is not found in the Word of God.

What is displayed at the cross is the high cost of this free gift. Grace cost Jesus. The Word who was with God and was God. "In the beginning was the Word, and the Word was with God, and the Word was God" (John 1:1, ESV). To save us, Jesus emptied himself. "Though he was in the form of God, did not count equality with God a thing to be grasped, but emptied himself, by taking the form of a servant, being born in the likeness of men. And being found in human form, he humbled himself by becoming obedient to the point of death, even death on a cross." (Philippians 2:6-8, ESV). He did not cling to his God-ness. We will not fully know or completely understand what this real emptying involved, but it was a costly exercise.

It meant He could be hurt and die. It also meant He could sin and be lost. He left something behind when He came to earth. When Paul describes Jesus as the resurrected mediator between God and men he calls Jesus a man. He paid a high price for this free gift.

Grace cost God the Father. "For God so loved the world that he gave his only Son, that whoever believes in him should not perish but have eternal life" (John 3:16, ESV). It cost the Father the death of His Son. The One He loved and who pleased Him. If you have children, you have an idea what this gift cost. I don't know if I could pay such a price, but the Father did.

The free gift of grace costs you. Jesus said, "If anyone would come after me, let him deny himself and take up his cross daily and follow me." (Luke 9:23-24, ESV). Paul calls on Christians, too. "I appeal to you therefore, brothers, by the mercies of God, to present your bodies as a living sacrifice, holy and acceptable to God, which is your spiritual worship" (Romans 12:1, ESV).

You cannot earn grace. You cannot buy grace. It is a free gift from God. That being said, you will never pay more than you do becoming a follower of Christ. We belong to Him. We die to ourselves. When we go to Golgotha, we see the display of self-sacrifice.

Today, I will…pray to the Father, "I ask you to keep helping me give up my life for your Son who gave up His life for me."

Table Meditation
Scripture: Philippians 2:6-8

What image comes to mind when you think about the cross? Maybe it's one of the famous classical paintings of the crucifixion. Perhaps it's a crucifix that hung around a loved one's neck or earrings fashioned into the image of a cross. For centuries, the cross has been revered and honored as a symbol of the great sacrifice that Jesus was willing to make on behalf of all humanity. However, in the first century, it was not so.

In the first century, the cross was a form of execution reserved for the most vile of criminals. Before being crucified, victims would be tortured; then, they would be forced to walk to the site of their crucifixion, carrying their cross. The victim would be stripped of their clothing before finally being crucified. Not only was crucifixion the most awful form of execution in the Roman world, but it was also an obscene and humiliating way to die. No one in the ancient world would have dared adorn themselves with an image of the cross.

We can only imagine the shame and disgrace the victim would have endured. It's easy to assume this was exactly what Paul had in mind when he wrote the words of Philippians 2:8, "And being found in human form, he humbled himself by becoming obedient to the point of death, *even death on a cross*" (ESV).

Our savior not only endured the physical torture of the cross, but he also endured its shame, disgrace, and humiliation.

A Table of Grace
Today's Scripture: 2 Samuel 9

Who doesn't love grace? Grace is desperately needed in this old, mean-spirited world filled with sin. That might seem harsh, but you get the point...WE LOVE GRACE because it goes completely against the grain of the world. When we see grace extended, it warms our hearts.

There is a beautiful story about King David extending an opportunity to Mephibosheth—the crippled son of his beloved friend Jonathan and grandson of the first King of Israel, Saul—to come and eat at his table continually (2 Samuel 9:12). This is nothing but an amazing act of GRACE to come to the table of the King.

Mephibosheth's disability limited his physical activities and relationships with others. This is true with most major disabilities like this. However, David looks beyond the disability and embraces the love he has for Mephibosheth's father, Jonathan. David's loyalty and love provide him the opportunity of a lifetime.

Mephibosheth's story is our story. We, too, are crippled by sin, a fall from our own choosing (Romans 3:23). We deserve to be separated forever from our God (Isaiah 59:1-2). God sends His One and only Son, Jesus Christ, to redeem us, reconcile us to Himself, and invite us to come to His table continually.

This story reminds us of the opportunity that we experience every Sunday when we get to eat at the King's Table of Grace (Matthew 26:26-29). Psalm 22:24 reminds us, "For he has not despised or abhorred the affliction of the afflicted, and he has not hidden his face from him, but has heard, when he cried to him" (ESV). The King invites us despite our flaws and hears us in our need.

Today, I will...start preparing my heart for the opportunity to sit at the Lord's Table of Grace on His day. I will remember the GRACE offered to me so that I can share a meal with the King, and I will consider it pure joy to eat with Him with gratitude in my heart! I will anticipate sharing this meal with all who are invited to the table.

TUESDAY
Everyone Is Invited to the Table
Today's Scripture: Luke 14:15-24

Sometimes, I struggle with people. And you probably do, too! There are good people, bad people, immoral people, religious people, political people, and even people who root for that other team. I struggle with people because they are successful. I struggle with people whose lives are an absolute mess. I get frustrated with people who can't seem to get it together and repeat the same old sins. I don't want to get messy, so I sit at my little corner table and stay away from everyone because they are all…sinners!

A concept that challenges me is that God loves the whole world! In the golden text of the Bible God shares that very fact (John 3:16). When I consider this truth about our amazing God, it gets me thinking… really? Does He really love the whole world? Resoundingly, yes!

Hebrews 2:11—quoting from Psalm 22:22—portrays Jesus among us in the assembly to stress that he is not ashamed to call us brothers: "I will tell of your name to my brothers; in the midst of the congregation I will sing your praise." (ESV). Let's remember to see others as part of God's people and as recipients of His grace. God really does love the people that we stand shoulder to shoulder and eyeball to eyeball with every day. He not only loves the people we love, He also loves the people we don't, and He invites them to share in His GRACE and sit at His table. He invites people who don't look like us, act like us, think like us, or behave like us to come and sit with us at His table and share in His meal! Why? Because everyone is invited to sit with the King at His Table.

Today, I will…remember with great appreciation and love that not only am I invited to the table of GRACE, but ALL SINNERS are invited to eat with the Lord of GRACE. I will try my best to develop a more Christlike view of people and see them through His eyes as I notice who is sitting at the table with me. I will appreciate the opportunity to break bread with all kinds of people who have been covered by the blood of Jesus!

WEDNESDAY
A Mirrored Table
Today's Scripture: 1 Corinthians 11:28

Recently, I was looking online at tables for sale, and I came across a mirrored table at a place called Decorations, Inc. I started thinking how awkward it would be to sit at this table and eat a meal. You would literally be looking at yourself every moment of the meal. You would see every bite, every drink, every spill, and every slippery, sticky, and messy moment you experience at this table.

While it would be awkward to eat at a mirrored table, in a very real and spiritual sense, we eat at a mirrored table every Sunday when we assemble with our Lord on His day to honor Him. Paul says that each of us should "examine" ourselves as we sit at the table of our Lord. According to the *Blue Letter Bible Outline of Biblical Use,* the word "examine" means to "test, examine, prove, scrutinize (to see whether a thing is genuine or not), to recognize as genuine after examination, to approve, deem worthy."[1] Psalm 22:14-15 prophesies a powerful image of Jesus' suffering: "I am poured out like water, and all my bones are out of joint; my heart is like wax; it is melted within my breast; my strength is dried up like a potsherd, and my tongue sticks to my jaws; you lay me in the dust of death" (ESV). This reminds us of the ultimate sacrifice made on our behalf and calls us to respond with genuine self-examination.

God desires for each of us to remember His Son Jesus and to walk as He walked (1 John 2:6). Each opportunity I have to sit at His table of GRACE, I will look at my own heart and life and repent when I need to get back on track and follow Him.

Today, I will...try my best to look at myself and not the spills, mistakes, and messiness of others who are eating at the table with me. I will try to look introspectively at my own heart and life and focus on the One Who sits at the head of the table and remember to reflect on Him alone!

---

[1] https://www.blueletterbible.org/resources/lexical/outline-biblical-usage.cfm

What Do You Experience at the Table?
Today's Scripture: 1 Corinthians 10:16-17

I can remember the experience of sharing a meal with my wife (at the time my girlfriend) for the very first time. It was on my birthday, February 13, 1991, at Bonanza Steak House in Paragould, AR. I was nervous, excited, and happy all at the same time. I will save you the time and guesswork…I have been sharing meals with her ever since that moment. I am still nervous, excited, and happy all at the same time and for the same reason. We have shared life together since that moment, and it has been beautiful. We have laughed, cried, and experienced the highs and lows that life has to offer. Being "together" is what made that first meal experience special, and it is what has made every meal since that moment special.

Our table is BIGGER now because we have added to it. We have seven (yes, seven) children (four biological and three adopted) and soon-to-be six grandchildren. Our table experience is loud, fun, chaotic, emotional, and most importantly, "together." Nothing is better than being together at the table! It represents love, shared experiences, support, community, and protection.

Jesus' table is no different. Psalm 22:27 says, "All the ends of the earth shall remember and turn to the Lord, and all the families of the nations shall worship before you" (ESV). Jesus' suffering and resurrection ensure that God's family grows, inviting all people to come to His table and share in His love. Paul said in 1 Corinthians 10:16-17 that when we sit with the Lord and eat from His table, we are taking part in all that He has to offer. That is what being "together" with Him is all about! He offers us forgiveness, mercy, grace, protection, and a BIGGER table with more family members to enjoy life. This also brings about an extreme caution to consider how we are living and those with whom we fellowship every day.

Today, I will…understand with great discernment the blessings I enjoy by being with the One Who created it all. I will consider the life He lived and the life He offers for me to share as I journey toward His home.

The Table...A Place of Connection
Today's Scripture: John 6

I remember someone saying something to this effect, that before we invite someone to church, Bible class, or to Jesus, we should invite them to dinner. Wow! I believe that it is spot on because your table is a place of CONNECTION, and it will give you a greater opportunity to invite them to Jesus and ultimately to His table!

We live in a time in which we are all very busy. It is just simply easier to invite someone to church, Bible class, or to come to know Jesus in some other place than our own table. If I invite someone to my table, it requires much effort to clean the house, buy groceries, prepare a meal, and give the kids a long lecture about how to behave. But when I do, the CONNECTION is so much better. We can talk about the St. Louis Cardinals or Alabama football—because who doesn't want to talk about those two teams? We can talk about jobs, kids, challenges, and joys while sitting at our table.

Being genuine at the table builds a strong CONNECTION that can last forever. Jesus, before He died on the cross for the sins of the world, didn't gather His disciples together to give them all the theology about religion. Instead, He gave them a meal (Matthew 26:26). In that passage, it says, "while they were eating"...they were sharing a meal together, making CONNECTIONS. This allowed Him to talk about greater and more spiritual things. He did this same thing in John 6 to help them to understand that He was God. David prophecies about the humiliating suffering of Jesus in Psalm 22:6-7, "But I am a worm and not a man, scorned by mankind and despised by the people. All who see me mock me; they make mouths at me; they wag their heads" (ESV). Through Jesus' suffering, God understands ours. Having this confidence, we relate to one another's struggles and challenges around our own tables. God gives us a beautiful pattern of breaking bread together, building relationships, and making a lasting CONNECTION for discussions that matter most.

Today, I will...prepare my table and invite others to come and share a meal so that I can build a CONNECTION to ultimately invite them to His Table and make a CONNECTION that will last for all eternity.

HIS FINAL WORDS
STATEMENTS FROM THE CROSS

Table Meditation
Scripture: John 1:4-5, 12

"In him was life, and the life was the light of men. The light shines in the darkness and the darkness has not overcome it" (John 1:4-5, ESV). Because of what happened on that terrible and wonderful day, there is light in a world that deserves darkness. Not only light but a light that cannot be defeated by sin or despair. So many in the world today cannot shake a sense of hopelessness. They cannot allow themselves to see his light as an anchor of hope Jesus provided through belief and faith. He is the light that stands as a beacon of our assured salvation!

Verse twelve goes on to say, "To all who did receive him, who believed in his name, he gave the right to become children of God" (John 1:12, ESV). Not only did Jesus provide a light, but he also gave us a safe place to abide while the tempests of life rage. He brought us into his family, his very bosom, as a sanctuary from the world. However, light and refuge are not without a price. The world covets these things while Christians are gifted them—they have an immeasurable cost…His blood. His pierced body was laid on the altar for our sin so that we can have the only true peace, peace that comes with the ultimate knowledge of where we will spend eternity.

MONDAY
"Father, Forgive..."
Today's Scripture: Luke 23:32-43

" *...them, for they know not what they do.*" (Luke 23:34, ESV)

Alexander Pope (1688-1744), an English poet, left us with this immortal quote: "To err is human; to forgive, divine." The first statement our wonderful Savior, Jesus, made while being nailed to the cross is the greatest evidence of this concise truth. His example inspired the first Christian martyr, Stephen, to pray with his dying breath, "Lord, do not hold this sin against them" (Acts 7:60, ESV).

Some people believe that only Jesus and Stephen prayed such prayers. I would love to have heard the dying prayers of Peter, Paul, and James—faithful apostles whose lives also ended in martyrdom for the world's greatest cause. Perhaps, like you, I have known saints who prayed similar prayers for attackers who intended for them to die. They, too, were inspired by the Lord's example. They, too, demonstrated a reality and strength of faith in Him that defined their lives, especially in the moments of life-threatening trial. We never know how strong we are, nor how weak we are, until we are tested. In such an unimaginable test, our precious Lord teaches us to forgive those who would rob us of life, as well as the myriad of matters far less significant. Our human tendency is to be unforgiving for even the smallest hurt or slight, while our divine Lord prayed, "Father, forgive them."

In doing so, Jesus has modeled what we should do when the need to forgive others appears. First, we *approach* the Father with the confidence He knows the burden of our hearts and listens to our cries. Second, we *appeal* for His help in being willing to forgive those who have hurt us. Third, we need to *analyze* the cause of the person's behavior who is hurting us, which is precisely what both Jesus and Stephen did. Fourth, we must *allow* our Father to answer our prayers in His own time and in His own way; what He does will be best for us.

Today, I will…praise the Father for the gift of His Son, for the grace of His forgiveness, and in partaking of the Lord's Supper each Lord's day, I will remember to forgive those who have brought hurt and harm to my life and those I love.

TUESDAY
"Father, Forgive Them..."
Today's Scripture: Psalm 22:1-31

"...for they know not what they do." (Luke 23:34, ESV)

Granting forgiveness is the hardest thing we do, and it is the most necessary. It is much easier for us to ask for forgiveness than to give it, but if we hope to be completely forgiven of our sins by God the Father, then we must be willing to forgive each other. Jesus made this abundantly clear, and we must take His warning most seriously (Matthew 6:14-15; 18:36).

To whom is Jesus referring when He prays for *"them?"* First, there were the Roman *soldiers* even while nailing crucifixion spikes into His sinless hands and feet. Second, there were the Jewish *mockers* who, in derision, passed by *"wagging their heads"* as they challenged Him to come down from the cross (Matthew 27:39-40, ESV). Third, they were led in this blasphemous mockery by the *chief priests, scribes, and elders* who claimed, "He saved others; He cannot save Himself" (27:42, ESV). This would include the High Priest, *Caiaphas* and members of the *Sanhedrin* who took the charge "Let Him be crucified!" directly to Pilate's door (Matthew 27:22-23, ESV). Fourth, "the *robbers* who were crucified with Him also reviled Him in the same way" (Matthew 27:44, ESV), although one later repented and received the Lord's pardon (Luke 23:43). Fifth, there was the cowardly Roman governor, *Pilate*. He listened to the voice of the people rather than the voice of his own conscience. Seeking to wash his hands of the matter, without mercy, he turned our Lord over to be scourged and crucified (Matthew 27:26), the greatest miscarriage of justice in history—past, present, and future!

It is easy for us to look at this horrific group of haters and lawbreakers and condemn them with our self-righteousness. As if we had been there, we would have stood up and defended Jesus, somehow preventing Him from such humiliating and excruciating torture. However, His apostles and disciples did not; we only feel we would have been bold and courageous because we know the rest of the story! Without exception, those who wear the name "Christian" today would have been in the same place as those the gospel writers describe. So, we should include ourselves in the *"them"* for whom Jesus prayed.

The only course for us is to remember our Lord came into the world to save sinners, to save *us*. We must respond to His unspeakable love with profound humility, gratitude, and surrender. He is our Savior, not ourselves. We are ever dependent upon His grace, mercy, and forgiveness born of selfless sacrifice.

Today, I will...meditate on the Lord's gracious invitation to feast with Him at His table. I will confess my sins and turn from them while demonstrating my undying love for Him.

"Father, Forgive Them, For..."
Today's Scripture: Isaiah 53:1-12

" ...they know not what they do." (Luke 23:34)

News reporters answer six key questions in telling their stories: *Who* did *what,* to *whom, when, where,* and *why?* One of the saddest statements in Scripture is, "He came to His own, and His own people did not receive Him" (John 1:11, ESV). Why, indeed, did the Jewish leadership hate Jesus to the point of contriving every possible plot to kill Him? He did not appear to be their vision of the Messiah. However, He fulfilled every Old Testament prophecy about Him (Acts 3:18). They knew the Messiah would not come from Nazareth. However, Jesus was born in Bethlehem (Matthew 2:1). Even Pilate knew it was "out of envy that they had delivered Him up" (Matthew 27:18, ESV). However, the main reason Jesus was rejected by His people was their willful ignorance (Acts 3:17) of His claims, being deaf to His lessons, and blind to His miracles. Yet, He died for them in the hope of their repentance and forgiveness.

In our current age, many are the reasons for unbelief in Jesus and our need for His cleansing blood to save us. This, in turn, develops a world not only of misunderstanding the urgency of the gospel message but also of an uncaring heart and mind toward others generally and those we hurt specifically. When we look at Jesus, we see not only His sinless character but also the depths of His genuine compassion for everyone He met: the lost, the hurting, the helpless, and the hopeless. And so must we if we are to be seen in His image (2 Corinthians 3:18).

How can we develop such compassion, especially the willingness to forgive as He forgave?

First, always remember the things we have done against God and others and that in being forgiven of so much, we must also be forgiving. *Second,* develop an understanding heart (1 Kings 3:9, 12), realizing there is usually a reason why people act as they do, even when our feelings are deeply hurt. *Third,* genuinely pray for God's help in granting forgiveness; call the person by name who has offended you in your prayers. *Fourth,* remember that hatred, ill will, and bitterness do far more harm to the *hater* than to the *hated*—mentally, emotionally, physically, and spiritually. This is well documented in medical journals, as well as our own experience. *Fifth,* remember that God forgives freely, abundantly, immediately, continually, and completely without reminding us over and over of the specific wrongs we have committed. Trust His grace and practice it.

No finer statement of "how" forgiveness is to be granted than this: "Be kind to one another, tenderhearted, forgiving one another, as God in Christ forgave you" (Ephesians 4:32, ESV).

Today, I will...remember that in coming to the Lord's table, I do so as one forgiven by Him of all sin, even as I sincerely strive to extend that forgiveness to others.

THURSDAY
"Father, Forgive Them, For They Know Not..."
Today's Scripture: 1 Peter 2:21-25

"...what they do." (Luke 23:34)

Joseph can be described as the most Christlike person in the Old Testament: he has no record of sin (Genesis 37-50), he was one in whom the Spirit of God lived (Genesis 41:38), and he is a preeminent example of genuine forgiveness. Joseph knew the hatred of his ten older brothers stemmed from their envy and jealousy of him, but his heart was touched with their repentance when he heard them confess, *"In truth we are guilty concerning our brother,* in that we saw the distress of his soul, when he begged us and we did not listen. That is why this distress has come upon us. And Reuben answered them, 'Did I not tell you not to sin against the boy? But you did not listen. So now there comes a reckoning for his blood'"* (Genesis 42:21-22, ESV). This led Joseph to reassure his sinful brothers of God's plan: "Do not be distressed or angry with yourselves because you sold me here (Egypt), for *God sent me before you to preserve life"* (Genesis 45:5, ESV). Though unjustly separated from his family for twenty-two years, Joseph did not seek retaliation, resentment, and revenge; instead, he greeted his penitent brothers with understanding, love, and forgiveness. Not everyone can do this, but Joseph did!

The meaning of *forgiveness* is "to release or set free." It is used for the cancellation of a debt or the release from a legal obligation. Forgiveness is described as a conscious decision on the part of the *offended* person to release the *offending* person from the penalty and guilt of their *offense.* Forgiveness not only frees the forgiven from guilt and punishment, but it also frees the forgiver of anger and bitterness. Again, this is the forgiveness God freely gives us (Romans 6:23) and that we are to offer each other (Colossians 3:13).

What do we learn from Joseph's forgiving spirit? First, Biblical forgiveness should be granted *promptly* (Genesis 45:7-8; 50:19-21). Second, forgiveness should be granted *privately* (Genesis 45:1). Third, forgiveness should be given *unconditionally* (Genesis 42:24; 43:30; 45:1-2; 50:17-21). Fourth, forgiveness must be granted *sacrificially.* Joseph's gift of grace came at great cost to him (Genesis 37:18; 39:19-20; 40:23). Fifth, genuine forgiveness must be given *permanently* (Genesis 45:9-12; 50:15-21). This is why forgiveness is the hardest thing we do and why it is the most necessary.

Author Archibald Hart (1932-2021) once wrote, "Forgiveness is giving up my right to hurt you for hurting me."

Today, I will...anticipate meeting the Lord at His Table each Lord's Day, thanking Him for His great sacrifice for each of us, and requesting His help for a more forgiving spirit.

"Father, Forgive Them, For They Know Not What They Do"

Today's Scripture: Philippians 2:5-11

Humanity's urgent need for forgiveness (salvation from sin) is the dominant theme of Scripture, from Genesis 3 to Revelation 22. Without it, we have no hope, but the good news is we love and serve a God who is "ready to forgive, gracious and merciful, slow to anger and abounding in steadfast love" (Nehemiah 9:17, ESV).

One of the saddest Old Testament episodes is when Samuel, the aging prophet/priest/judge of Israel, was rejected by his people in favor of a king, breaking his heart. God comforted him by saying, "They have not rejected you, but they have rejected Me from being king over them" (1 Samuel 8:7, ESV). When the day came for Samuel's farewell address, after 40 years of faithful and successful leadership, the people asked him to pray for them because they had added to their sins the evil of asking for a king (1 Samuel 12:19). In a remarkable display of his forgiving spirit, Samuel assured them, "Far be it from me that I should sin against the Lord by ceasing to pray for you" (1 Samuel 12:23).

The greatest example I have known of genuine Biblical forgiveness in my lifetime is that of an outstanding Christian couple from Hopkinsville, Kentucky—Frank and Elizabeth Morris. Their story of forgiveness in the early to mid-1980s made national news. Frank and Elizabeth's only child, Ted, a sterling young man of 18, was killed by a drunk driver, Tommy Pigage. Ted was home for Christmas break in his first year of college when Tommy's car crossed the center line and hit Ted's car head-on. Crushed and outraged for two years, Frank and Elizabeth hated Tommy as they sought every avenue for justice, adding further torment to Tommy's guilty conscience and broken heart. When they realized what their hatred was doing to them and their spiritual life, Frank and Elizabeth decided the only way they could conquer the hatred was by forgiving Tommy completely. He had a sensitive heart and was open to studying the Bible with them. In time, Frank baptized the killer of his only son into Christ at the Hopkinsville Church of Christ, where Tommy is still a faithful member forty years later. Frank died in December of 2006, and Elizabeth passed in December of 2023. At her request, Tommy delivered the eulogy as her "adopted" son. Amazing grace, indeed!

Forgiveness is not easy; it's not natural. But when we forgive, we find that a prisoner has been set free. And that prisoner is us. "Father, forgive them, for they know not what they do."

Today, I will…humble myself in the sight of the Lord, confessing my sins and seeking His forgiveness, that I might meet Him at His table in purity and holiness.

Table Meditation
Scripture: Isaiah 53:3-7

What an honor it is to partake of this Memorial Feast each first day of the week (Acts 20:7). A lot of folks wonder why we do so because of redundancy, claiming it becomes habitual and loses its meaning. My question is, why wouldn't we want to partake of this every first day of the week to help us focus on that wonderful gift we have received from our Creator and Sustainer? Jesus, in the form of a man, came, bled, and died for OUR sins! He was blameless, yet he took the sins of the world on his shoulders and endured the shame, pain, and suffering of the most horrific ordeal anyone could go through. He loved us so much that he suffered these things so that we could inherit the ETERNAL LIFE that was promised to us.

We know of the prophet Isaiah foretelling of our Savior's suffering (Isaiah 53:3-7); that He was oppressed and afflicted but did not open His mouth (Isaiah 53:7); that He was pierced for our transgressions (Isaiah 53:5). Christ could have come down from the cross, but because of His Love, He endured all the pain, humiliation, and suffering for you and me. It's hard to be overjoyed that a human being, even though he was God in the flesh, endured the scourging and awful, awful agony of the cross for me. This is one of our acts of worship each week that Christ Himself instituted and should be considered an honor and privilege.

MONDAY
Numbered Among Transgressors
Today's Scripture: Luke 22:37 & Isaiah 53:11-12

The religious elite criticized Jesus for actively living among "sinners" (Luke 5:30; 7:39; 15:1-2). He responds—in all three passages—that he lived among sinners because he cared about saving sinners (Luke 5:32; 7:47-50; 15:3-32). It is no surprise, then, that Jesus actively died "with sinners."

When he was nearing his arrest, he reminded the disciples, "This Scripture must be fulfilled in me: 'And he was numbered with the transgressors.' For what is written about me has its fulfillment" (Luke 22:37, ESV). Jesus was quoting Isaiah 53:12. He knew that his suffering would involve interacting with evil and bloodthirsty men.

The context of Isaiah 53:11-12 indicates that his "numbering among the transgressors" is directly connected to his mission of saving transgressors. Because he would be "numbered with transgressors," he would bear their "iniquities" (Isaiah 53:11) and "sins" (Isaiah 53:12). His vicarious suffering and death "make many to be accounted righteous" (Isaiah 53:11, ESV).

Jesus' suffering and death with sinners perfected him so that he might: confidently call us brothers, destroy the devil's influence, release us from the fear of death, serve God faithfully, represent us mercifully, and be the source of our forgiveness. "He is able to help those who are being tempted" (Hebrews 2:10-18, ESV).

Today, I will…picture Christ at the throne of God serving on my behalf and give thanks for the help he gives when I struggle.

TUESDAY
Be Humbled By the Certainty of Death
Today's Scripture: Luke 23:39-43

Funeral and memorial services increasingly show up in social media timelines, thanks to live streaming. It is uniquely "21st century" to watch real-time tributes about people we've never met.

Thinking about the deaths of others moves us to assess our own deaths. Thinking about dying changes how we think about living. Ecclesiastes 7:1-2 emphasizes that we only fully consider our "good names" when we choose to think more about death. Early in life, we must not sabotage the future with reckless foolishness. Later in life, we must not succumb to passions that would ruin years of a godly reputation.

The second criminal experiences this awareness as he hangs on the cross. He knows that his death is imminent. The Romans had perfected crucifixion, and he understood that no pardon would come. He is in the place where he will take his final breath.

Out of this awareness, he rebukes the first criminal (who, like the crowd, mocks Jesus and demands he bring him down from the cross): "Do you not fear God, since you are under the same sentence of condemnation?" (Luke 23:40-41, ESV). Arrogant mockery is not fitting in a time of imminent, humiliating death.

Today, I will…think about death—Jesus' death and my own. I will allow Jesus' death to humble me, to strengthen my love for him, and increase my enthusiasm for his return.

WEDNESDAY
Be Crucified with Christ
Today's Scripture: Romans 6:6-8 & Galatians 2:20; 5:24

Obeying Jesus is not "safe." In 2023, about an hour from where I live, 31 cows were struck dead by lightning. They were all found underneath the shade of a large tree. When the storm arose, they all moved to what seemed to be the place of protection. But a tree in a lightning storm is not safe. We cannot follow Jesus while also remaining "safe."

The second criminal is not the pattern for how Christ saves today. God saves through immersion into Jesus Christ for the forgiveness of sins (Acts 2:38; Romans 6:3-4). This criminal does, however, foreshadow a specific aspect of salvation: being crucified with Christ.

During this man's few hours on the cross, he repents. Matthew 27:44 says he was mocking Jesus along with the criminal on the opposite side of Jesus. Something touched his heart and changed his mind. He understood that Jesus was innocent. More so, he knew that Jesus was innocent while he was guilty. Jesus was suffering unjustly while he was suffering justly. When he declared Jesus' innocence, he became the fourth person to do so (joining Pilate, Pilate's wife, and Herod).

This thief reminds us that no one is saved except by God's grace. Jesus kept the law fully and perfectly yet received what he did not deserve—death. Likewise, we who do not keep God's law perfectly receive that which we do not deserve—eternal life (Romans 3:23-25).

We receive the blessing of eternal life when we join him in his death. We are crucified with Christ. Jesus said we must "deny self, take up our cross daily, and follow him" (Luke 9:23, ESV). We die to sin through Jesus' death for sin.

Today, I will…list the sins, thoughts, and habits that died when I was crucified with Christ.

THURSDAY
Be Transformed by His Salvation
Today's Scripture: Romans 6:3-4 & 2 Corinthians 5:17

On February 29, 2024, 46-year-old NFL legend Tom Brady ran the 40-yard dash faster than he did as a 22-year-old at the 2000 combine. This unthinkable feat highlights Brady's longevity and commitment to fitness. After suffering a devastating knee injury in 2008, Brady revamped his health regimen, prioritizing pliability, diet, sleep, and recovery. His post-injury focus led to four more Super Bowl wins, cementing his legacy as one of the greatest athletes in history. When he retired, he had spent more than half his life in the NFL. Brady's 2024 40-yard dash is an extreme anomaly because even the most physically fit athletes lose a step as they age. Brady's transformation overcame natural deterioration.

"Transformation that overcomes deterioration" is the promise of Jesus Christ's covenant of salvation. We die to sin and are buried into death. God raises us to "walk in newness of life" as "new creations" (Romans 6:3-4; 2 Corinthians 5:17).

The second criminal hanging near Jesus knew the following: (1) Jesus was a king with a kingdom, (2) his kingdom had not yet begun, (3) Jesus would be conscious and alive following his death, and (4) the kingdom would come following Jesus' death.

The criminal has no hope for his own soul, but he is confident in Jesus' power after death. It is not a stretch to suggest that this criminal understood the promise of the kingdom and resurrection more clearly than the majority of Jesus' disciples.

Today, we enjoy the covenant of transformation in the kingdom of Christ. Our sin deserves the humiliation and suffering of death. Jesus has given us continual glorification over sin's carnal and eternal consequences.

Today, I will…place a verse about Christ's transformation in clear sight (phone background, the mirror, the steering wheel, etc.) to remind me of His promise of spiritual renewal.

FRIDAY
Be With Jesus in Paradise
Today's Scripture: 1 Thessalonians 4:17-18

In 1999, 45-year-old Michael May received a groundbreaking stem-cell transplant to correct his blindness. He saw for the first time since the age of three. He worked with the hospital so that when he first opened his eyes, he saw those most precious to him—his wife and sons.[1]

What did the second criminal behold when he opened his eyes immediately following death? What will we behold when we open our eyes for the first time on the other side of eternity? We are thankful for the promise that it will be a "Who?" and that He is Jesus.

When Jesus hears the criminal's contrition and belief, he does more than vow to "remember him"—he promises his presence. Being "with Jesus" after death is the ultimate promise and supreme comfort. Even in death, Jesus is still "seeking and saving the lost" (Luke 19:10).

Jesus promises to "be with" the criminal in "paradise." This is where God lives (2 Corinthians 12:3). The criminal is in his darkest hour and deepest pain. Jesus promises companionship in paradise, filling the man's greatest need and strongest hope.

John 14:3, "I will come again and will take you to myself, that where I am you may be also" (ESV).

1 Thessalonians 4:17, "and so we will always be with the Lord" (ESV).

Today, I will...write out the lyrics of William Cowper's 1772 song "There Is a Fountain Filled with Blood," especially verses 1, 2, and 5, and bring them Sunday to the assembly to meditate upon during the Lord's Supper.

---

[1] https://www.npr.org/templates/story/story.php?storyId=10382528

Table Meditation
Scripture: Luke 22:14-23

Before His crucifixion, Jesus Christ instituted the Lord's Supper—directing that we eat unleavened bread and drink the fruit of the vine to remember His sacrificial death on the cross.

It is a distinct point of remembrance, never to be forgotten, that the God of heaven came to earth and offered a sacrifice that only He could offer. We do not have the ability or the goodness to replicate what needed to be done to alleviate the stain of sin. It is God, and God alone, who could design and implement this sacrifice. Jesus was willing to offer himself as the sacrifice because of His love for the Father and through the Father's love for us.

In the Lord's Supper, we remember the most cruel, inhumane, and repulsive killing that Jesus endured for us. We are thankful, to the depths of our ability, that Jesus was obedient to the Father's will. We are thankful to participate in the most important event in human history, when sinless perfection took upon Himself our sins and reconciled us to our Father. Only through His death can we have life.

"This do in remembrance of Me." (Lk. 22:19, KJV)

MONDAY

Different Kinds of People Gather at the Cross

Today's Scripture: John 19:24-25

As we consider sections of Scripture that help us to remember and refocus our hearts on communing with the Lord each week at "His Table," we turn our attention to one of the seven sayings of Jesus from the cross: when He spoke to His mother and the apostle John. Although only three verses are recorded (John 19:25-27), there is much to glean from these words.

Pause long enough to consider the first word (in the ESV) in verse 25, "But." Why the word of contrast? What or who is being contrasted?

There were different groups of people gathered at the cross. The assigned text for this week focuses on the four women and the apostle who gathered there, but verses 23-24 first focus on a very different group—the Roman soldiers. They were gathered at the cross, but their focus was much different than the women and John. After crucifying Jesus, their attention was centered on the Messiah's garments and their self-centered greed to have them. They "took," "divided," and "cast lots" for them. "So the soldiers did these things" (John 19:24b), "but" (the first word in verse 25) shows that the women and John were focused on the cross.

When we gather to remember the cross each Lord's Day, there will be different kinds of folks there, who are focused on a variety of things. Some will be looking at garments (like those soldiers)—maybe their own or what someone else is wearing. Some might even be wishing that they had someone else's outfit (or shoes or purse or car or phone). Their focus, like the soldiers, may be everywhere else but the cross.

May God help us to not worry about what others think or what others have, especially when we gather at His Table. Instead, let us be focused on "discerning the body," as we "examine" ourselves next to our suffering Savior (1 Corinthians 11:23-30).

Today, I will…circle the word "but" (or "now" in KJV/NKJV) in verse 25 and determine that I will be more like the women at the cross and not the soldiers.

Mary's Heart

Today's Scripture: John 19:25

Does it surprise you that Mary was at the cross of Jesus? Can you imagine her not being there in her Son's final moments? What must have been going through her heart?

Approximately thirty-three years (and nine months) earlier, an angel announced to Mary that she would "bear a son" and that He "will be called the Son of the Most High...the Son of God" (Luke 1:26-37, ESV). Certainly Joseph would have told her that an angel told him that their Son would "save his people from their sins" (Matthew 1:21). These things must have sunk deep into her heart.

Nine months later, the Child was born. Shepherds came to see the "Savior, who is Christ the Lord," and then went out and "made known" what they learned about "this child" (Luke 2:11, 17, ESV). And, "Mary treasured up all these things, pondering them in her heart" (Luke 2:19, ESV). Forty days later ("according to the Law" in Leviticus 12:1-8), Joseph and Mary brought Jesus "to Jerusalem to present him to the Lord" (Luke 2:22, ESV). Simeon took Jesus in his arms and thanked God to "have seen [His] salvation," and he told Mary that "a sword will pierce through your own soul also" (Luke 2:30, 35, ESV). What mother would ever forget those words? Twelve years later, her preteen declared, "I must be in my Father's house" (Luke 2:46-47, 49, ESV). She "did not understand" it all, but again, she "treasured up all these things in her heart" (Luke 2:51, ESV).

After 33 years, how many "treasures" do you suppose she had stored up in her heart? A popular song asks, "Mary, did you know?" Yes! Yes, she did! When her son went to the cross, her heart must have been torn into pieces, but it was also seeing all of those "treasures" coming together in a grand crescendo. Seeing her Son on the cross (for her!) must have struck her more than anyone else!

Today, I will...a treasured list of what Mary must have known when she was at the cross and reflect upon it when I commune.

WEDNESDAY

Mary Had Been Standing And Standing By the Cross

Today's Scripture: John 19:25

The text states that Mary was "standing by the cross of Jesus" (John 19:25, ESV). The Greek tense of the word "standing" is interesting— this particular tense is not used very often in the Greek New Testament. It is called the pluperfect tense, which indicates that an action occurred in the past and the results or effects of that action continued to exist and to be felt in the past. It is not that she merely "stood" there in the past, but her "standing by the cross" in the past was something that continued to be felt. Being there and seeing and experiencing all that she did while there had an ongoing impact on her.

At what point, do you suppose, in the suffering that Christ endured did Mary begin to follow and watch what was happening to her precious Son? We do not know, but it is reasonable to believe that she entered the scene long before Golgotha. When did her "standing by" Jesus in those final hours commence?

She was not in Gethsemane, but would news that her Son had been arrested and put on trial have reached her? Would she have left her home to go and be with Him? Is it possible that she was in the crowd when Pilate brought Him out and said, "Behold the Man!" and personally witnessed the vicious mob shouting, "Crucify Him!" (John 19:5-6)? Is it not likely that she was among the women who "followed...mourned and lamented" as He was marched to Golgotha (Luke 23:27)? Did she watch in horror and shudder when spikes were driven into her Son and the scornful crowd mocked and spit upon Him?

Her "standing by the cross" indicates she had been there for a while and it continued to be felt. When you stand by the cross every Sunday, visualize and feel what Mary saw and felt in those hours.

Today, I will...make a list of what this closest eyewitness saw and felt as Jesus suffered, and I will reflect on it as I commune on Sunday.

Mary Was Not Alone at the Cross
Today's Scripture: John 19:25

How lonely would it have been for Mary if she was standing there at the cross all by herself? But she did not go to the cross by herself. No doubt she would have loved to have her husband there with her, but many suppose that he died earlier. It would have been truly comforting if her own children (her sons and daughters, Mark 6:3) had been with her as her oldest son was murdered, but they "did not believe" (John 7:5), which may explain their absence (but not justify it).

She went to the cross with others who shared her love and devotion to this Man named Jesus. She was there with her sister, who may have been Salome (Mark 15:40), the mother of Zebedee's sons (Matthew 27:56). She was there with another Mary, the wife of Clopas, who may have been "the mother of James the younger and of Joses" (Mark 15:40, ESV). And, she was there with Mary Magdalene. At one point, these women were "looking on from a distance" (Mark 15:40, ESV), but now they are all "standing by the cross of Jesus" with the Lord's mother. She was not alone!

Fast forward to that Lord's Day, not many weeks later, when Mary would partake of the unleavened bread and the fruit of the vine "in remembrance" of her Son and her Savior (Luke 22:19). On that occasion, again, she would not be alone. She was surrounded by disciples who shared her love, devotion, and deep faith in Christ and were bound together by His blood. She would engage every Lord's Day in "a participation in the blood of Christ" and "the body of Christ" (1 Corinthians 10:16-17, ESV), when she "gathered together" with fellow disciples (Acts 20:7, ESV).

Remembering the cross is not a place where the Lord wants us to be alone. Mary needed those other followers of Jesus at the cross just as much as we need them when we partake every Sunday.

Today, I will...thank God for my fellow Christians, with whom I get to commune as one body every Lord's Day.

Jesus Loved Unto the Very End

Today's Scripture: John 19:26

When Jesus was getting ready for that last evening together with His disciples before His betrayal and crucifixion, John 13:1 states, "When Jesus knew that his hour had come to depart out of this world to the Father, having loved his own who were in the world, he loved them to the end." *He loved them to the end!* That was not talking merely about the Passover Feast that night. It was looking to His end on the cross, almost 24 hours later.

In His final moments before Jesus drew His last breath, He loved His own to the end! How much pain must He have endured in those final minutes? How excruciatingly awful must it have been for Him to take a breath and exhale it? Yet, as easy (and natural) as it would have been for Him to focus on self, Jesus still watched out for others (which was the very reason He was on the cross).

Through His sweat-drenched and blood-caked eyes, "Jesus saw his mother and the disciple whom he loved standing nearby" (ESV). He did not ask them for something. He did not figure that He would wait three days to have this conversation. He did not trust that His unbelieving brothers would step up. No! In a last selfless, others-focused, love-defining act, Jesus ensured that His precious mother would be cared for and protected by His dear friend, John. "Woman, behold your son!" (ESV).

In one statement in one moment, Jesus expressed His purpose and desire not only for one soul but for every soul who would ever live! The message that was being shouted from this horrific scene of the Creator dying for His creation was, "World, behold your Savior!" Jesus wanted to protect His mother, but more, Jesus was dying to protect His people from eternal hell. He loved His disciples (ALL of us!) unto the very end!

Today, I will…meditate on the tender care that Jesus extended from the cross, and I will prepare myself to commune with Him this coming Lord's Day.

Table Meditation
Scripture: Galatians 3:1

"This Do in Remembrance of Me"

Jesus' words when he instituted the Lord's Supper are so familiar that we could say them without giving proper attention to their profound meaning. We are drawn to the death of Christ on Calvary. We remember His body and his blood when we partake of the bread and the fruit of the vine.

"This do" tells us to do it not once, but regularly. "Remembrance" signifies it as a memorial, we draw our thoughts to what happened. "Me" is the person of our thoughts, Jesus.

Paul warned the Galatians, who had been bewitched and led away from following Christ (Galatians 3:1). How could this have happened? Before their very eyes, Jesus had been publicly crucified. How was it possible for them to have seen the crucifixion when Jesus had been crucified years beforehand? The answer is found in the Greek word translated as "clearly portrayed" in the NKJV. Other versions say "publicly portrayed." The translated word is a word picture, one that had been publicly painted through preaching for them to see.

Contemplating this picture of Jesus crucified should draw us to Him and keep us from being led astray. These thoughts should be in our minds:

> Jesus loved me and gave himself for me.
> He died *because* of my sins.
> He sacrificed himself *for* my sins.
> His death means I can live.

MONDAY
Memorizing the Cross
Today's Scripture: Matthew 27:46; Mark 15:34

Under the stress of His crucifixion and approaching death, Jesus turned to Scripture, quoting the opening words of Psalm 22: "My God, my God, why have you forsaken me?" (ESV).

Students sometimes regard memorizing Scripture as "make work," merely a mechanical task inappropriate for thinking adults. Yet, filling our minds with Scripture stores up for ourselves a treasury from which we can draw wisdom, comfort, and courage in times of crisis.

Jesus made Scripture so much a part of His thinking that He returns to it again and again throughout His ministry—from His temptation after His baptism until the very end on the cross. About one-tenth of all His recorded speech is a quotation from the Old Testament. He taught and exemplified the principle that we should live "by every word that comes from the mouth of God" (Matthew 4:4 (ESV), quoting Deuteronomy 8:3).

We cannot live by what we do not know. To know the Scriptures thoroughly enough truly to live by them requires that we be like the blessed man described in Psalm 1, whose "delight is in the law of the Lord, and on his law he meditates day and night" (Psalm 1:2, ESV).

Jesus said of His death, "And I, when I am lifted up from the earth, will draw all people to myself" (John 12:32, ESV). The heart of Scripture is Christ. The heart of His story is the cross. Each Christian should learn that story so well that we constantly have the true picture of His love before our minds. By focusing on His love as both our grounds of confidence and our goal for our own character, we fulfill His will. "And we all, with unveiled face, beholding the glory of the Lord, are being transformed into the same image from one degree of glory to another" (2 Corinthians 3:18, ESV).

Today, I will…read again slowly and thoughtfully the Scripture record of Christ's crucifixion.

TUESDAY
Courage in Communion
Today's Scripture: Matthew 27:46; Mark 15:34

On the cross, when Jesus quotes the opening words of Psalm 22, he is using the words of David. When David wrote those words a thousand years before, whatever prophetic meaning they may have had, they also described David's sense of doubt and abandonment in the moment he was living then. We do not know the specific events that gave rise to this Psalm, but the life of David included many times in which he must have felt that "trouble is near, and there is none to help" (Psalm 22:11, ESV).

Psalm 22 as a whole, though expressing genuine agony in David's crisis, is a work of faith. Though God has seemed not to hear his prayers, David appeals to the proof of God's steadfast love in the past: "In you our fathers trusted; they trusted, and you delivered them" (Psalm 22:4, ESV). David has confidence in God, "For he has not despised or abhorred the affliction of the afflicted, and he has not hidden his face from him, but has heard, when he cried to him" (Psalm 22:24, ESV).

In quoting David, Jesus echoes David's agony and his faith, as well as the grounds of that faith. God reassured His people through the prophet Malachi, "For I the Lord do not change" (Malachi 3:6, ESV). "But this I call to mind, and therefore I have hope: The steadfast love of the Lord never ceases; his mercies never come to an end, they are new every morning; great is your faithfulness" (Lamentations 3:22-23, ESV).

Much of the Bible is history for powerful reasons. We draw strength from those who have gone before us, who have suffered, doubted, renewed their faith, and come through the crisis with God's help and to His reward. Jesus was, and is, divine, but also a human being. It was natural and fitting for Him to remember David and use his words as His own.

Today, I will…reflect on how communion expresses the shared struggle and faith of all God's people as they find their fellowship in Christ.

WEDNESDAY
Faithful Doubt
Today's Scripture: Matthew 27:46; Mark 15:34

Did Jesus doubt? The Bible condemns the doubt of being undecided in our commitment to trust God, describing the "double-minded man" as "unstable in all his ways" (James 1:6-8, ESV). In that sense, Jesus represents the very opposite of a doubter, never wavering, "who for the joy that was set before him endured the cross" (Hebrews 1:2, ESV). On the night before His death, Jesus prayed earnestly and repeatedly that He be spared from crucifixion, yet concluded three times with the resolve that God's will be done.

If by doubt, however, we do not mean indecision in our commitment to God's will, but some measure of uncertainty in the working out of God's will, we are describing an inherent part of the human condition, "for we walk by faith, and not by sight" (2 Corinthians 5:7, ESV). We have some knowledge in this life, but not perfect knowledge. Paul looks forward to someday seeing God "face to face" and "then I shall know fully, even as I have been fully known" (1 Corinthians 13:12, ESV). In this life, however, Paul describes Christians as "perplexed, but not driven to despair" (2 Corinthians 4:8, ESV).

As a fully human being, Jesus shared the human experience of doubt. People in agony do not pray pointless prayers. Jesus would not have asked God to let the cup of anguish pass from Him if He knew its inevitability. It would not be true that we have a high priest "who in every respect has been tempted as we are" (Hebrews 4:15, ESV) if He had never known doubt. He could not be the "pioneer" of our faith (Hebrews 12:2, CSB, NIV) if He never had to walk by faith Himself.

"My God, my God, why have you forsaken me?" is a genuine question that Jesus could ask in all seriousness and faith, just as David asked it long before, and as we may ask it in our darkest days.

Today, I will…face my doubts and focus on Jesus as my example in maintaining my faith through them.

THURSDAY
Truly Forsaken
Today's Scripture: Matthew 27:46; Mark 15:34

Genesis 22 records God testing Abraham by asking him to sacrifice his only son. Abraham passes the test by proceeding to the act of lifting the knife to strike, and God spares him by sparing his son.

Nearly two thousand years later, God demonstrated His love by sacrificing His only Son. There was no last-minute reprieve. God demanded of Himself the tragic loss which He spared Abraham.

God's demand on Himself makes bearable His demands on us. Just as with our response to any merely human leader, the knowledge that He asks nothing of us which He is unwilling to exemplify is a crucial part of winning our trust and loyalty. Jesus did not die on the cross so that God would love us, but because God loved us, and so that we would love Him.

God's purpose was accomplished at the price of real suffering by His Son. In the words, "My God, my God, why have you forsaken me?" Jesus questioned the reasons for His abandonment, not the terrible reality of being abandoned. Paul writes that Jesus "emptied himself" and "humbled himself" not just to die, but "even death on a cross" (Philippians 2:7-8, ESV). That emptiness and abasement for the Prince of Heaven are an experience beyond our imagination, but for a Father who could stop it at any time, letting His Son endure such agony, that can touch our hearts. "For our sake he made him to be sin who knew no sin, so that in him we might become the righteousness of God" (2 Corinthians 5:21, ESV).

We find ourselves in Christ, but only by losing ourselves and taking up the cross. "For to this you have been called, because Christ also suffered for you, leaving you an example, so that you might follow in his steps" (1 Peter 2:21, ESV). Yet, Paul describes Christians as "persecuted, but not forsaken" (1 Corinthians 4:9, ESV), using the same Greek word for "forsaken" as is used to translate Christ's cry from the cross. Even bearing our cross, compared to His burden and suffering, his yoke for us is easy and His burden is light.

Today, I will…remember God's presence in my life as made possible by Christ on the cross.

FRIDAY

Mysterious Love

Today's Scripture: Matthew 27:46; Mark 15:34

Jesus asked, "My God, my God, why have you forsaken me?" There is an answer to His question, both straightforward and certain, clearly and repeatedly stated in Scripture. God sent His Son to the cross because He loves us. Paul writes that God "did not spare his own Son but gave him up for us all" (Romans 8:32, ESV) and that this "shows his love for us" (Romans 5:8, ESV). John writes that in Christ's sacrifice, "the love of God was made manifest among us" (1 John 4:9, ESV). In the language of everyday life, the Greek term translated "made manifest" means "made obvious:" it is obvious that Christ died because God loves us.

What is not obvious is why God loves us so much as to sacrifice His Son.

Sometimes love has reasons. As Jesus pointed out, "Even sinners love those who love them" (Luke 6:32, ESV). In the light of His character and actions, our love for God needs no further explanation: "We love because he first loved us" (1 John 4:19, ESV). Paul exhorts the Romans to present their bodies as a sacrifice to God because "the mercies of God" make it our "rational service," as the alternative rendering of the ESV footnote correctly expresses the literal meaning of his words. (Romans 12:2). None of us can ever do anything in our lives more truly rational than to love God and Christ.

But God calls us to a love that goes beyond reason, at least as our reason is limited in this life to things we understand. To love our enemies as ourselves implies acknowledging a kinship that our enemies deny and that is often far from obvious.

In the mystery of His will, God has chosen to claim a kinship with us, to love and to care for us as His children, and not just as His creatures. We cannot know why in this life, and perhaps there is no answer other than His own gracious will.

Today, I will…I will accept God's love for me as needing no explanation and share His love with others without requiring any reason.

Table Meditation
Scripture: Matthew 18:20

I would like to ask you to be very quiet. Clear your mind. Now, take a deep breath and focus on Jesus. You know he is here; His spirit is among us. We know He is here because he promised us He would be here. In Matthew 18:20, Jesus said: "For where two or three are gathered together in my name, there am I in the midst of them" (KJV). Listen to your heart as you focus on Jesus. Imagine you're holding His nail-scared hand.

Jesus sacrificed himself for us. He didn't have to do it; he chose to do it. He knew what would happen even before He came to earth. He knew he would suffer and die a horrible death, but He came anyway. He came from heaven to earth to live as a man, just like us. He lived a perfect life without sin. He showed much compassion to everyone, even those who would hang him on that cruel cross. They tortured his body and broke his heart. But He forgave them. He even forgave you and me.

The Lord's Supper is before us. Our hearts and minds are filled with Jesus; let us partake of the emblems he chose for us to remember him at that last Passover meal. The bread represents his body, and the fruit of the vine represents his blood.

Jesus loves you. He died and rose again. He is here.

Thirsting for Righteousness
Today's Scripture: Psalm 23:5

I am humbled and honored to be asked to be a part of this work of encouragement. I have been asked to do five lessons on the phrase of Jesus, "I thirst." These lessons are related to the Lord's Table. Life, and even scripture, in particular, views the table as a special place for special things.

The Psalmist would say, "You prepare a table before me in the presence of my enemies" (Psalm 23:5, ESV). As our Lord and Savior hung on the cross dying, Jesus would call to the Father and also announce to those who could hear, "I thirst" (John 19:28, ESV).

We must remember that on the cross, Jesus was the Son of God but still fully living in human form with all aspects of humankind. It should not surprise us that in that moment, Jesus would express the need of thirst.

For us, who live daily in our humanity, thirsting is a regular attribute. We overcome that thirst in many different ways.

When we approach the Lord's Table on the first day of the week, we would do well to remember the great sacrifice that Jesus made. We must also remember our great need, what should be a "thirst," for what God has offered through his Son.

At the Lord's table, we gather to remember. At the Lord's table, we gather to honor. At the Lord's table, we gather to quench a "thirst." Each first day of the week, we reattach ourselves to our Lord and Savior.

On the first day of the week, as on every day of the week, we ought to thirst after righteousness. We should also thirst in remembering our Lord and Savior and His great sacrifice for us.

Today, I will…focus on the human reality of thirst. But I will relate it to how I should thirst to be more grateful for the great offering that our Lord and Savior made on my behalf. I want to thirst after righteousness on the first day of the week and every day of the week.

TUESDAY
Jesus Accepted the Cup
Today's Scripture: Luke 22:39-36

On the first day of the week, the early saints gather together to worship. An integral part of that worship was to gather at the Lord's table. The Lord's table is not a literal table, but rather a time and place where the Lord's Supper is offered.

The Lord's Supper consisted of unleavened bread and the fruit of the vine. Our whole hearts should be involved in the statement of Jesus: "I thirst." We, too, should thirst in a manner that we desire strongly to partake in this remembrance of him through the fruit of the vine.

God loved us so much that he sent His Only Begotten Son. In turn, we should show our love to God and Jesus Christ in our adherence to the great call of the Lord's table. At the Lord's Table, we memorialize Jesus. At the Lord's table, we are to honor him. Even to the point of offering our praise by remembering his great sacrifice for us.

All of God's people are blessed because Jesus was brought to the point of saying, "I thirst." As Jesus prayed to the Father while in the garden, he begged God to remove this cup. In his great request, he stipulated that he wanted whatever was God's will to be done.

As the time drew closer, and Jesus himself got closer to the cross, our Lord and Savior knew beyond a shadow of a doubt that the only way was the cross. For this great love, for this great commitment, I draw near to the Lord's Table. And "I thirst."

Today, I will...think more about God's goodness. For today, I will think more about Jesus' obedience and his example of what I should be more and more like.

Thirsting for God's Will
Today's Scripture: John 19:28

On the first day of the week, we gather to remember God's goodness. On the first day of the week, we gather to honor the great sacrifice of Jesus. On the first day of the week, our hearts should be drawn closer and closer to the goodness of the Father and the willingness of the Son to go through with this great plan of salvation for mankind.

As we gather at the Lord's Table, our hearts should be softer than clay and focused on taking in everything that followed the words of Jesus, "I thirst."

Have you ever taken time to think what might have been had Jesus not gone to the cross? It would've been full-blown disobedience from the Son toward the Father and would've divided the greatest unity in existence. God be thanked that Jesus went to the Cross. God be thanked, that Jesus said, "I thirst."

When we gather around the table that Jesus has provided for us by his sacrifice, may God give all of us the strength to want to thirst for God's will; to thirst for our compliance to God's will; to thirst for a full love of God's will that is so strong it will not allow us to turn away from it.

Today, I will…think of the Lord's Table as a shining example of the importance that God's will should have in my life. The strength of our Lord and Savior Jesus shines brightly in His statement, "I thirst." Even more so when we gather at His Table.

THURSDAY
Jesus Fulfilled God's Will
Today's Scripture: Hebrews 4:15

As we draw closer to the conclusion of this five-lesson series, the words of Jesus should still be ringing loudly in our ears, "I thirst." It is al hope that every time we hear the phrase from scripture, "I thirst," it turns our hearts and our minds to the Lord's Table and to Jesus' death on the cross.

God is the one who designed salvation for mankind in the church and what the church should be like and look like. Jesus is the one who took the blueprint, fashioned it, and delivered it.

The word of God says of Jesus, "In every respect has been tempted as we are, yet without sin" (Hebrews 4:15, ESV). Our Lord and Savior Jesus Christ is the only one to live on this earth without sin. The apostle Paul reminds us in Romans 3:23 that all have sinned and come short of the glory of God.

Our Lord and Savior Jesus Christ, left the indelible mark of obedience, love, and endurance, whatever the cost, in the will of God for us. As we gather to His Table on the first day of the week, let us always remember the indelible mark that Jesus has left for me in the phrase, "I thirst." Those words have a stronger meaning than ever before.

Today, I will…learn how to couple Jesus' phrase, "I thirst," with the great purpose the Lord's supper should mean for all of us. We call it the Lord's Supper because first, he instituted it, and then, in his death, he magnified those two figures—the unleavened bread and the fruit of the vine—to represent his humanity and sacrifice.

Thirsting for God's Strength
Today's Scripture: John 19:28

"I thirst" has a new meaning in my life. I hope the same can be said by each one who is participating in this study.

Since Jesus is our Lord and Savior, what better example can be found than from Him? As we seek out his will for us and fasten our willingness to obey that will to him, we get closer and closer to what God would have us to look like. In this study, we have been encouraged to be more and more like Jesus. In the weakest of times, Jesus was still the strongest ever. He was tempted in all points like us, yet he was without sin.

In his weakest physical moments, we see him cry, we see him beg to the Father, and we see him remain faithful in obedience. As Jesus hung on the cross, he called out, "I thirst." Although the men at his crucifixion tried to diminish His greatness in their attempt to give him vinegar to drink, Jesus did not falter.

May God give all of us the strength to take this one moment at the end of Jesus' life and use it for strength, courage, and hope.

Today, I will…thirst for words that bring new courage. May the gathering at the Lord's Table rejuvenate my determination to draw closer to God through his beloved and only begotten Son, Jesus Christ.

Table Meditation
Scripture: Matthew 28:5-6

I have heard many wonderful approaches to prepare for communion over the years: the reading of beautiful hymns like "Ten Thousand Angels," articles from various authors that bring a deep and eloquent perspective, as well as personal stories intended to take our minds from the cares of the moment to the foot of the cross.

Yet nothing "takes me there" better than simply walking with Jesus in the last hours before His death, and then three days later, to the one moment in time that changed everything for everyone... including me!

> While He was still speaking, Judas came, one of the twelve, and with him a great crowd with swords and clubs... Then they seized Him and led Him away...
> (Matthew 26:47, ESV & Luke 22:54, ESV)

> But Pilate said to them, "Why, what evil has He done?" But they shouted all the more, "Crucify Him!"... So he delivered Him over to them to be crucified...
> (Mark 15:14, ESV & John 19:16, ESV)

> And He went out, bearing His own cross, to the place called The Place of a Skull... There they crucified Him...
> (John 19:17-18, ESV)

> And about the ninth hour Jesus cried out with a loud voice, saying, "Eli, Eli, lema sabachthani?" that is, "My God, my God, why have you forsaken me?"... When Jesus had received the sour wine, He said, "It is finished," and He bowed His head and gave up His spirit.
> (Matthew 27:46, ESV & John 19:30, ESV)

> But the angel said to the women, "Do not be afraid, for I know that you seek Jesus who was crucified. He is not here, for HE HAS RISEN..."
> (Matthew 28:5-6, ESV)

For God so loved the world that He gave His only begotten Son!

Jesus Finished What He Set Out to Do
Today's Scripture: John 12:20-27; 19:30

Early in Jesus' ministry, we find Mary telling Jesus at a wedding that the host had run out of wine. His response was, "Woman, what does this have to do with me? My hour has not yet come" (John 2:4, ESV). This phrase becomes a bit of a theme throughout John's gospel (John 7:6, 30; 8:20). Yet, we finally see Jesus proclaim, "The hour has come for the Son of Man to be glorified" (John 12:23, ESV). He knew that He was ready to finish what He set out to do. He was going to die for the sins of the world.

As anyone who knew that they were about to die would feel, Jesus felt greatly troubled by the impending agony. Yet, it would not stop Him from finishing His purpose. "Now is My soul troubled. And what shall I say? 'Father, save Me from this hour'? But for this purpose I have come to this hour" (John 12:27, ESV).

On the night of the Passover, Jesus "knew that His hour had come to depart out of this world" (John 13:1, ESV). So He gave His Apostles some bread and said, "This is My body" (Luke 22:19, ESV). And then He took the fruit of the vine and said, "This cup that is poured out for you is the new covenant in My blood" (Luke 22:20, ESV). It was His hour to do what He set out to do.

The following day, Jesus hung upon the cross, having His body excruciatingly tortured and nailed to a wooden cross for several hours as His blood poured out. Before Jesus died, He proclaimed, "It is finished" (John 19:30, ESV). Everything that He had set out to do in His ministry was finished. He had completed it and it was now time to die.

Today, I will…stand in awe of the remarkable purpose that Jesus held Himself to. And I will remember that selfless purpose. He purposed to die an agonizing death for us. I will be thankful that He finished what He set out to do.

Jesus Finished What Others Prophesied Would Happen
Today's Scripture: Psalm 22; John 19:30-36

Jesus hung on the cross and proclaimed, "It is finished" before He died (John 19:30, ESV). What was finished? His selfless purpose to die was finished, yes. Yet, also the plethora of prophecies written in the Old Testament about His death was finished as well. Here are a few examples:

Jesus would have known that Isaiah prophesied that He would be like "a lamb that is led to the slaughter, and like a sheep that before its shearers is silent, so he opened not his mouth" (Isaiah 53:7, ESV). Because of this, Jesus allowed the Sanhedrin and the Romans to mock Him before His death.

Jesus would have remembered that David prophesied, "They divide my garments among them, and for my clothing they cast lots" (Psalm 22:18, ESV). He witnessed the Romans do this to His clothes when He was nailed to the cross. Jesus would have known the words, "My God, my God, why have you forsaken me?" (Psalm 22:1, ESV). He proclaimed these words as He hung with the agony of death and the weight of the sins of the world on His shoulders. Jesus would have known the prophecy, "He keeps all his bones; not one of them is broken" (Psalm 34:20, ESV). So, Jesus knew His death had to be finished before the soldiers broke the legs of the surviving victims at the end of the long day (John 19:31-36).

Jesus knew Scripture. This knowledge helped Him combat temptation (Matthew 4:1-11). After each temptation, Jesus combated it with "It is written" and then quoted Scripture. Jesus knew that His selfless purpose to die for us could not be completed until He finished the many prophecies written about Him.

Today, I will…reclaim my love for Scripture. Knowing that Jesus loved Scripture and wanted to complete what was prophesied about Him (even the agony of death). I, too, can love Scripture and want to finish what He wants from me.

Jesus Trusted in What Would Happen After He Finished It All
Today's Scripture: Matthew 26:26-29

As Jesus gave the Apostles the Lord's Supper, He made the point that He would partake in it again, "I tell you I will not drink again of this fruit of the vine until that day when I drink it new with you in my Father's kingdom" (Matthew 26:29, ESV). Jesus is saying that He will live one day to do this again.

Jesus made this claim a lot. In Matthew 16:21, we read, "From that time Jesus began to show his disciples that he must go to Jerusalem and suffer many things from the elders and chief priests and scribes, and be killed, and on the third day be raised" (ESV). He knew that He would live again!

As Jesus was hanging on the cross, He was confident in the fact that a resurrection was going to take place. Did He want to go through terrible torture and death? Not always. Matthew 26:39 shows us Jesus in the Garden of Gethsemane the night before, saying, "My Father, if it be possible, let this cup pass from me; nevertheless, not as I will, but as You will" (Matthew 26:39, ESV). Jesus decided to go through with His selfless purpose. Were there questions about the pain? Yes. Yet, did He have questions or doubts about His resurrection? No. He knew that He would be raised!

As He proclaimed, "It is finished," He knew He wasn't eternally finished. He knew He would rise again. What a wonderful reminder for us. If Jesus holds off on coming back for many more years, all of us reading this will die. Might we be anxious about that moment of death? Yes. Do we have to be anxious about our eternity? No. Thanks be to Jesus for the body that hung on the cross and the blood that was shed, we do not have to!

Today, I will...be thankful that Jesus finished the task of dying for my sins so that I can be confident in my eternal salvation!

THURSDAY
The Pain Is Finished
Today's Scripture: 1 Peter 1:3-9; James 1:2-4

Precious metal often goes through fire to meet its full potential. Through the cross, Jesus figuratively went through the fire for us so that we could meet our potential. Jesus also had to die before He could be raised.

As Jesus hung on the cross and said, "It is finished," His pain was almost finished. The hard part was done, and now it was time to die. The beatings from the guards, the spikes in the wrists and feet, the crown of thorns shoved in His head, the falling beneath the cross as He walked toward the place of His death, the emotional pain of the mocking crowd...It was all finished. And it was finished for you and me.

We will probably never have to go through a death as gruesome and painful as Jesus'. But we will go through the fire. Do we realize that when we have to go through hard times, those times can make us stronger? Those times can help us reach our full potential. Peter says, "In this you rejoice, though now for a little while, if necessary, you have been grieved by various trials, so that the tested genuineness of your faith—more precious than gold that perishes though it is tested by fire —may be found to result in praise and glory and honor at the revelation of Jesus Christ" (1 Peter 1:6-7, ESV). As Jesus told us to remember His body and blood, we picture that moment on the cross when He knew that the pain was nearing the end. We can celebrate with Him that the pain was almost done and that He would be raised a few days later. We can also celebrate when we are going through hard times, knowing that they can make us stronger and that those times will be finished forever one day!

Today, I will...consider times of fire as a blessing.

Racing to the Finish
Today's Scripture: 2 Timothy 4:6-8

The Christian life is not a sprint, it is a marathon. The road can be long and hard. There will be wonderful moments and there will be difficult moments. As Christians, we know that because our Lord finished what He set out to do, we have a wonderful finish in store for us no matter how difficult the race is. Are you racing to that finish?

There is a man in the New Testament who raced with all the ability he had. We know him as the Apostle Paul. Life was not easy for Paul. He was beaten, imprisoned, and faced scary situations because he loved and proclaimed Christ. Those bad times didn't stop him from running the race. Near the end of his life, we read these words, "For I am already being poured out as a drink offering, and the time of my departure has come. I have fought the good fight, I have finished the race, I have kept the faith. Henceforth there is laid up for me the crown of righteousness, which the Lord, the righteous judge, will award to me on that day, and not only to me but also to all who have loved His appearing" (2 Timothy 4:6-8 ESV).

Jesus had a goal: save you and me. Paul had a goal: finish this race faithful to Jesus and help others do the same. What is my goal? Am I running in such a way as to be able to confidently say that I have finished the race?

Today, I will…check my goals. I will check my focus in life. There are so many distractions in the world, so I will refocus my life on the body and blood of Jesus. I will be thankful for that sacrifice that He set out to do and that He finished.

Table Meditation
Scripture: Matthew 26:36-56

During the Lord's Supper, our minds often gravitate toward the Last Supper, a moment rich with profound meaning behind what we do every week. While this focus is natural, it can sometimes eclipse the events that followed—in particular, those in the Garden of Gethsemane. Although this was a time of immense suffering for Jesus, it was a time that truly reminds us of his humanity.

Consider first that Jesus, fully aware of the suffering and death that would await him after Judas' betrayal, chose to pray. He did not face this moment alone; he invited some of his closest friends to be with him.

This act alone should be a source of comfort for us. How often have we felt that we must confront our fears in isolation, especially when it comes to sharing them with those that we love? Yet here is Jesus, the greatest of all, choosing to have his friends nearby in his darkest hour. If he were only divine, he might have faced this ordeal alone. But being human, he needed the company of his friends. The next time I am afraid, I need to remember that he was too.

Jesus also knew the pain of being let down by those closest to him. Those friends he thought he could rely on in his greatest time of need? They fell asleep as he prayed. It must have felt as though his friends cared nothing about him at all. The next time those I love fail me in my time of need, I need to remember those he loved failed him too.

We remember that Jesus turned to God in fervent prayer, only to have his pleas go unanswered. If anyone's prayers deserved to be heard and answered, it was s Jesus.

Yet, in his greatest trial, he asked to be spared from this horrible event—not once, not twice, but three times. How many times have we also pleaded to be freed from our own struggles, only to receive a "No" from God? The next time I feel the pain and disappointment from an unanswered prayer, I need to remember that Jesus did, too.

Next, in the moments when loyalty was needed the most, Jesus was betrayed. And not just by Judas—who selfishly gave Jesus up for nothing more than silver valued at about $500 in today's value—but also by Peter, one of his dearest disciples. The next time I feel betrayed by the fear and selfishness of those who I value the most, I need to remember that Jesus did, too.

But the next time I feel so alone and that no one cares, I need to remember this: Jesus willingly endured every second of his suffering. He didn't have to come to us. He didn't have to go to the cross. But he did anyway. He died so that we might have life.

As we partake in the Lord's Supper, we are called to examine ourselves soberly and honestly. Sometimes, our selfishness gets in the way. But we know that Christ, whose blood covers our sin, has felt the same things we feel. We know that he endured the cross for us, leaving no doubt about His love for us. Being loved so deeply and having the privilege to honor and remember him each first day of the week—through our partaking of the bread and the cup—is so unbelievably special that we should never take it for granted.

MONDAY
The Darkness and the Light
Today's Scripture: Luke 23:44-46

On April 8, 2024, a small but significant portion of the continental United States experienced the phenomena of a solar eclipse. People drove from near and far to place themselves in the "path of totality."

If you have ever experienced such an event, you know how incredible and eerie it can be. Animals get confused and act strange, some even prepare for sleep even though it is the middle of the day. There can be rapid changes in weather with temperatures dropping more than 20 degrees. Wind changes direction and radio frequencies can be interrupted. In short, the sun being darkened during otherwise normal daylight hours is so unusual that it makes a significant impression. And all of this happens in just a matter of moments! In most places, the eclipse lasted less than 4 minutes.

It is hard to fathom three hours of miraculous darkness at the brightest time of day (noon to 3 pm). Yet, that is exactly what Luke 23:44 says took place.

Make no mistake, this was a miracle. The darkness was divine intervention to mark the seriousness and magnitude of the occasion.

In Scripture, darkness can indicate judgment for sin and rebellion (note Joel 2 and Amos 8). That is fitting here. When Jesus was on the cross, the world was being judged, and satan was being defeated (John 12:31).

Without question, the darkness made a powerful impression on those who experienced it. This particular cosmic event had a profound effect on all of the witnesses. It must have a profound effect on us as well.

Imagine yourself in Jerusalem and being close enough to the place called The Skull (Luke 23:33) that you hear Jesus cry out with a loud voice to the Father. Then, at that moment, after three hours of darkness, the light returns.

Jesus is the light that conquers darkness (John 1:5, 9)! He is the light of the world who offers us life (John 8:12; 9:5; 12:46).

Today, I will…remember that thanks to the cross of Christ, all darkness is dispelled, and we can dwell in the light.

TUESDAY
More than Flesh
Today's Scripture: Luke 23:46

All of us will be somewhere forever. This life is not all that there is to our existence.

When Jesus called out with a loud voice, "Father, into your hands I commit my spirit!" He was communicating multiple profound truths. Among them was the fact that even though His body was about to experience death, His existence would continue. Like Jesus, when we draw our last breath here on earth, it is not the end for us!

We will either be with the Lord (Luke 23:43), or we will be cast out of the presence of God to a place of agony (Luke 16:24).

Consider other examples from Scripture concerning our dual nature:

> "Do not fear those who kill the body but cannot kill the soul. Rather fear Him who can destroy both soul and body in hell" (Matthew 10:28, ESV).

> "For as the body apart from the spirit is dead, so also faith apart from works is dead" (James 2:26, ESV).

The skeptic and nonbeliever think that humans are mere flesh—only material beings and nothing more. They are under the impression that when we die, we are finished…out like a light. What a tragic, pitiful, and depressing worldview. Thankfully, this is false! We were created for something more! We are endowed with eternal souls.

Jesus was more than flesh. We are more than flesh.

Today, I will…remember that I do not merely have a body that must be cared for…I have a soul that must be nourished, strengthened, and prepared for eternity. Thanks to the love of Jesus and His work on the cross, I have confidence that my soul is secure and I will reside in the presence of God forever.

WEDNESDAY
An Evening Prayer
Today's Scripture: Psalm 31:3-5

Tucking our children into bed in the evening is a sweet and precious time. For many years, parents have taught their children an easy-to-remember prayer that goes something like this: "Now I lay me down to sleep, I pray the Lord my soul to keep. If I should die before I wake, I pray the Lord my soul to take."

This type of prayer has a long and rich tradition. For centuries, Jewish parents have used the Psalms to tuck their children in at night and teach them bedtime prayers.

Specifically, Psalm 31 has been used to calm little hearts and minds and to prepare them for sleep.

> "For you are my rock and my fortress; and for your name's sake you lead me and guide me; you take me out of the net they have hidden for me, for you are my refuge. Into your hand I commit my spirit; you have redeemed me, O Lord, faithful God" (Psalm 31:3-5, ESV).

Did you catch that?

At the time of the crucifixion, Jewish parents had been teaching their children for many years to say this as they prepared to rest for the night and go to sleep.

Here, in this most significant and painful moment, Jesus utters the same precious words.

It is the image of a child who trusts God with what will happen during the night…whatever that may be.

When we partake of the Lord's Supper and remember these words spoken by Jesus from the cross, we give thanks for the One who has redeemed us. We give thanks for the One who is faithful to us. We give thanks for the One who guides us and hides us.

Today, I will…remember that I am but a child who relies on my heavenly Father to protect me. In my most vulnerable time, I commit my soul to the eternal Redeemer.

THURSDAY
Aware of My Sin
Today's Scripture: Luke 23:46-48

Imagine with me...let's put ourselves in the place of those gathered around the cross. We are standing among those who have assembled for the spectacle of the execution of Jesus of Nazareth. We can see the looks on their faces and hear the anger in their words.

Some six hours have passed. Now they have witnessed the execution of the One they used to hate.

They have heard what He said. They have seen the way He courageously faced and handled death. They have experienced the darkness and the earthquake.

The Bible says of that crowd, "When they saw what had taken place, returned home beating their breasts" (Luke 23:48, ESV).

Could it be that they were now disturbed and emotionally shaken up?

Could it be that they were now in a state of grief because they were now convicted that Jesus was innocent and that they were the guilty ones?

This is exactly what should happen to each one of us when we hear the words of Jesus and see the heart of Jesus. You and I should walk away from the cross beating on our chests.

But it cannot end there! When we realize our sin, when the cross has made it clear that we are sinners in need of salvation, we must seek rescue.

"The tax collector, standing far off, would not even lift up his eyes to heaven, but beat his breast, saying, 'God, be merciful to me, a sinner!'" (Luke 18:13, ESV).

When the crowd in Acts 2 were convinced that Jesus was Lord and Christ (Acts 2:36), and they were convicted of their sin (Acts 2:37), they were instructed to repent and be baptized (Acts 2:38). May we not merely stand among them, may we follow them in sincerity.

Today, I will...see the cross...I will hear the words of Jesus...and I will be aware of my sin. But I will not dwell there! I will give thanks that the Lord loves me and gave Himself for me so that I might be forgiven and live.

What Comes Next
Today's Scripture: 1 Peter 2:23-25; 4:19

Maybe more than anything else, when Jesus loudly proclaimed, "Father, into your hands I commit my spirit" (Luke 23:46, ESV), He was saying, "Father, I trust you."

Jesus has been agonizing on the cross for some six hours. Yet He trusted the Father with what comes next. Put simply, Jesus trusted the promises of the Father.

For example, Psalm 16:10 is a prediction that the coming Messiah would die but would be raised from the dead. Jesus trusted prophecies such as this one! Remember how He told the disciples over and over that everything written about Him would be accomplished, specifically that He would be killed but resurrected on the third day (Luke 9:22; 18:31-33)? Jesus knew that He could trust the Father with what came next. Even from the cross, He "continued entrusting Himself to Him who judges justly" (1 Peter 2:23, ESV).

He knew He was going to die, but He knew He would not be forgotten. He knew He was going to die, but He knew He was going to continue to live.

Jesus has finished the necessary work for you and for me to be saved and have hope. The question is, do we trust Him? Do we trust the Lord with our souls?

May we all believe like Jesus and trust the Father—even when things seem bleak and ugly!

"Therefore let those who suffer according to God's will entrust their souls to a faithful Creator while doing good" (1 Peter 4:19, ESV).

When it comes to partaking of the Lord's Supper, our joint participation in this meal is a bold declaration that we are not only thankful for what has been done but that we trust God with what comes next. "As often as you eat this bread and drink the cup, you proclaim the Lord's death until He comes" (1 Corinthians 11:26, ESV).

Today, I will…remember how Jesus entrusted His soul to the Father and follow His example. I may be scared or hurt, but I will trust the Lord with what comes next!

HIS DEATH
FRIDAY
3:00 PM-5:00 PM

Table Meditation
Scripture: Luke 22:19 & 1 Corinthians 11:23-26

"Do this..." are words spoken by Jesus and recorded for us by Luke in Luke 22:19 and Paul in 1 Corinthians 11:23-26. These two words are imperatives. Therefore they form a command, instruction, and direction.

"Do this" references two elements that we understand to be the vital elements of the Lord's Supper. The first element is the eating of unleavened bread. This means the bread is made without yeast. It represents to us the holy and sinless body of Jesus, given as the sacrifice for our sins. The second element is the drinking of the fruit of the vine or the juice of the grape. This represents to us the blood of Jesus Christ, which God accepts as the payment for all our sins when we believe in his Son and put our trust in him.

These two elements comprise the Lord's Supper, where he introduced to his disciples the deeper meaning of the Passover. God passes over our sins because of our faith in the death, burial, and resurrection of Jesus. His body and his blood are accepted by God as payment for all the sins of those who put their faith in him.

To help us remember, Jesus introduced us to this Lord's Supper and told us, "Do this in remembrance of me." To put it another way, "Do this remembering me."

MONDAY
Broken Legs

Today's Scripture: John 19:31-33

Do you ever feel that you rush through communion? As if it is, "sip and a chip" and on to the next part of worship? We are commanded to take the Lord's Supper weekly, but there is no direction on the amount of time we give to this act of worship. So we rush on through. It has to be done, but for how long is a matter of opinion. Bible people focus on the regularity of the Lord's Supper, but the quality of the time spent seems to be an important but less-debated topic. Over the years the people of God have talked about the weekly observance of the Lord's Supper and whether we can observe it more or less frequently, but rarely about the meaningfulness of the time spent remembering our Lord. We have focused on getting the rule of frequency right, but should that be highlighted more often than the right focus?

The Jews in Jesus' day were worried about keeping the Sabbath holy. The religious leaders asked that the soldiers break the leg bones of the criminals so that the dead bodies would not be hanging on the cross during the Passover. The normal practice of the Romans was to leave the crucified men on the cross until they died which could take days. The rotting bodies would hang there until the vultures would devour them. To speed up the process, soldiers would smash the legs of the victims with an iron mallet. This stopped the victim from pushing up with their legs to get a breath and the person quickly suffocated shortly after.

The Jews wanted to speed up this process so they could keep their holiness. But if the soldiers broke the bones of Jesus, this would have been in violation of divine prophecy. Psalm 34:20 says, "he protects all his bones, not one of them will be broken" (NIV). If they had done so, their need to speed up his death to appear holy would have invalidated Jesus as Messiah. Let us not merely seek to check the box of "weekly communion" and rush remembering the greatest event in history—the sacrifice of our Lord for our salvation.

Today, I will… partake of the Lord's Supper with patience.

TUESDAY
The Spear of Memory
Today's Scripture: John 19:34

Imagine being the man who slid the spear through the skin of Jesus. Imagine you are the one holding that wooden pole with a pointed metal tip at the top, walking up to his flesh, and pushing the sharpened object into the side of Jesus until you feel the pressure of his bloody skin give way and puncture his flesh. As the blood and water gush out of his side, maybe you attempt to avoid the splash of fluid onto your feet. At that moment you might have been more worried about becoming dirty than guilty.

Imagine being that soldier and meeting Jesus on the Day of Judgment and he says to you, "Remember me? You pierced my side, and here is the scar that you left." For years, it was common to hear people say, "I would rather be the person that drove the spear through the body of Jesus than the person that divides the Lord's Church." This line is alarming. First, hopefully, none of us would want to be either!

The reality is that most people do not realize what they are doing until it is all over and the dust has settled from their actions. People who cause division typically feel it is justified. People who fight believe the cause is worthy. In the moment, people have little reflection on the impact of their actions.

The soldier might plea to Jesus that he was only following orders. There is little chance this soldier believed he was fulfilling scripture. Zechariah 12:10 mentions the side of Jesus being pierced. Imagine Jesus looking at the soldier and saying, "No worries. You helped fulfill the messianic prophecies." Too often, we cannot see the grander impact of our actions. We can only look back and realize what our actions caused. It is wise to think about the ramifications of what we did long ago.

Today, I will... reflect on times when my actions blessed or harmed others.

Care for the Body
Today's Scripture: Mark 15:42-43

One of my most memorable experiences is seeing two brothers hugging during the Lord's Supper. I was new to church and saw the two brothers get heated in bible class over a topic I don't remember. But I do vividly remember how they raised their voices, magnified their passion, and flared their tempers. The argument escalated until one of the brothers walked out of the room angry. He could no longer be in the same room as his brother. I remember sitting there thinking, "Wow. This is how Christians act?"

During the evening service, one of the brothers was giving some communion thoughts, and here came the other brother. He walked into the back through the brown, double-folding doors. They seemed to open magically to reveal him standing there. Everyone (or perhaps just me) turned around to see what would happen next. Maybe a fight, punches thrown, or a shouting match. But that is not what happened. The brother doing the thoughts for the Lord's Supper stepped down and walked toward his brother who was likewise walking towards him and they embraced one another with a massive bear hug. I heard them say, "I am sorry." And I once again sat there and thought, "Wow. This is how Christians act."

Making peace is evidence of courage. Anyone can hold a grudge, but the person who restores peace in the body of Christ is a true hero. All of us are called to figuratively protect the body of Jesus. Joseph of Arimathea made himself vulnerable in order to care for the body of Jesus. Mark 15:43 (ESV) states that he "took courage" and asked Pilate for the body.

The Lord's Supper is concerned about maintaining fellowship with one another. When there is conflict, the person who makes peace is the most courageous. There are always a thousand excuses not to go, but one reason to go—to make peace with your brother or sister. Establishing peace is an act of courage, while staying in conflict is an act of a cowardice.

Today, I will… go and make peace.

THURSDAY
Unlikely Partners
Today's Scripture: Mark 15:44-46

What "great partnerships" can you list? A boy and his dog; ketchup and mustard; peanut butter and jelly; Frodo and Sam; Chewy and Han Solo. Our spouses, best friends, and business associates are crucial relationships which increase our success. No one accomplishes anything much alone. We all need good partnerships.

Often during the Lord's Supper, my wife and I partake of the emblems at the same time. I hold the tray, and she takes the emblem and we eat and drink together. She has been my partner for over 20 years now. My life is better because of her. My partnership with Charity has shaped my life more than any other relationship here on earth. I also think about countless partnerships and mentors in the gospel that have blessed me and remain valuable to me.

Some partnerships just make sense. Other partnerships seem to be a stretch. Pilate and Joseph of Arimathea coming together seems pretty farfetched. Joseph asked Pilate for the body of Jesus. Maybe Pilate considered saying, "No." But he agreed and Joseph cared for Jesus' body and buried him in his tomb. Sometimes help comes from an unlikely source.

During the Lord's Supper, think about partaking with all of the partners in the gospel that you have. Our congregations are filled with people who are contributing to the work of the Lord. Your greatest partners could be the people most unlike you. It could be the people who seem like the most unlikely friends who end up being the most helpful relationships you have in sharing the gospel.

Today, I will... be thankful for the people who have partnered with me.

FRIDAY
Part of the Group
Today's Scripture: Luke 23:55-56

Consider the countless unknown names involved in major events in history. Thousands of men stormed Normandy Beach right into the line of fire in order to defeat Germany. How many of these men can you name? Thousands of people died on 9/11, but the individual names are almost completely forgotten. We have had thousands of missionaries go out with the good news of Jesus, but how many of those people can you recall? A lot has happened in this world, but the names are forgotten.

Luke 23:23 starts with one phrase, "the women." Who are these women? We perhaps get some insight into the names from Luke 8:2-3, "And also some women who had been healed of evil spirits and infirmities: Mary, called Magdalene, from whom seven demons had gone out, and Joanna, the wife of Chuza, Herod's household manager, and Susanna, and many others, who provided for them out of their means (ESV)." This group is an interesting collection. Some have been healed from evil spirits and infirmities, some appear to have been wealthy and powerful and therefore provided funds for the mission of Jesus. They were a crucial group to Jesus' ministry. In Luke 23:23, we do not know these ladies' names or their stories of discipleship.

In America, people typically desire to stand out, be noticed, and make an impression. But in this text, it is about the group of women. No one rises above the others. All are equal at the gravesite of Jesus. It is a powerful dynamic when groups come together for the work of the Lord.

One of the best aspects about the Lord's Supper is that we are part of the group. We are one among many. The Lord's Supper is not just about me, it is about us. Sometimes it is best to look around the room and see the group and not just yourself.

Today, I will… blend in at the table, not stand out.

Table Meditation
Scripture: 1 Corinthians 11:28-29

When we come together to partake of the Lord's Supper, we do so in remembrance of our Lord and Savior. His death on the cross made the new covenant possible. He shed His blood for the remission of our sins. When we partake each week, we have a fresh and loving encounter with Jesus. We pause to reflect on the blessings we enjoy through Christ. Because of His blood, we can walk in the light.

Partaking of the Lord's Supper is a serious occasion. We eat it with reverence to God. The Supper is intended to create a clear spiritual vision of our Savior and His sacrifice. It is human to forget. So, it is the place of the Lord's Supper to keep our memory straight, clear, and focused. What we discern serves as an anchor to our faith. Let's never lose sight of the significance of the Lord's Supper and what it means to our spiritual life. He provided the way of salvation for those who follow His plan. He endured the pain and agony of the cross for us. He loves us so much. He is all we need. We should be thankful and humbled by what He has done for us. Let's give thanks.

* Give **thanks for the bread**, which represents the broken body of our Lord.

* Give **thanks for the fruit of the vine,** which represents the shed blood of our Lord.

MONDAY
He Still Shakes the World
Today's Scripture: Matthew 27:51-53

When Jesus "died for our sins according to the scriptures" (1 Corinthians 15:3, ESV), amazing, earth-shattering events took place. The curtain of the temple split in two. The earth shook. Rocks split. Resurrection occurred.

What else would you expect? The very God of the universe…the One who inhabited heaven…the One whose wisdom and holiness are so vast that our perceptions of Him seem so small as to be blasphemy of His glory…the One who has life in Himself…has just died. How could the world that bore His fingerprints not quake and break at the moment of His sacrifice? Mankind may have forgotten its Creator, but the universe never would.

In His life, Jesus raised the daughter of Jairus, the Nain widow's son, and Lazarus. These miracles confirmed the truth that He was the Lord over life and death. When He died, He raised many more who came out of their tombs and walked the streets of Jerusalem. These were not the walking dead. They were the risen living who showed a message to those who were spiritually dead people walking. Even in His death, Jesus was still the Lord of life.

As we come to the table of the Lord, we proclaim the Lord's death until He comes (1 Corinthians 11:26), but we do not proclaim a dead Lord. As His spirit left His body, it tore down the temple veil, broke the ground with the force of an earthquake, and infused the righteous dead with life.

Today, I will…remember what the world often forgets. Our Lord still shakes the world.

TUESDAY
The Barrier Was Taken Away
Today's Scripture: Matthew 27:51-53

The curtain of the temple was the veil that stood between the Holy Place and the Most Holy Place (the Holy of Holies). It was in the Most Holy Place that the Spirit of God was present. No one could enter the Most Holy Place except for the High Priest, and then only on the Day of Atonement. The curtain separated God from sinful people.

That meant that for the people of Israel, God was hidden and distant. The idea of a personal relationship with Him seemed improbable if not impossible.

But when Jesus died, the curtain of the temple was torn from top to bottom—-not from bottom to top. The meaning is clear. Man could not cross the barrier to God, so God, because of His love, and through the sacrifice of Jesus, tore the veil from top to bottom.

It is not the righteousness of men that gives us access to the presence of God. It is His love! Love sent Jesus for our sins (John 3:16). Love makes us children of God (1 John 3:1). Love gives us access to the throne of God in prayer (John 16:26-27). Love gives us the power to love (1 John 4:19). Love makes us more than conquerors (Romans 8:31-39). Love will bring us home.

Today, I will…thank God that He loved us enough to open Himself to us through the death of Jesus.

WEDNESDAY
The Tombs Were Opened
Today's Scripture: Matthew 27:51-53

Death is an enemy (1 Corinthians 15:26). It has been ever since Adam and Eve opened the door to it through sin (Romans 5:12).

When it takes the life of the elderly piece by piece it is unmerciful. When it robs a wife of the husband she loves it is cruel. When it destroys the life of a child it is a monster. We fear death. We hate it. We fight it. We seek to postpone it, even though we know it is relentless and inevitable.

When Jesus died the tombs were opened and the dead were raised. What could it possibly mean? It means that Jesus "abolished death and brought life and immortality to light" (2 Timothy 1:10, ESV). The tomb has lost its power. It means that through death Jesus will "destroy the one who has the power of death, that is, the devil" (Hebrews 2:14, ESV). When satan thought that he had destroyed Jesus, he destroyed himself. It means that through death Jesus delivered "all those who through fear of death were subject to lifelong slavery" (Hebrews 2:15, ESV). The grave has lost its terror. And it means that we will rise as surely as the dead rose in Judea (1 Thessalonians 4:13-18). Death has lost its tragedy.

Because the tombs were opened, you and I can now see death as a doorway and not a doom.

Today, I will…thank God for the death of Jesus which takes away the sting of death for me.

After His Resurrection
Today's Scripture: Matthew 27:51-53

It is significant that the dead who were raised at the death of Jesus went into the holy city AFTER His resurrection. While we focus on the death of Christ at the table of the Lord, that death would have no impact on our lives without the resurrection.

The death of Jesus, if had remained permanent, would be no gospel at all. It would simply be the tragic death of another good man. He would only be one in a long line of martyrs for a great cause. But we remember the death of Jesus with great reverence because His resurrection declares its value.

Listen to the words of Paul:

> "Now I would remind you, brothers, of the gospel I preached to you, which you received, in which you stand, and by which you are being saved, if you hold fast to the word I preached to you—unless you believed in vain…Christ died for our sins in accordance with the Scriptures…he was buried…he was raised on the third day in accordance with the Scriptures." (1 Corinthians 15:1-4, ESV)

Listen to the words of Jesus Himself:

> "These are my words that I spoke to you while I was still with you, that everything written about me in the Law of Moses and the Prophets and the Psalms must be fulfilled… Thus it is written, that the Christ should suffer and on the third day rise from the dead, and that repentance for the forgiveness of sins should be proclaimed in his name to all nations." (Luke 24:44-47, ESV)

Today, I will…proclaim the Lord's death and look forward to His coming.

FRIDAY
His Death and His Return
Today's Scripture: Matthew 27:51-53

The death of Jesus was an ending and a beginning with seismic impact and cosmic consequences. It was the ending of one era and the beginning of a better one. It was the violent shaking of the old to bring in the new. It was the awakening of the dead to a new life.

As we gather at the table of the Lord, we remember that He will come again. "For as often as you eat this bread and drink the cup, you proclaim the Lord's death until he comes" (1 Corinthians 11:26, ESV).

In many ways, the events surrounding the death of Jesus foreshadow of His return. When He comes, it will be an ending and a beginning with seismic impact and cosmic consequences. It will be the ending of one era and the beginning of a perfect one. It will be the awakening of the dead to a new life.

> "The day of the Lord will come like a thief, and then the heavens will pass away with a roar, and the heavenly bodies will be burned up and dissolved, and the earth and the works that are done on it will be exposed… All these things are thus to be dissolved… The heavens will be set on fire and dissolved, and the heavenly bodies will melt as they burn! But according to his promise we are waiting for new heavens and a new earth in which righteousness dwells" (2 Peter 3:10-13, ESV).

Today, I will…remember that, because of the death of Jesus, I am moving toward a future full of hope.

Table Meditation
Scripture: 1 Corinthians 12:12-13

We enjoy a special and unique blessing when we gather with our physical families for celebration meals! You know, we eagerly anticipate these times together, when we draw closer to each family member and when we become better than before. We realize how important it is to be part of a great and unique fellowship. This family experience sustains us and unites us in a bond of togetherness! This is a blessing from God!

When our spiritual family meets together on the first day of a new week, we share an even greater special blessing and unique bond of fellowship: God, Christ, and the Holy Spirit are in our presence. Individually and collectively, we are in partnership, communion, and fellowship with the divine family when we remember and celebrate at His Table! This table is not physical, but it is a spiritual table—where Christ's followers' hearts and minds unite with the godhead.

Through the body and blood that Christ gave, we remember and understand that we are part of the divine family and the divine nature when we participate together at His spiritual Table. We know that we belong to Him! And that is worth remembering our partnership!

MONDAY
A Personhood Like No Other
Today's Scripture: Matthew 27:54

As we gather weekly to remember the love and sacrifice of our Lord Jesus, our hearts remember many incredible truths. We reflect upon the agony Jesus experienced, the love and forgiveness He provides, and the noble way He endured his trial and crucifixion. Yet, the one thing we might miss is an attribute observed by an eyewitness to those events: His personhood.

A centurion, complicit in the execution of Jesus, looked upon our crucified Savior and the events that took place surrounding His death and proclaimed, "Truly this was the Son of God!" (Matthew 27:54, ESV). The earthquake, darkening of the sky, and resurrection of the dead impacted the soldier. However, the astonishment that led to his statement was influenced by Jesus' character on the cross. Jesus endured his torture without a word, showed mercy to a fellow criminal, and cried out for God to forgive his murderers. The Centurion had seen all of this, and along with the miraculous events surrounding Jesus' death, Christ's character changed him.

The historian Will Durant once observed that the person of Jesus, with such lofty character and impeccable ethics, could not have been invented by man. Simply put, Jesus is not like anyone else. He is better. He is more loving. He is divine. While Jesus' miracles and teachings were decisive, the most significant factor that drew so many to Him was His incredible character. His personality caused fishermen to leave their possessions and careers to follow Him, massive crowds to sit for hours and hang on His every word, and multitudes to give up everything to serve Him.

Today, I will...reflect upon the character of Jesus, who endured the cross for me, and rededicate myself to model my life after His.

TUESDAY
All Are Welcome at the Cross
Today's Scripture: 1 Corinthians 11:28

The Lord's Supper is designed to have a powerful impact on believers when we gather to commune with Christ and one another. We remember the sacrifice of Jesus and the redemption purchased for us through His substitutionary sacrifice. Still, there is another point of reflection essential to the communion: self-examination. Paul emphasizes this aspect of the Lord's Supper, saying, "Let a person examine himself, then, and so eat of the bread and drink of the cup" (1 Corinthians 11:28, ESV).

Self-reflection can be hard, particularly considering Jesus's incredible sacrifice on the cross. Paul instructs the Philippians to "Only let your manner of life be worthy of the gospel of Christ" (Philippians 1:27, ESV). In this regard, we all feel inadequate. Who among us lives worthy of the death, burial, and resurrection of Christ Jesus? We all know that we are unworthy of His blood. This reminder is part of the reason Jesus instructed us to remember His sacrifice regularly!

The events surrounding Christ's death, particularly the witnesses that were present, provide us comfort. Matthew writes, "There were also many women there, looking on from a distance, who had followed Jesus from Galilee, ministering to him, among whom were Mary Magdalene and Mary the mother of James and Joseph and the mother of the sons of Zebedee" (Matthew 27:55-56, ESV). In their faith and love for Jesus, they witnessed His crucifixion. They certainly did not feel worthy. Did they self-examine themselves and determine they were righteous enough to witness the most significant self-sacrifice in human history? No, any self-reflection reinforced why they were there in the first place: they loved Jesus and were grateful for how He had changed their lives and wanted to be as close to Him as possible. Perhaps Paul instructs us to self-examine during the Lord's Supper so that we might reach the same conclusion.

Today, I will…reflect upon the sacrifice Jesus made for me and thank Him for saving me despite my imperfections.

WEDNESDAY
Proclaiming His Death
Today's Scripture: John 12:32

Paul's instructions on the proper administration of the Lord's Supper include this explanation of what we accomplish through our participation, "For as often as you eat this bread and drink the cup, you proclaim the Lord's death until he comes" (1 Corinthians 11:26, ESV). Why does Paul describe communion in this way? How do we "proclaim" his death through partaking in the bread and the fruit of the vine?

In John 12:32, Jesus proclaims, "And I, when I am lifted up from the earth, will draw all people to myself" (ESV). His statement certainly addresses the appeal of His sacrifice on the cross as His divine love has transformed the world. Yet there is also a sense in which we lift Jesus as we proclaim all that he did for us in His death, burial, and resurrection. There is never a time when we more vividly pronounce His death than when we intentionally and publicly remember it.

As Jesus hung there suspended between heaven and earth, pouring out His blood and his life for the very people who were murdering Him, the scene had a profound impact on those who witnessed the event. Some wept, some mocked, a thief begged for mercy, and a centurion proclaimed, "Truly this was the son of God!" (Matthew 27:54, ESV). Seeing Jesus there, lifted up in all of His sacrificial glory, was transformative. The Lord's Supper should have a similar impact on those of us who understand everything communion represents. Every week, our hearts are transported back to Golgotha as we witness again a love that is no equal. Does it impact us? Does it change us? If not, we need to examine ourselves and recommit to once again "lift Him up."

Today, I will…focus on exalting Christ through my communion to lift Him us as my Savior and King.

THURSDAY
An Event Like No Other
Today's Scripture: Matthew 27:51-54

As the Roman Centurion looked upon Jesus after the King of Kings cried out and gave up His spirit, the soldier proclaimed, "Truly this was the Son of God" (Matthew 27:54, ESV). As a warrior and a commander, he had undoubtedly witnessed many executions. Yet, this one profoundly impacted him in ways the others had not. Jesus' character played a part in his astonishment, as the Lord forgave His accusers and offered kindness to a fellow condemned man. The circumstances also contributed to his proclamation, with the crowd vilifying an innocent man. However, would those factors alone explain the profound statement of this hardened soldier?

The previous verses add context to why he said what he did. Matthew writes, "And behold, the temple curtain was torn in two, from top to bottom. And the earth shook, and the rocks were split. The tombs also were opened. And many bodies of the saints who had fallen asleep were raised, and coming out of the tombs after his resurrection they went into the holy city and appeared to many" (Matthew 27:51-53, ESV). Yes, the Centurion saw this execution as different than others he had witnessed *before* Jesus succumbed to His wounds. Still, the events that transpired the moment Christ died confirmed his suspicions: deity was killed on that cross. The death of any man, regardless of how innocent or good he may be, does not cause the sky to darken, the earth to shake, and the dead to climb from their tombs and walk again.

As we partake of the Lord's Supper and remember that moment, are we impacted the way the Centurion was? Do we go through the motions as we have countless times before, or do we memorialize the most significant moment in the history of the universe?

Today, I will…consider the significance of the cross as the central event in all human history.

FRIDAY
Filled With Awe
Today's Scripture: Matthew 27:54

Matthew 27:54 tells us, "When the centurion and those who were with him, keeping watch over Jesus, saw the earthquake and what took place, they were filled with awe and said, 'Truly this was the Son of God!'" (ESV). The Roman Centurion and other onlookers had a surreal experience as the dead came out of their graves, the sun hid, and the earth shook. The Man on the cross triggered these supernatural events before them, breathing his last breath. He must have surveyed the scene with confusion, fascination, and soul-shaking fear.

The Bible says they were "filled with awe" (Matthew 27:54, ESV). According to a simple Google search, the word "awe" denotes an array of mixed emotions, including fear, respect, and wonder. It is a consuming emotion that pushes away all other concerns and focuses on the spectacle and grandeur of the moment. This is precisely what the Centurion, and every other observer that day, felt as God expired on the cross. It was overwhelming.

We use the word "awe" loosely in our society. Everything seems to be potentially "awesome" according to our present vocabulary. We say, "This ice cream is awesome," then sing in church, "I stand in awe of You." Have we lost the sense of what "awe" is all about? Suppose we casually use the word for anything we like or enjoy. What words do we reserve for events and scenes that are genuinely soul-inspiring and all-consuming?

It is unlikely that we can change the watered-down usage of the word, but what we can do is distinguish in our hearts that some things indeed are "awesome." We come together every Sunday to experience again an awe-inspiring event as we focus our minds back in time and witness the cross again. When we do, we can truly sing, "I stand in AWE of You."

Today, I will...focus my heart on the majesty of Christ's death and determine never to forget the awesome sacrifice He made for me.

HIS BURIAL
SATURDAY

Table Meditation
Scripture: Ephesians 5:1-2

What do you think about during the Lord's Supper? Some people say that during the breaking of the bread that represents Christ's body, they think about the spear in his side or his crown of thorns and the nails through his hands and feet. When partaking of the fruit of the vine, we may concentrate on the blood he so freely gave so that we may be forgiven. But perhaps the thing that we could easily overlook is the reason for this sacrifice: LOVE!

The Lord's Supper not only reminds us of the sacrifice that Jesus made for us but also the love that God has for us. A.W. Tozer said, "God's love is an incomprehensibly vast, bottomless shoreless sea."[1] Ephesians 5:1-2 tells us to "be imitators of God as dear children. And walk in love, as Christ also has loved us and given himself for us" (NKJV). Romans 5:8 goes on to say, "God demonstrates His own love toward us, in that while we were still sinners, Christ died for us" (NKJV). Jesus said in John 15:13, "Greater love has no one than this, than to lay down one's life for his friends" (NKJV). Probably the best-known verse, John 3:16 emphasizes, "God so LOVED the world that he gave his only begotten Son, that whoever believes in him should not perish but have everlasting life" (NKJV). So, while we remember Christ's body represented by the bread and his blood represented by the fruit of the vine, let's remember the reason for that great sacrifice, God's love for us!

---

[1] *The Knowledge of the Holy.* Harper & Row, 1961. 98.

Not All Safeguards Are Equal
Today's Scripture: Matthew 27:62-66

After Jesus had been killed and buried, the chief priests and Pharisees worried that His disciples would steal the body, so they went to Pilate and asked that a guard be placed on the tomb until the third day. Pilate agreed to their request, and he left it to them as to how the guard should be deployed. They refused to accept that Jesus was the Christ, the Son of the Living God. That unbelief kept them from thinking that Jesus might rise from the grave. So they set a guard because Jesus' body was more valuable to them in the tomb.

Matthew's inspired record, however, gives no indication that the disciples ever gave thought to stealing the body. They were in shock over the events that had occurred and were simply trying to figure out what was going to happen to them next. To them, the guard was an unnecessary inconvenience because all they wanted was to make sure that Jesus' body was treated with the dignity and respect that it deserved.

But no guard could keep Him there. No amount of unbelief could keep Him there. No amount of confusion, shock, or inconvenience could keep Him there. In reality, Jesus went into the tomb so that He could come out of it (1 Corinthians 15:4; Acts 2:32; Acts 3:15; Acts 13:30)! Unbelieving man has given it their best shot by killing Him (Acts 2:23); by burying Him and sealing the tomb (Matthew 27:66); and by denying Him (Acts 19:9). And yet He lives (Revelation 1:18).

Today, I will…not permit the schemes of unbelieving man to hinder my faith in God, and I will boldly speak of my risen Savior.

TUESDAY
"That Deceiver" Said...
Today's Scripture: Matthew 27:62-66

Throughout the generations, some tactics have remained consistent. One of those is this: whether in a courtroom before a grand jury or in a lunchroom surrounded by second-grade classmates—if you can't beat them, insult them. When words begin flying, and we feel like we're not getting our point across, we feel like we're losing an argument, or even if we simply feel like we're being ignored, our strategy can quickly turn to insults. And too frequently, being on the receiving end of insults leads us to counter them with more insults.

We read in Matthew 27:63 that the chief priests and Pharisees referred to Jesus as "that deceiver." That is insulting. It was an insult to Jesus then, and it is an insult now to us who believe. They called Him that to try to get sympathy from Pilate, a kind of self-assurance to themselves and to the man who had permitted His death. But they also did so as a provocation to Him and His disciples. If someone referred to Jesus as a deceiver today, we would respond.

It is wonderful that we have sufficient passion for our Savior to be angry when someone blasphemes His Holy Name. But our response needs to be love, not anger. Jesus said, "Blessed are you when others revile you and persecute you and utter all kinds of evil against you falsely on my account" (Matthew 5:11, ESV). And also, "But I say to you, Love your enemies and pray for those who persecute you, so that you may be sons of your Father who is in heaven"(Matthew 5:44-45, ESV).

Today, I will…resolve to love. I will not follow the course of men, but I will let God's grace shine above the insults, slurs, and doubting of others. I will bless the name of Jesus for His example of meekness and obedience to the cross (Hebrews 5:8).

WEDNESDAY
Combinations
Today's Scripture: Matthew 27:62-66

Like most people, I have several full key rings that I never use. Some of them go to other people's houses (like our children or neighbors); some of them go to locks for things like trailers and storage units, and those keys are important but seldom ever get used; then there are some keys that I have no idea where they came from or what they go to. I hesitate to throw those away because they might be important, but without knowing the right key for the right lock, they are useless.

The guard was set on the tomb of Jesus. They knew where to guard, and they knew when to guard, but they didn't know what to guard. They had a lock, but they didn't have the right key, and that made the guard useless.

Paul wrote, "And the peace of God, which surpasses all understanding, will guard your hearts and your minds in Christ Jesus" (Philippians 4:7). Our hearts have a lock on them, and the peace of God is the key that seals them. Don't lose this key! satan wants you to leave your heart open to temptation, hatred, worldliness, humanism, greed, lust, and evil desire (see Colossians 3:5; Ephesians 5:3-6; 1 Corinthians 6:9-10). He wants unrestricted access to the secrets of your heart so that he may gain control.

Jesus went to the grave so that we might lock satan out. We have to know what to guard and how to guard it because the value of our souls is simply too high to leave at risk. Jesus said, "The thief comes only to steal and kill and destroy. I came that they may have life and have it abundantly" (John 10:10, ESV).

Today, I will…not leave myself open to the attacks of satan, and I will constantly be on guard against his temptations and wickedness.

The Last Fraud
Today's Scripture: Matthew 27:62-66

It seems like every week, banks and other financial institutions issue warnings concerning fraud. Scammers prey on two things—emotions and greed. They either present something that is designed to tug on the heartstrings, or they present an apparent opportunity for easy gain, and often they present them together. Also, frequently, there is a twist in their scheme where you can feel good about yourself by helping to right some wrong and frustrating evil by doing good. And it's all a scam, a fraud, and a deception where you are the loser.

"And the last fraud will be worse than the first." Isn't it ironic that the chief priests and Pharisees were so worried about the possibility that the disciples of Jesus would commit fraud by stealing His body when they were the ones who had been deceived? They probably felt good about going to Pilate and asking for a guard to be placed on His tomb. There was a film in 1939 called "You Can't Cheat an Honest Man." I doubt that the apostle Paul influenced that production, but he wrote in 2 Timothy 3:13, "While evil people and impostors will go on from bad to worse, deceiving and being deceived." There has always been a connection between deceiving and being deceived. It's easier to deceive a deceiver than it is to deceive a righteous person.

"Again Jesus spoke to them, saying, 'I am the light of the world. Whoever follows me will not walk in darkness, but will have the light of life'" (John 8:12, ESV). Over and over, Jesus gave this message: Come into the light. "He committed no sin, neither was deceit found in his mouth"(1 Peter 2:22, ESV).

Today, I will...walk in the steadfast assurance that everything about Jesus is true. I will live my life knowing that He is risen and that He will raise me up. No amount of deception in this world can move me from that confidence.

"Make It As Secure As You Can"
Today's Scripture: Matthew 27:62-66

Jesus was in a tomb, and a great stone was set in the entrance to the tomb (Matthew 27:60; Mark 16:3). The stone was sealed, and a guard of Roman soldiers was posted. The chief priests and Pharisees had "made the tomb secure," as secure as they knew how. But how secure is secure enough?

If you desire eternal salvation, you are going to be obedient to the Word of God. Following the instructions of Jesus, you are going to believe in Him (John 3:36), confess His name (Matthew 10:32), repent of your sins (Luke 13:3), and be baptized in His name (Mark 16:15-16). And having done those things, you will know that you have been forgiven of your sins and that eternal life is yours. You are secure in Him.

But life throws a lot of different things at us. Sometimes our faith grows weak, sometimes we yield to temptation, sometimes we hate instead of love, and sometimes the root of bitterness springs up. We want to be like Christ. We want to live for Him. We want to be holy. But something happens that destroys our confidence in salvation. We need our salvation to be as secure as it can be.

Paul wrote, "But thanks be to God, who gives us the victory through our Lord Jesus Christ. Therefore, my beloved brothers, be steadfast, immovable, always abounding in the work of the Lord, knowing that in the Lord your labor is not in vain" (1 Corinthians 15:57-58, ESV). We cannot afford to quit, nor can we afford to forget that the promises of God are sure. The proof is that even though they made the grave of Jesus as secure as they knew how, it was empty on that Sunday morning.

Today, I will…make my salvation as secure as I can. I will serve the Lord with gladness, and I will not permit life's discouragements to erode my salvation.

HIS RESURRECTION SUNDAY

Table Meditation
Scripture: Hebrews 10:1-4

Under the Old Testament law, 80,771 Burnt and Sin Offerings of bulls, rams, lambs, and goats would have occurred publicly on my behalf from the day of my birth until the end of 2024.[1] You can read the details in Leviticus 1, 4-6, 16; Numbers 15, and 28-29. Those sacrifices did not include additional voluntary, free-will offerings I could have made.

The writer in Hebrews 10:1-4 says that these mandatory and time-consuming sacrifices reminded me of my sins, shortcomings, and failures. That it is impossible "for the blood of bulls and goats to take away sins."

Contrast this with the New Testament sacrifice of Jesus in verses 9-18, His sacrifice is "once and for all time" and that there is "no more need for a sacrifice for sins."

I thank God that the burnt and sin offerings are replaced with the weekly communion feast of Jesus remembering His sacrifice. I thank God that the imperfect sacrifice is replaced with the perfect and I no longer must be burdened by the memory of previous transgressions.

Today I am thankful for the death, burial, and resurrection of Christ Jesus. I am thankful that I can eat the bread and drink the cup that remind me of Christ's sacrifice. I am thankful that my sins are forgiven and forgotten by God. That God loves us enough to provide the perfect and one-time sacrifice of His only Son.

---

[1] https://crossward.org/bullsandgoats/

MONDAY
Why Don't We Tell Them About Jesus?
Today's Scripture: Matthew 28:1-10

Many years ago, my oldest daughter Ashley and I went out to eat. She was about six years old, and this was to be a little father/daughter time. We walked into the restaurant, sat down, and ordered. A couple came in and sat down at the table next to us. They started using words that we don't use in our home. Bad words, ugly words, four-letter words. So I said to her, "Ashley, let's move." We got up from our seats and moved to the far side of the restaurant.

She said, "Daddy, why did we move"? I said, "Well, do you see that couple? They were using some words that we don't use at home. Bad and ugly words." She said, "Daddy, why were they using those words?" I said, "Honey, I don't know. Probably because they're not Christians. You know, Mom and I are Christians. We're trying to be like Jesus. And they're probably not Christians." She said, "Daddy, why aren't they Christians?" I responded, "Sweetheart, I don't know. Probably because nobody has ever told them about Jesus." She then asked me this question: "Daddy, why don't we tell them about Jesus?" I just sat there. She asked the second time, "Daddy, why don't we tell them about Jesus?" Again, I was silent. But she broke the silence and said, "Daddy, why don't we tell them about Jesus?"

Well, I want to ask you the same question my daughter asked me many years ago: Why don't we tell people about Jesus? The angel said to the women who visited the empty tomb: "Go quickly and tell his disciples: He has risen from the dead." And did they do it? "They ran to tell his disciples" (Matthew 28:8). When we come to the Lord's table to remember his body and blood, may we also remember that

others need to know the crucified Christ and the resurrected Lord.

Today, I will…think of someone that I could tell about the risen Savior.

TUESDAY
Why Are You Crying?
Today's Scripture: John 20:10-18

Mary was asked the same question twice. Once by two angels and once by Jesus. First, read John 20:13. The angels of God asked Mary, "Why are you weeping?" Thinking that someone had moved Jesus' body, Mary answered, "They have taken away my Lord, and I do not know where they have laid him" (ESV).

Second, read John 20:15. Jesus said to Mary, "Why are you weeping?" Thinking Jesus was the gardener, Mary said to Jesus, "Sir, if you have carried him away, tell me where you have laid him, and I will take him away" (ESV). Mary was crying over the body of Jesus.

Question: Have you ever cried over the body and blood of our Lord?

The week before his resurrection, Jesus took bread, gave thanks, broke it, and said, "Take and eat, this is my body." He then took the cup, gave thanks, and said to his followers, "This is my blood." Every Sunday, we remember the body and blood when we eat the bread and drink the fruit of the vine. When you observe communion, do tears ever come to your eyes? Do you ever get a lump in your throat? Do you see his agony? Do you feel his loneliness as he cried, "My God, my God, why have you forsaken me?" Do you see Jesus during communion? Or, is the Lord's supper just something that we do to cover a check-list? Is it just something that we do to fulfill the requirements? Honestly, when was the last time you cried as you searched for Jesus' body?

"Whoever, therefore, eats the bread or drinks the cup of the Lord in an unworthy manner will be guilty concerning the body and blood of the Lord. Let a person examine himself, then, and so let him eat of the bread and drink of the cup. For anyone who eats and drinks without discerning the body, eats and drinks judgment on himself" (1 Corinthians 11:27-29, ESV).

Today, I will…consider what I will think about on Sunday as I participate in communion.

WEDNESDAY
Worship God
Today's Scripture: Matthew 28:8-10

Only God is worthy of worship. Not money. Not pleasure. Not fun. Not cars. Not houses. Not popularity. Not church leaders. Not even angels. When the prophet of Patmos, John, saw the angel, he fell down to worship him. The angel said, "Don't do it. Worship God" (Revelation 19:10).

When Jesus arose from the dead, the women at the tomb were told by the angel that Jesus had been raised. "So they departed quickly from the tomb with fear and great joy, and ran to tell his disciples. And behold, Jesus met them and said, 'Greetings!' And they came and took hold of his feet and worshiped him" (Matthew 28:8-9, ESV).

Did you catch them? The last two words in the passage? I'll help you… WORSHIPED HIM. If only God is worthy of worship (and he is—Revelation 19:10), and if Jesus was worshiped with God's approval (and he was—the wise men came to worship him when he was born, Matthew 2:1-11), that tells me something about Jesus. Jesus is God. He's supreme. He is the King of kings and Lord of lords. Jesus (just like the Father and the Holy Spirit) deserves our very best. To Him be honor and glory forever and ever!

First, we need to worship God with reverence and fear. When the women left the tomb, they left with fear. "Therefore let us be grateful for receiving a kingdom that cannot be shaken, and thus let us offer to God acceptable worship, with reverence and awe" (Hebrews 12:28, ESV).

Second, we need to worship with great joy. When the women left the tomb, they left with great joy. "Make a joyful noise to the Lord, all the earth! Serve the Lord with gladness! Come into his presence with singing!" (Psalm 100:1-2, ESV).

This coming Sunday, when we gather to sing and pray, bring your best. When you give your money to God, do what our money claims, "In God we trust." When we assemble around the table to remember the body and blood, fully focus on the cross.

Today, I will…worship Jesus in "spirit and truth" (John 4:24).

THURSDAY
Running
Today's Scripture: John 20:1-9

I used to run. But I've gotten old, so now I walk. Back in the day when I was a runner, I didn't enjoy it. I made myself do it for health reasons.

The resurrection of Jesus caused some people to run. When Mary Magdalene went to the tomb and saw that the stone had been moved, she ran to Peter and John to tell them the news. Then Peter and John ran to the tomb, "Both of them were running together, but the other disciple outran Peter and reached the tomb first" (John 20:4, ESV).

Why do people run? Fear. Fun. Freedom. Frustration. Fitness.

I think about the time that Philip ran. Remember the story? An Ethiopian eunuch was reading about the slaughtered sheep and the silenced lamb. And what did Philip do? Philip ran up to the chariot (Acts 8:30). Some say that the reason Philip ran is because that's the only way to catch a moving target. Maybe so. But could it be that Philip ran for the same reason that Mary Magdalene, Peter, and John ran? Not because of fear, or fun, or freedom, or frustration, or fitness…but because of faith? Could Philip have run because he was excited about telling someone about Jesus? Could Mary, John, and Peter have run because of the hope that burned within them?

All four gospel writers say the stone was rolled away (Matthew 28:2, Mark 16:4, Luke 24:2, John 20:1). Why was the stone (which was very large—Mark 16:4) moved? I used to think it was removed so that Jesus could get out. But then it occurred to me, wait a minute, did God need help getting out of the tomb? Perhaps the stone was removed, not so that Jesus could get out, but so that man could look in. And when we look in, what do we see? Clothes, but no body (John 20:6-7). The body is gone. He arose! He arose! Hallelujah, He arose!

Today, I will…with hope and excitement in my heart, run and tell somebody about Jesus.

Money Is the Answer for Everything
Today's Scripture: Matthew 28:11-15

Is money the answer for everything? Wait. Pause. Think. Don't be too quick with your answer. If you believe the Bible, you must believe that money is the answer for everything. Read Ecclesiastes 10:19. My mother's Bible, the King James Version, says it like this: "Money answereth all things." The New International Version says, "Money is the answer for everything." The English Standard Version says, "Money answers everything." One Bible puts it like this: "Money solves a lot of problems."

And it does, doesn't it? Now it can't get you to Heaven, but money solves a lot of problems. It would be hard to own a house or drive a car without money. It would be difficult to eat or get an education without money. It would be hard to pay your preacher (and that would be a terrible thing, wouldn't it? Let all the preachers say "Amen.") without money.

On the other hand, money causes a few problems. When Jesus was raised from the dead, the religious leaders in Jerusalem paid a lot of money to the soldiers to say that the disciples stole the body at night when everyone was asleep (Matthew 28:12-13). The lie lasted for years, even till the time that Matthew wrote his gospel (Matthew 28:15). Judas betrayed Jesus for thirty pieces of silver (Matthew 26:14-16). The son of Luke 15 ("the prodigal son") wasted all his money on wild living (Luke 15:13). Jesus often warned about how hard it is for rich people to be saved (Matthew 19:23-24). Paul simply said, "Don't be greedy, which is the same as worshiping idols" (Colossians 3:5, CEV).

In most congregations of churches of Christ, the communion and the contribution are back-to-back. The men who "wait on the table" are the same guys who gather the offering. This coming Sunday, when you remember the body and blood, focus on the price that Jesus paid for you. Perhaps this will help you be a happy giver (Acts 20:35).

Today, I will…trust more in God than I do in money.

Table Meditation
Scripture: Luke 9:23

Jesus Christ of Nazareth was crucified on the cruel cross of Calvary, not for any sins of His own, but for all of ours. He had nails driven through His hands and feet for our sins. Jesus wore a crown of thorns so that we might die to our sins. Christ allowed Himself to be slain so that we might have forgiveness of our sins.

We take the Lord's Supper with every other saint present. We take it with all our brothers and sisters throughout the world. This communion has a very special meaning and ties together all baptized believers in fellowship with Christ.

The Lord's Supper is an appointed, weekly, and mental trip back to Christ's death on the cross. We must remember Jesus being wounded on the tree and the saving blood flowing from His body.

Communion is a time for appreciation and thanksgiving. Jesus suffered extreme pain and agony and died so that we can have eternal life. He bowed His head and gave up His spirit, allowing Himself to be slain for you and me.

As we partake of the Lord's Supper, we need to hear the voice of Jesus and make it personal. As Jesus said, "If anyone would come after me, let him deny himself and take up his cross daily and follow me" (Luke 9:23, ESV).

MONDAY
Seven Miles with Jesus
Today's Scripture: Luke 24:13-35

Near the end of Luke's gospel account, Jesus walks seven miles with a couple of disciples. The two individuals share the local news with Him about the one they hoped was their Messiah…and yet the rulers had executed Him. They also add the reason for their shock: the report of His empty tomb…the possibility of His resurrection from the dead!

Jesus answered by showing them, from Moses and the Prophets, that this suffering and exaltation is precisely what had to happen. The Messiah's suffering, death, and resurrection are the point of the story of God and Israel. We see specific predictions from the Hebrew texts realized in Him, and we also see an overarching narrative of suffering and vindication. We see the continued need for a Savior…a true King. Paul echoes this same idea as he notes that these events occurred "in accordance with the Scriptures" (1 Corinthians 15:3-4, ESV).

"'O foolish ones, and slow of heart to believe all that the prophets have spoken! Was it not necessary that the Christ should suffer these things and enter into his glory?' And beginning with Moses and all the Prophets, he interpreted to them in all the Scriptures the things concerning himself" (Luke 24:25-26, ESV).

The two appear to realize they need to spend more time with this "man," so they beg Him to stay with them. They enjoy a meal together. Jesus then reveals to them exactly who he is…they soon go back to the city, straight to the apostles. They inform of their confirmation of the recent report…"The Lord has risen indeed, and has appeared to Simon!" (Luke 24:34, ESV).

We are not unlike these two disciples when we gather around the Lord's Table in memory of the suffering Messiah. Communion is like attending a memorial service for the One who is no longer dead! We join the long list of disciples over the centuries to enjoy knowing the risen Jesus.

Today, I will…share in the "Emmaus experience" by remembering the suffering of our risen Lord Jesus.

TUESDAY
Breaking Bread
Today's Scripture: Luke 24:28-30

This account of Jesus and the two on the road reminds us of the Lord's Table in a few related and yet different ways. One of those ways is Jesus breaking bread, giving thanks for (blessing) the bread, and giving it to those present with Him.

"So they drew near to the village to which they were going. He acted as if he were going farther, but they urged him strongly, saying, 'Stay with us, for it is toward evening and the day is now far spent.' So he went in to stay with them. When he was at table with them, he took the bread and blessed and broke it and gave it to them" (Luke 24:28-30, ESV).

As we reflect on this passage/event, we also remember earlier times when Jesus broke bread: the miraculous feeding of thousands and partaking of feasts like Passover. Jesus institutes the Lord's Supper during a Passover meal the same night of His betrayal and arrest. These events set His crucifixion in motion.

> "I have earnestly desired to eat this Passover with you before I suffer. For I tell you I will not eat it until it is fulfilled in the kingdom of God" (Luke 22:15, ESV).

> "And he took bread, and when he had given thanks, he broke it and gave it to them, saying, 'This is my body, which is given for you. Do this in remembrance of me'" (Luke 22:19, ESV).

When we weekly break bread, we join in this pattern set by Jesus (Acts 20:7; 1 Corinthians 11:26). Eating the bread and drinking the juice provides a strong link with our Lord and with one another. Each time we partake, we hold the bread and juice in our hands and consume them. These acts are the most visual and physical aspects of our Sunday worship assembly.

Today, I will...take note of the value of meal sharing, especially the way communion gives us such an impactful reminder of our King.

Going to the Scriptures
Today's Scripture: Luke 24:25-27, 32

When Jesus takes a walk with the two disciples, it is no mere accident that He "takes" them to the Scriptures. Later, after they discover Jesus' identity, they remember how His exposition of the Scriptures affected their hearts.

> "They said to each other, 'Did not our hearts burn within us while he talked to us on the road, while he opened to us the Scriptures?'" (Luke 24:32, ESV).

To help them understand, the Lord exposed them to a journey through the Scriptures—the Law and all the Prophets. Along with the Psalms, these were the basic divisions (of that time) of the Hebrew Scriptures (see Luke 24:44). This collection is called "the Old Testament" today.

Likewise, the way we observe communion should follow the teachings in the Scriptures. The reason we partake is because of the commands and examples we have from Jesus and His apostles. May we do so with the elements and in the frequency we see in the Divine record.

As we remember Jesus and His work on our behalf, we do so by the knowledge of how He is revealed in the inspired word. We guard our minds against being improperly influenced by the words of mere humans. These (potentially dangerous) sources are informal, like conversions with others, and formal, like commentaries, books, or sermons. Our personal thoughts and feelings about Jesus can get us in trouble if we are not watchful.

One practical suggestion during communion is to turn to a passage and contemplate how it teaches about Jesus. Jesus' story is throughout the Bible. There are specific passages that might be especially beneficial. Isaiah 52-53, for example, can prove very helpful for meditating while partaking together.

Today, I will…embrace the value of God's holy words and allow them to shape my time at the Table of the Lord.

THURSDAY
Darkness to Light
Today's Scripture: Luke 24:13-35

Jesus stops the two on the road and asks about their conversation. They react first by standing still, "looking sad." When they speak, they express their shock that He is (seemingly) unaware of the local events. As they explain what has happened, they share the way their hopes were dashed as their supposed Messiah died.

As we add it all up, Jesus initially finds them in the darkness of despair, and yes, with the shadow of doubt…"foolish" and "slow" hearts. By the time He departs from them, they are excited and relieved with joy. Even their hesitance at the claim of His resurrection (Luke 24:22) has now turned into confident hope (Luke 24:32-35)!

The Table is about the Lord and His suffering; it is centered around His excruciating death. He gave His body and shed His blood for us. We participate with sobriety and sadness over His sacrificial love.

Yet, He did not stay dead; He arose on the third day and lives to never die again! The cleansing power of His blood and His hope-giving resurrection bring intense gladness to our hearts. Communion is a sorrowful-joyful time to commune with the One who is both our Savior and our Master.

From one standpoint, the account in Luke 24 is about the way two disciples came to know their Messiah all over again (Luke 24:31). When we eat and drink the communion meal, may we grow closer to Him, seeing Him with the eyes of faith. Communion is not meant as an item to check off our list of religious duties; it is to play a key role in our ongoing "walk" with the Lord of glory. As we walk with the Lord, our doubt and despair are turned to joy and hope. One day…to borrow from the hymn, "He will take us by the hand, and lead us through the promised land."[1]

Today, I will…allow Jesus to grant me His peace, joy, and love, even as I solemnly contemplate His sinless suffering.

---

[1] "What a Day That Will Be," Jim Hill, 1955.

You Are a Preacher
Today's Scripture: Luke 24:31-35

After Jesus walks and eats with the two disciples in Luke 24, what do we see them doing? Based on what they had seen and heard, they spread the news about the risen Lord!

"And they rose that same hour and returned to Jerusalem. And they found the eleven and those who were with them gathered together, saying, 'The Lord has risen indeed, and has appeared to Simon!' Then they told what had happened on the road, and how he was known to them in the breaking of the bread" (Luke 24:31-35, ESV).

Can we learn from their example? Is there a pattern here of communing with the Lord and communicating to others about Him? When we consider the church, the two endeavors of communion and telling others about Him are inseparable.

We share in the Lord's Table, and each time we do, it sends the message about who we are. More than that, it sends a message about the One to whom we submit. He is the true Ruler of heaven and earth, but many in our world do not yet know that as a reality. We make this known to each other and our society as they observe us.

By our weekly meeting and partaking of the supper as His body, we "proclaim the Lord's death until he comes" (1 Corinthians 11:26, ESV). Communion is the one activity that makes us all proclaimers. It is also the one time that the Bible refers to an act (no words required) itself as a form of preaching.

At the Table, we focus on His death as we look to His return because He is the risen Judge. We know that all will bow to Him and confess Him as Lord, sooner or later, one way or another (Philippians 2:9-11). May our eating and drinking in communion encourage us to share Jesus in various ways!

Today, I will…remind myself of the significance of partaking in weekly communion, taking seriously the way God includes it in announcing His Son's work.

Table Meditation
Scripture: John 19:28-30

Our Lord, You were willing to be alone, holding the weight and embarrassment of our sins for all the world to see. You heard words hurled at You no one should ever be exposed to. We're so sorry You had to hear them! You witnessed behavior no parent would want their child to ever be associated with. We're sorry we offended You so many times with behavior just like You had to absorb on the way to Calvary. And You accepted in our stead the unjust judgment for acts that You never did. With Your perfect love, You gave up your life in hopes that we would someday know Your everlasting kindness. Lord, it pains us to know You suffered and agonized for us. But now, knowing there is no other way to be with you, to be embraced by you, we thank you! Hallelujah! What a Savior!

Lord, we long for the day we will be together. We don't know if what we're doing to glorify You is enough here on earth. We want to be right with You and honor You as a King should be honored. Until we are home, we want to never forget your love for us. Continue to write that song of redemption on our hearts. Continue to guide us in Your ways. We pray we're forever motivated to hear You say, "Well done." May we never forget Your voice trembling the words on the Cross, "It is finished." When in Heaven, our Lord, we don't know if we'll be loud enough to be heard. We're hoping our new bodies and voices will beautifully shout out the praise You deserve throughout eternity with all Your children in harmony, rejoicing Your Holy Name. Until then, we don't want voices that fade, rather, we want voices that praise Your name and echo Your Words without shame and hesitation. And finally, Lord, we want to remember some souls need to know Your eternal saving power so they get the chance to say... Hallelujah! What a Savior!

MONDAY
Luke and John "Set the Table" for Us
Today's Scripture: Luke 24:36-43; John 20:19-25

When Sunday comes around, and the elements of the Lord's Supper are passed, the mind thinks in many directions. Assuming we are centered on the meaning behind the Supper, we contemplate the horrible scenes of Calvary, with its pain and cruel humiliation. We tie that suffering to our sin and wrestle with shame and guilt. We also experience and embrace gratitude and thanksgiving for such love and sacrifice offered for us. It shows the great value we have to God. Yet, we also anticipate because the object of our commemoration is the risen Christ!

The scenes depicted by the gospel writers Luke and John are both in their "resurrection chapters." They overwhelmingly emphasize Jesus's appearances to His disciples after He is risen from the dead. In both narratives, Jesus meets with and communes with them. While He looks back, He is as interested in the present and the future! He spends time eating a meal with them (Luke 24:42; paralleled in John 20:19ff). As He stated at the last supper before His crucifixion, He would eat the commemorating meal with them in the kingdom. He would soon ascend to take His seat at God's right hand! As much as there is majesty, there is also intimacy. He allows us to enter boldly into God's throne room (Hebrews 4:16)!

Today, I will…prepare my mind to see a cross and a throne room when I partake of the Lord's Supper. I will also see my Savior sitting across a table, who joins me as friend to friend.

TUESDAY
Almost Too Good to Be True (Part One)
Today's Scripture: Luke 24:36-43

We often hear that the gospel is defined as "good news." It is God's good news, meant to be shared. That's exactly what the women and the two disciples do with the larger group of disciples when Jesus makes His final appearance before returning to heaven. But there are a few things He wants to impress upon them before He goes.

He reminds them of His identity (Luke 24:36-43). The predominant reminder in this last appearance is of His humanity, the identity He took on to save us from our sins. He shows them His hands and feet (Luke 24:40) and then eats a meal before them (Luke 24:41-43). While He will appeal to His Deity in His final instructions, referencing His Father in heaven (Luke 24:49), He did not want them to forget the brotherhood He shared with them.

How often do I benefit by remembering, as I live as His disciple, that Jesus fully understands what I am going through? Read Hebrews 2:9-18, for example. He was, for a little while made lower than the angels to taste death for everyone (Hebrews 2:9). He was perfected in His work as our great High Priest by suffering as a human (Hebrews 2:10). He is not ashamed to call us "brethren" (Hebrews 2:11). He partook of sharing our flesh and blood (Hebrews 2:14). He had to be made like His brethren in all things to become a merciful and faithful High Priest (Hebrews 2:17). He was tempted in His suffering, which helps Him come to our aid as we suffer (Hebrews 2:18).

Today, I will...remember the resurrected Jesus' humanity, as he stressed to His disciples before ascending to heaven.

WEDNESDAY
Almost Too Good To Be True (Part Two)
Today's Scripture: Luke 24:44-53

He reminds them of His history (Luke 24:44-48). The truth that Jesus' history goes back to his preexistence before He became human boggles the mind. Sacred history of greatest interest to Him. So He opened their minds to understand the Scripture (Luke 24:45). He appealed to the three major divisions of the Hebrew Old Testament: the Law, the Prophets, and the Psalms (Luke 24:44). We might call them the books of history, prophecy, and poetry. They are saturated with the themes He elaborates upon in verses 46-47: His suffering, His resurrection, and His plan of salvation. By looking to God's past revelation, they would be equipped for their present mission and fortified for their future reward. So it is for us today. We have the verification of Scripture—fulfilled prophecy.

He reminds them of His destiny (Luke 24:49-53). It included ascending to heaven to carry out the promise of His Father upon them, to be His witnesses, "clothed with power from on high" (Luke 24:49, ESV). Luke gives us additional details about this discussion in Acts 1:4-8, and it includes His marching orders and an elaboration of what we read Him telling them about being His witnesses starting in Jerusalem (Luke 24:46-47). His immediate destination is heaven (Luke 24:50), and theirs is Jerusalem (Luke 24:52-53). They went there with great joy and, once there, "were continually in the temple praising God" (Luke 24:53). They were mentally preparing for their earth-shattering, world-changing mission. Heartache was overwhelmed by hope. Disappointment was conquered by determination. They were about to turn the world upside down, an intention they made good on from Jerusalem to Judea, to Samaria, and to the rest of the world (Acts 1:8; 17:6). Lest we forget, their role in His destiny is the same as ours. We are standing on their shoulders, carrying on their mission today. Jesus needs us to help fulfill His destiny in our world just as He needed them. They rose and met the challenge! What about us?

Today, I will…prepare for my time at the table of the Lord, to look back at Scripture, and then look ahead at the destiny we share with Him when we are members of His body.

Peace Be With You (Part One)

Today's Scripture: John 20:19ff

After appearing to Mary Magdalene Sunday morning, Jesus was present at the evening assembly of His disciples behind their closed doors (John 20:19). They were fearful of the Jews, but His simple message to them was, "Peace be with you" (John 20:19). To facilitate this peace, He proved that He was risen and among them. They examined His wounds and rejoiced at His presence (John 20:20). He has a perfect sense of what they need most: the conquering of inner disturbances.

So, three times, as John records it, Jesus uses the phrase with them, "peace be with you" (John 20:19, 21, 27, ESV). It is more than a greeting. One commentary observes, "Those familiar with theophanies in the Old Testament will soon recognize the various elements of a theophany/Christophany (an appearance of God or Christ) here…The basic elements of a theophany are (1) fear, (2) the calming word of 'peace' or 'do not be afraid' from God or Christ, and (3) a word of commission for the task to be performed."[1] (Borchert, NAC, 304).

Jesus was there with His disciples in fellowship, together as they examined His wounds and rejoiced at His presence. He overcame their momentary qualms and future uncertainties.

Today, I will…prepare for my time in the Lord's Supper by examining his wounds and blood and rejoicing over his presence. I will allow this to give me lasting inward peace.

---

[1] Borchert, Gerald L. "John 12–21." Vol. 25B. *The New American Commentary*. Nashville: Broadman & Holman Publishers, 2002. 304.

FRIDAY
Peace Be With You (Part Two)
Today's Scripture: John 20:19ff

His peace would transform them from cowardice to courage. He also equips them with God's Spirit to aid their mission (John 20:22-23). They are renewed and reinvigorated. But, as John notes, one of the apostles was not present. He was unwilling to believe that Jesus had risen and had appeared to them unless and until he could see so for himself (John 20:24-25). Eight days later, Jesus appears again, and this time, Thomas is present. Jesus offers him the same greeting of peace (John 20:26-27). Seeing His scars, Thomas confesses, "My Lord and my God" (John 20:28).

Thomas had determined to withhold faith until proven by sight. Jesus uses this to extend an even greater blessing to those "who did not see, and yet believed" (John 20:29). It is in this context that John utters the sentence that is the overarching theme of the gospel of John. "Therefore many other signs Jesus also performed in the presence of the disciples, which are not written in this book; but these have been written so that you may believe that Jesus is the Christ, the Son of God; and that believing you may have life in His name" (John 20:30-31, ESV).

You and I are among those who have not physically seen the risen Lord but have believed the things written in this book. When we commune, we are seeing with eyes of faith. We are those Jesus blesses in Thomas' presence, those who have not seen yet believe. What is the effect of our faith? Even in this troubling world, we can take possession of Jesus' promise: "Peace I leave with you; My peace I give to you; not as the world gives do I give to you. Do not let your heart be troubled, nor let it be fearful" (John 14:27).

Today, I will…turn my troubles and fears over to Him who is risen and rest in His peace.

HIS PEOPLE

Table Meditation

Scripture: Matthew 27:15-26; Mark 15:6-15; Luke 23:18-25; John 18:38-40

Have you ever thought about being like Barabbas? We know very little about him, but he provides an image of man's relationship to Jesus. Barabbas was in jail for a capital offense. Death was his deserving fate. Jesus stepped into his path and took his place on the cross. Although Barabbas did not deserve it, Jesus loved him. Barabbas accepted Christ's gift by walking away totally free, pardoned from his previous bad decisions. The name Barabbas in Hebrew means "son of the father." We are all sons or daughters of the Father.

I always thought of Barabbas as a terrible person who received such an underserved gift of freedom. And then I realized that I am just like him. We see our sins as smaller and declare ourselves better than Barabbas. Our sin enslaves us until Jesus frees us from our selfish decisions. He offers freedom that cannot be provided in any other way. Barabbas received the same gift we are all offered: freedom from the captivity of sin, freely given by the Son of God. In a lost position, we all deserve the death penalty. God's gift of freedom from sin does not come because we have earned it or because we deserve it. We are all Barabbas, a flawed human standing in the need of someone to step in front to free us from the sin that destroys our freedom and future. As we meditate on the Lord's Supper this morning, let us remember what a great price was paid for our undeserving souls.

MONDAY
Resurrection

Today's Scripture: 1 Peter 1:10-12

Oh that morning. Like a kid at Christmas, you remember the feeling, don't you? You were sure you knew what was coming but could hardly wait. I could be wrong, but in my mind, that's what I think the angels felt like in 1 Peter 1:12. I heard my dad describe it as if they were "standing on tiptoes just looking at it all unfold."

To get the full import, start in verse 10: "Concerning this salvation, the prophets who prophesied about the grace that was to be yours searched and inquired carefully, inquiring what person or time the Spirit of Christ in them was indicating when he predicted the sufferings of Christ and the subsequent glories. It was revealed to them that they were serving not themselves but you, in the things that have now been announced to you through those who preached the good news to you by the Holy Spirit sent from heaven, *things into which angels long to look*" (1 Peter 1:10-12, ESV, emp dj).

"...things into which angels long to look." They had waited so long. How long? We don't know, but we do know this plan was in the works for at least 4,000 years. Maybe they knew the whole time. The prophets, too. They knew what was going to happen but still did not fully understand. Who, but God, would have? "You're going to send Your Son. He's going to die. And He's going to be glorified." As much as the "sufferings of Christ" cut my soul (it was my sin that caused them), I love the phrase "subsequent glories."

It had been "announced," now came the waiting. And when it all happened, it appears all of heaven stood to watch.

RESURRECTION!

Today, I will...strive to live joyfully in light of the reality of the resurrection of Jesus.

TUESDAY
No One Thing?
Today's Scripture: Ephesians 3:9-11

We seem to like saying, "There was really no one thing," I suppose, most of the time, we are right. While a touchdown pass on the last play of the game may seem like the one thing, what about the 2-yard rush up the middle on a 4th down to keep that drive alive? While a perchance meeting walking out of the library that led to a relationship may seem like the one thing, what about when you signed up for the class that required that you be at the library in the first place?

No one thing. Many, many steps led us to THE ONE THING. But THE one thing that changed history more than any other one thing is the resurrection of Jesus Christ from the dead. Many things set up that event, dating back before time existed (Ephesians 3:9-11), but there is a very real sense in which all of history hinges on that Sunday morning 2,000 years ago. The resurrection. Yes, there is the vicarious death of Jesus on the cross; what love, what injustice, what sacrifice, an event that could never have happened, except it did. But "people" die every day. And if Jesus had stayed in the tomb, He would have only been an amazingly powerful rabbi who tragically died. BUT He did not stay in the tomb!

And if Jesus had stayed in the tomb, Paul makes clear, we would be of all most to be pitied. Yes, a few others were brought back from the dead, but each of them had a second memorial service on down the road. As the song says, "Jesus lives no more to die."[1] In this case there was really ONE THING.

RESURRECTION!

"But in fact Christ has been raised from the dead" (1 Corinthians 15:20, ESV).

Today, I will…when faced with adversity, praise God for the One Thing that changed all of history and my personal history.

---

[1] "Jesus Lives." George Romanacce and Bob Kauflin. © 2011 Sovereign Grace Worship/ASCAP, Sovereign Grace Praise/BMI (adm. by Integrity Music).

The Lord Is Risen and Goes Before You
Today's Scripture: Matthew 28:7

"He has risen from the dead, and behold, he is going before you" (Matthew 28:7, ESV). Can you imagine how their hearts must have rushed when they heard these words? Put yourself there that Sunday morning. It appears all hope had been lost—we hear it in the words of the two on the road to Emmaus: "But we had hoped that he was the one to redeem Israel. Yes, and besides all this, it is now the third day since these things happened" (Luke 24:21, ESV). But here they were, and there he was. A strong angel (are there even "weak" angels?) moved the stone, apparently so they could see there wasn't a body there, and perhaps frightened the Roman Soldiers off. He had a message. It makes me wonder…did the angels fight to get this blessed assignment? Did God or Jesus tell them who to look for? How long had he been sitting there? The message is pretty clear.

- Don't be afraid (typically the first line each time angels encountered humans)
- I know who you are looking for.
- He's not here.
- He has risen.

And then my favorite part: *He goes before you.*

In most of our lives, we have to walk into spaces, places, situations, and encounters where we are unsure, fearful, not knowing what is before us, or scared to death! I have found that if I repeat this great truth, it comforts me more than any other thing I know: *He goes before you.*

And it is true for all of God's children: the Lord is risen and goes before you. Where you are going, He has gone. Whatever the situation, He is already there. He knows what is on the other side of that door, line, or encounter. And we have his unbreakable promise (Titus 1:2) that He will be with us and not forsake us (Matthew 28:20; Hebrews 13:5).

Today, I will…remember whenever I am uncomfortable, the Lord is risen and has gone before me.

THURSDAY
A Little Fun
Today's Scripture: Luke 24:13-34

You know the story. It may be my favorite story related to Jesus' resurrection. For the sake of brevity let me just hit the highlights, but I do hope today you'll read the whole text:

> "That very day two of them were going to a village named Emmaus, about seven miles from Jerusalem, and they were talking with each other about all these things that had happened…Jesus himself drew near and went with them. But their eyes were kept from recognizing him. And he said to them, "What is this conversation that you are holding with each other as you walk?" …Cleopas, answered, "Are you the only visitor to Jerusalem who does not know the things that have happened there in these days?" And he said to them, "What things?" And they said to him, "Concerning Jesus of Nazareth…we had hoped that he was the one to redeem Israel. …some women of our company amazed us. They were at the tomb early in the morning, and when they did not find his body, they came back saying that they had even seen a vision of angels, who said that he was alive. …And beginning with Moses and all the Prophets, he interpreted to them in all the Scriptures the things concerning himself…So they drew near to the village to which they were going. He acted as if he were going farther, but they urged him strongly, saying, "Stay with us, for it is toward evening and the day is now far spent." So he went in to stay with them. When he was at table with them, he took the bread and blessed and broke it and gave it to them. And their eyes were opened, and they recognized him. And he vanished from their sight." (Luke 24:13-31, ESV)

It may be my favorite story related to the resurrection. Why? I don't think He needed the company. He didn't need help finding Jerusalem. These weren't future apostles. This doesn't appear to be something from His spiritual checklist. I hope I'm not outside the lines in saying this, and I know it is speculation, but I wonder if the Lord wasn't just having a little fun! As I read the text there are several places I can't help but believe Jesus had to hold back a giant grin or muffle a laugh.

We know, even if we can't fully process it, that He knows all, all the time. That He hears every conversation. Was He eavesdropping on these two joyously confused, hope-filled disciples? Was He busting all over just wanting to tell someone the Good News? Did He hear them talking and think, "This will be fun?" I can't prove any of my speculation, but I hope I'm right. I think of it as "the day Jesus preached the Gospel."

Today, I will…remember that my message about Him is as true as His message about Him is.

After the Memorial
Today's Scripture: Mark 14:25

For years, I've heard people talk about "celebrating the Lord's Supper," and I know what they mean. I know the word "celebrate" has more than one meaning. But in my mind, a celebration is a party. And let's be very sure to remember, even though it may not be in vogue, the partaking of the supper is a somber remembrance of the death of Jesus. It is a remembering of what He gave for us. The Lord Himself set it up before His crucifixion and asked us to remember it the way He set it up. It is a remembering of His body and of His blood given in my stead. It is a remembering of the lengths He went through to save us. It is a reflection of that. In fact, "anyone who eats and drinks without discerning the body eats and drinks judgment on himself" (1 Corinthians 11:29, ESV). It is a misinterpretation of the verse to think the "unworthy" reflects on our worth, for who among us would claim to be worthy of such a sacrifice? It is the manner we partake that is in question. The manner is: the bread, the fruit of the vine, and our own thoughts. And it works. Each week, I remember what the Lord did for me. It calls me to higher living, it keeps me from becoming haughty. He did for me what no one else could. So, as much as I'd like to celebrate, this is deeper than a party.

Yet.

I have for years asked song leaders to select a song of celebration, praise, and joy as the song to be sung *immediately after* the Supper. For it is all I can do to keep my mind from racing ahead during that sad remembrance to the resurrection. So I want to come right out of that time with a time to rejoice! Jesus did die for me. He in fact "gave it all." BUT he arose! He arose! After we remember together, let's rejoice together!

RESURRECTION!

Today, I will…begin preparing for the Sunday by remembering that it all began on a Friday.

Table Meditation
Scripture: 1 Corinthians 11:24-28; Acts 20:7

As we prepare for communion on this Lord's Day, we reflect on the death, burial, and resurrection of our Lord. We are to examine ourselves (1 Corinthians 11:28). This is a special event, and we should focus all our thoughts on the cross. We are in the presence of God, practicing what He commands of us. We have the emblems of bread and wine, and we are told in 1 Corinthians 11:24-25 that these emblems represent the Lord's body and blood. We are told that by doing this we proclaim the Lord's death until He comes (1 Corinthians 11:26). We do this each Lord's Day or Sunday, the first day of the week.

But why do we do it every Sunday? The apostle Paul sets the example of what day the Lord's Supper is observed. In Act 20:7, Paul demonstrates that the Christians at Troas met to take the Lord's Supper on the first day of the week, Sunday. The inspired Apostle does not say "which" first day of the week, just that on the first day of the week the disciples worshipped and observed the Lord's Supper. If we look a bit deeper in this passage of Acts 20, we can see more clearly that the Lord's Supper was to be observed every first day of the week. We learn that Paul arrived in Troas and stayed there seven days, he met with the disciples on the first day of the week. Then, being ready to depart Troas on the next day, Monday. This means he arrived on Monday and waited seven days to observe the Lord's Supper. If the disciples decided they would only observe the Lord's Supper only once a month, Paul would have had to stay in Troas for a month to break bread. Saying "the first day of the week" sets the frequency of observance to every week. A frequency different than every week comes from man and not God.

MONDAY
The Church Comes Together
Today's Scripture: Acts 20:5-7

Over the years, we have rightly contended that the Bible authorizes by direct command and approved example. In our text for today, we have an example of the early Christians assembling regularly, specifically on the first day of the week. The apostle Paul approved of this, for he waited seven days to meet with the brethren at Troas. "...where we stayed for seven days. On the first day of the week, when we were gathered together..." (Acts 20:6-7, ESV). Years prior, Jesus rose from the grave on the first day of the week (Matthew 28:1-8). Also, the Lord's church was established on the first day of the week. "When the day of Pentecost arrived, they were all together in one place" (Acts 2:1, ESV). Pentecost always fell on Sunday (Leviticus 23:15-16). In Acts 2, we read that the church was established on earth when 3,000 souls were saved and added to it. Paul acknowledged that Christians come together "as a church" (1 Corinthians 11:17-18). He knew that on the "first day of every week" (1 Corinthians 16:2), they would be meeting to worship God.

Those early Christians wanted to meet together. "And they devoted themselves to the apostles' teaching and the fellowship, to the breaking of bread and the prayers" (Acts 2:42, ESV). No wonder the early Christians came together every Sunday to worship God. Every first day of the week was an opportunity to be with brethren of like-minded faith. To worship with brethren, I must be with them. That takes place in the corporate assembly of the church. There are several questions I must ask myself. Do I want to meet with other Christians as much as those early Christians did? Do I look forward to this marvelous opportunity? Do I take it for granted? Is it a joy?

Today, I will...pray that my attitude about coming together in worship with my fellow Christians will be one of anticipation, joy, and thanksgiving.

The Church Comes Together Every Sunday
Today's Scripture: Acts 20:7

The heart of worship for those early Christians was eating the Lord's Supper. They "gathered together to break bread" (Acts 20:7, ESV). Sometimes, the phrase "break bread" refers to a common meal. That's what we read in Acts 2:46, where it says, "And day by day, attending the temple together and breaking bread in their homes, they received their food with glad and generous hearts." This was something they did "day by day," and there was no question they enjoyed regular meals together. On the other hand, the phrase "break bread" sometimes means the Lord's Supper that Jesus instituted before His death on the cross. "Now as they were eating, Jesus took bread, and after blessing it broke it and gave it to the disciples, and said, Take, eat; this is my body" (Matthew 26:26, ESV). And that's exactly what the early Christians were doing when we read, "And they devoted themselves to the apostles' teaching and fellowship, to the breaking of bread and the prayers" (Acts 2:42, ESV).

Eating the Lord's Supper was an avenue of worship the early Christians did together every Sunday. In his letter to the church at Corinth, Paul acknowledged they came together to eat the Lord's Supper (1 Corinthians 11:17-18), and even though they were not doing it correctly, he recognized they meet "on the first day of every week" (1 Corinthians 16:1-2). The apostle Paul waited seven days so he could eat the Lord's Supper with the brethren at Troas because he knew they would be doing that on a Sunday. "On the first day of the week, when we were gathered together to break bread..." (Acts 20:7, ESV).

Today, I will...pray that I will anticipate meeting with my brethren every Sunday so we can eat the Lord's Supper together in worship to God.

WEDNESDAY
The Church Eats the Lord's Supper Together
Today's Scripture: Acts 20:7

Every Sunday, early Christians "gathered together to break bread" (Acts 20:7, ESV). Note the text says the purpose of meeting was "to break bread." That's the heart of New Testament worship. That does not minimize the other acts of worship, but the Lord's Supper was central in their worship every Lord's Day. The Lord's Supper was not eaten on any other day of the week. On other days, we can worship God through preaching, singing, and praying, but the Lord's Supper was only observed on Sunday.

Note in Acts 20:7 that Paul and the other brethren were "together." Paul wanted to be with his fellow Christians. He was willing to wait seven days so he could assemble with the brethren at Troas. That togetherness is expressed in the eating of the Lord's Supper. Paul described it as a participation or a communion (NKJV). "The cup of blessing that we bless, is it not a participation in the blood of Christ? The bread that we break, is it not a participation in the body of Christ (1 Corinthians 10:16, ESV). The word "participation" is sometimes translated as "fellowship" or "sharing." In 1 Corinthians 11, Paul says when we eat the Lord's Supper, we should remember what Jesus did for us on the cross. and we should also be "discerning the Lord's body" (1 Corinthians 11:29, NKJV). The "body" in this text is both the Lord's body offered for our sins and the spiritual body of Christ, the church. The Lord's Supper should help us be grateful for the Lord's church, for it was purchased with the blood of Christ. It should cause us to love each other more and care more deeply for one another. By being together every first day of the week, we grow closer to one another and the Lord.

Today, I will…pray that when I eat the Lord's Supper not only will I reflect on the death of Jesus for my sins, but also express appreciation for my church family.

The Church Preaches a Sermon

Today's Scripture: Acts 20:7-12

The proclamation of God's Word is closely connected to the church's assembling to eat the Lord's Supper together. In our text, the apostle Paul "talked with them" (Acts 20:7, ESV). He is publicly teaching the Word. This verse is rightly used to show that preaching or the teaching of God's Word is an act of worship in the assembly. But often overlooked is the fact that in eating the Lord's Supper, everyone preaches a silent sermon.

Paul tells us that when we eat the Lord's Supper together, we "proclaim the Lord's death until he comes" (1 Corinthians 11:26, ESV). Even though in our text Paul is doing the public teaching, everyone still preaches. It is a declaration, a sermon, a proclamation. A sermon to the world that Jesus died for its sins. The gospel must be proclaimed to the world (Mark 16:15-16). The Lord's Supper is one way every Christian proclaims the death, burial, and resurrection of Christ. Therefore, we ought not to forsake the assembly (Hebrews 10:24-25).

The sermon of the Lord's Supper helps to teach people who are lost that Jesus has provided for their salvation. Charles Hodge, in his commentary on 1 Corinthians, made the excellent observation: "Those who come to it, therefore, should come not to satisfy hunger, nor for the gratification of social feelings, but for the definite purpose of bearing their testimony to the great fact of redemption, and to contribute their portion of influence to the preservation and propagation of the knowledge of that fact."[1]

The Lord's Supper as a proclamation to the world suggest: (1) A Sermon of God's love, grace, and salvation that every Christians can preach every week, and (2) The Christian virtue of faith is exhibited every time we observe it.

Today, I will...pray that I every time I eat the Lord's Supper, I will be aware of the sermon I'm preaching to the world.

---

[1] Hodge, Charles, "1 Corinthians." Volume 11. *Crossway Classic Commentaries*. Edited by Alister McGrath and J. I. Packer. Crossway, 1995

The Church Eats Two Different Meals
Today's Scripture: Acts 20:7-12

The early church believed the Lord's Supper was a covenant meal. It was an agreement between God and the Christians participating in this meal. The following by Dan Owen is worth considering: "Only covenant participants ate the covenant meal. Early Christians saw the Lord's Supper as a covenant meal. Baptized believers who had accepted the New Covenant by contacting the blood of Christ ate the meal to demonstrate the covenant relationship that existed between each Christian and God and between each Christian and all other Christians."[2]

In our text, "we [disciples] were gathered together to break bread." They shared this spiritual feast together that not only served as a memorial to the death of Jesus but also symbolized their unity and togetherness. "Because there is one bread, we who are many are one body, for we all partake of the one bread" (1 Corinthians 10:17, ESV). We "discern" the Lord's body (1 Corinthians 11:29), which includes both the body of Jesus and His spiritual body, the church. Eating this Lord's Supper meal shows we are united together in Christ. We have a special bond in the Lord. What a blessing that is.

In our text, the early Christians also ate a fellowship meal or a common meal (Acts 20:11). Eating the spiritual meal, the Lord's Supper, provides a basis for great Christian fellowship when we eat a common meal together. During this meal, Paul "conversed with them." This means he had a relaxed conversation with them. They enjoyed each other's company. What a great example for us today. There is no way I can properly eat the Lord's Supper and not want to have table fellowship with my brethren whenever possible. "...and breaking bread in their homes, they received their food with glad and generous hearts" (Acts 2:46, ESV).

Today, I will...pray that when I eat the Lord's Supper, I will remember the covenant I entered with Christ and the relationship it provides with fellow Christians.

---

[2] *Gospel Advocate*, April 2010.

Table Meditation
Scripture: 1 Corinthians 11:23-30

In Joshua 5, the children of Israel are finally at the edge of the promised land. Even though they were ready to take Canaan, God had other plans. The males that were born in the wilderness had not been circumcised. Circumcision was the sign of the covenant that Israel entered with God. Before God allowed them to accept his promise, he had to enforce the promise they made to him when Israel entered the covenant. We see that Israel was circumcised "for a second time" and then they celebrated Passover. Circumcision was required to celebrate the Passover. God only wanted those who were committed to him to celebrate it.

In the gospels, we see Jesus celebrating the Passover, but he did something different. He took bread and gave it a new meaning to represent his body. He then took the cup and gave it a new meaning to represent his blood. The nation of Israel had a feast that would remind them of God saving them from bondage, and we Christians have a feast that represents God saving us from the bondage of sin. In the same way he required the Israelites to be circumcised to take the Passover, we are required to enter a covenant relationship with God through baptism to partake of the Lord's Supper.

In 1 Corinthians 11:23-30, Paul stressed the importance of examining ourselves to see if we are honoring the covenant that we agreed to, that is the covenant that Jesus paid for with his death.

MONDAY
Seeing the Unseen

Today's Scripture: 1 Corinthians 10:16-17

For some believers, participation in the Sunday gathering feels similar to brunch at the local café—nostalgic and comfortable. Perhaps the greatest threat the Church perceives is the leaning tower of communion trays. But as we gather together to break bread (Acts 20:7), there are unseen spiritual realities. We are at war. And, have you noticed the devil never skips church?

The Corinthian church also seemed to lose sight of the spiritual significance of participating at the Lord's Table. Paul addressed their problems of division, sexual immorality, and idolatry. As a mostly Gentile church in an ethnically eclectic, business-centric, and pagan culture, perhaps we should not be surprised. Do we not also suffer from the influence of contemporary culture in our churches?

The Corinthian church found ways to rationalize their hypocrisy. They wrongly reasoned the physical body was of no eternal significance, so sexual immorality was of no consequence. Idols were false gods, so participating in idol worship to participate in the local trade and social circles seemed permissible as well. But false gods are not fake, and participating in their feasts that involved drunken carousing is, likewise, improper for believers whose bodies house the Holy Spirit (1 Corinthians 3:16). It seems the Corinthians misunderstood the connection between things that are visible and invisible. They had failed to discern the divine from the demonic.

The classic hymn "Night with Ebon Pinion" tells of that night when darkness hovered like black wings over the Kidron Valley through which Jesus and His disciples walked to the garden where He would be betrayed. The disciples did not discern the imminent spiritual danger that would soon sift their souls. They slept, while Jesus prayed and wept.

The Table of Jesus is more than a ritual act. It involves the communing of our spirits with Jesus and with our brothers and sisters. At the Table, we share in Jesus' victory over sin, darkness, and death through a covenant relationship with Him.

Today, I will... look with discernment beyond the surface to the unseen spiritual realities as I share in the table of Jesus.

Flee to the Cup

Today's Scripture: 1 Corinthians 10:16-17

The blessings of and commitment to covenant have become foreign in modern culture. We have replaced the relational "covenant" with the transactional "contract." In Jewish tradition, betrothal involves the groom offering a cup to the woman. In America, the groom places a ring on the finger of his fiancé. To share in the cup or accept the ring is to pledge exclusive allegiance to the covenant for life. Paul connected the cup of the Lord's table to the covenant of Jesus in 1 Corinthians 11:25. But here, Paul's focus addresses the church betraying Jesus by drinking the cup of idolatry and immorality. To both temptations, Paul issues the same imperative—"flee" (1 Corinthians 6:18; 10:14).

Jesus drank the cup of anguish to redeem man from sin and offer us the cup of blessing through loyalty to His name. Paul contends that believers share in the blood of Christ by drinking the cup of blessing. The cup of blessing reminded Jewish readers of the Passover cup of thanksgiving to God. Psalm 23 paints a beautiful picture of the cup overflowing, poured by the hand of the Lord. The cup is not a mere symbol of past events. It represents the continual sharing in the fellowship offering Jesus provided on the cross which creates peace between God and men, as well as a new identity as His redeemed covenant people.

Tragically, humanity also drinks from another cup, the cup of idolatry and immorality. Paul says there is no room for mixed allegiance. We cannot share in the table of Jesus and demons (1 Corinthians 10:21). 1 Corinthians 10:1-15 connects the church to Israel who also drank the cup of Christ yet perished because of their persistent unfaithfulness. The hymn "There Is a Fountain Filled with Blood" says in verse 3, "Dear dying Lamb, Thy precious blood / Shall never lose its power / Till all the ransomed church of God / Be saved, to sin no more."[1]

Today, I will…flee to the cup of Jesus in whole-hearted allegiance when I feel tempted to turn back to the world to experience peace, identity, and belonging.

---

[1] William Cowper, 1772.

WEEK 50   PARTICIPATION IN
THE BLOOD & BODY   Kent Berman
WEDNESDAY

Flee to the Bread

Today's Scripture: 1 Corinthians 10:16-17

People rescued from poverty sometimes continue to hide food based on survival instinct, even after it is no longer necessary. Their experience has trained them to fear. While in the wilderness, God continually provided Israel's needs. He would give manna with instructions to gather only enough for the day (Exodus 16). Yet, Israel struggled to trust God's provision. Our human nature is to trust in what we can see, control, and measure. Some gathered extra food only to find it rot. God desired that Israel learn to trust Him fully. Their worrying, complaining, and unfaithfulness led to their destruction. Some of the Corinthian Christians were tempted to participate in idolatry and immorality to increase their social standing, wealth, and pleasure. In the face of such temptation, Paul implored them to flee to the bread of Jesus.

From the beginning, man was made to live one day at a time. Ever since the fall, mankind has faced difficulties such as famine, unemployment, disease, injury, loss, and death. No matter how hard we work, all of our efforts to overcome our dependence and mortality fail. Over thousands of years, little has changed. Do we not still worry? Do we not still tirelessly labor to lay up security on earth? But in the face of our mortality, such attempts to transcend the human condition are in vain.

Only by sharing in the bread at the table of Jesus are we promised continual strength and provision for the day. He promises to satisfy every need of our soul by offering the greatest gift of all—Himself. Time and again, He has proven faithful. He cares for us as His own body. We do not need to worry or strive in foolish self-sufficiency. The hymn, "We Plow the Fields and Scatter" says in the second verse, "The winds and waves obey Him, / By Him the birds are fed; / Much more to us, His children, / He gives our daily bread."[2]

Today, I will…flee to the bread of Jesus in complete surrender and trust in His daily provision knowing He cares for me as His own body.

---

[2] Matthias Claudius, 1782.

Kent Berman

Flee to the Community

Today's Scripture: 1 Corinthians 10:16-17

In spite of the disappointment many have experienced in church, Jesus has designed our souls to thrive in community. We need each other. The Church began as a unified community joyfully praising, breaking bread, and sharing together (Acts 2:42-47). But by the time Paul wrote to the Corinthian church, human nature had led to religious and social division. No wonder the church also struggled with vulnerability to idolatry and immorality.

The human body is amazing. In a healthy body, every part of the body works to care for and protect the other parts of the body. When injured, the body's systems work to heal itself. No invention of man has been able to mimic these fascinating qualities of organic life. It is God's design that the many members of the body of Christ likewise function as one (1 Corinthians 12:12).

Sometimes, Christians have been known to "shoot their own wounded." The culture becomes one of pretense. Those tainted by public sin withdraw in shame. But James 5:16 says when we confess our sins, we find healing—not humiliation. Many attend every assembly faithfully while making no progress spiritually. Many feel alone among hundreds each Sunday. Many timidly seek healing without confessing. The church ought to be the safest place on earth to confess any struggle. We must endeavor to make it so. If we fail to be vulnerable to one another, we will find ourselves vulnerable to the enemy, as were the Corinthians.

Only by sharing the bread with other believers at the table of Jesus may we experience oneness, healing, and belonging as His body. The hymn, "The Church's One Foundation," proclaims in verse two, "Elect from every nation, / Yet one o'er all the earth; / Her charter of salvation, / One Lord, one faith, one birth; / One holy name she blesses, / Partakes one holy food / And to one hope she presses, / With every grace endued."[3]

Today, I will… flee to the community of Jesus by sharing my struggles with another believer and praying together for strength and healing in Christ.

---

[3] Samuel John Stone, 1866.

FRIDAY
At the Table Through Trials
Today's Scripture: 1 Corinthians 10:16-17

To struggle with sin and temptation as we flee to the table of Jesus for strength may not be hypocritical, but it is human. Judas reclined at the table with Jesus, dipping his bread in the same dish while premeditating His betrayal. But I imagine most believers gathering at the Table deeply desire to be loyal to King Jesus. Though we struggle and fail, few are outright traitors as Judas was. But many may relate to Peter or the other disciples who momentarily forsook the Lord. A classic hymn pleads, "In the hour of trial, / Jesus, plead for me, / Lest by base denial / I depart from Thee. / When thou seest me waver, / With a look recall, / Nor for fear or favor / Suffer me to fall."[4]

Peter intended to follow Jesus, even to death. He shared in the table of Jesus, having sacrificially left all to follow Him. But in his humanity, he fell. Tradition says Peter later overcame his weakness and valiantly endured his own martyrdom. But at this moment, his allegiance to Jesus was not complete. Jesus looked upon Peter with compassion, knowing the man he would become, and called him back to the table (John 21:15-19). Perhaps it was such marvelous grace that gripped Peter's heart and compelled him to persevere.

We must flee to the table of Jesus moment by moment as the enemy presses in upon us. Paul asks, "The cup of blessing that we bless, is it not a participation in the blood of Christ? The bread that we break, is it not a participation in the body of Christ?" (1 Corinthians 10:16, ESV).

Paul's searching questions challenge our flawed reasoning, redirect our thoughts, clarify our reality, cut through our deception, and rebuke our compromise by calling us to the table of Jesus.

"With forbidden pleasures / Would this vain world charm, / Or its sordid treasures / Spread to work me harm, / Bring to my remembrance / Sad Gethsemane, / Or, in darker semblance, / Cross-crowned Calvary."[5]

Today, I will… memorize 1 Corinthians 10:16-17 and practice reciting it when tempted.

---

[4] James Montgomery, "In the Hour of Trial," 1834.

[5] Ibid.

Table Meditation
Scripture: Matthew 26:28

In Genesis 3, we read about the sin of man creating a separation from God. Thankfully, we also see God's plan to reconcile man to Him through the ultimate coming of Christ.

In Isaiah 53, we read of the expected Messiah and the suffering and sacrificial price He would pay for our redemption. Twice, the prophet speaks of the promised Messiah being bruised and wounded as an offering for sin, pouring out his life (his blood) as a sin offering (Isaiah 53:5, 10).

In Matthew 26, we read of Jesus instituting the "Lord's Supper" as a planned memorial for what he was about to do in carrying out the prophecy of Isaiah. When the Lord was speaking of the fruit of the vine, a symbol of his blood, he said: "This is my blood of the covenant, which is poured out for many unto the remission of sins" (Matthew 26:28, ASV).

In Acts 20, we read about the first-century church participating in this memorial every week.

In 1 Corinthians, we learn that it can become commonplace lacking its intended solemn meaning for those partaking in it. The Lord's Supper is a memorial service that looks back toward the cross and reminds us of the deed accomplished there for us.

In Hebrews, we read about how much better Christ and His sacrifice is than any before. And how His death provides complete sanctification and remission of sins, establishing a new covenant.

In Revelation, we see its completion when we are in Heaven with God and sin is no more.

MONDAY
Examine Yourself
Today's Scripture: 2 Corinthians 13:5

It has been observed that we live in the most self-unaware generation ever. What we hear continually is to "be true to yourself" and "love who you are." While on the surface that may sound helpful, it is not. People no longer seek to better themselves but have learned to accept their flaws and shortcomings as "just who I am." Yet, several experts oppose this notion and argue that self-examination is healthy and beneficial. Listen to this example: "To be able to make progress in any area of your life, you need to know who you are, what you want, and what steps to take to get there. Asking yourself the necessary questions before you start will allow you to go down the correct path. This is what self-examination is all about. There's no worse feeling than to put a bunch of time and effort into something to discover it led to the wrong outcome!!"[1]

As we consider the inspired words of 1 Corinthians 11:28, God issues this command: "But let a man examine himself." This statement is in the context of partaking of the Lord's Supper. Let us consider two questions: What does it mean to examine yourself? What is the purpose of this self-examination?

First, what does it mean to "examine yourself?" As we prepare to partake of the emblems of the Lord's Supper, the bread and fruit of the vine, we should examine our hearts and minds. We examine our hearts: are we partaking for the right reason? We examine our minds: do we understand the purpose of the Lord's Supper and why we do this?

Second, what is the purpose of this self-examination? By doing this we remind ourselves of the importance of this wonderful act of worship!

Obeying this command does not have to be a long, drawn-out process. Remember that no one is worthy to partake because all have sinned (Romans 3:23). Thus our hearts are filled with gratitude and love. What a blessing to partake!

Today, I will…make sure I'm partaking of the Lord's Supper for the right reasons.

---

[1] simplyrenewedliving.com

TUESDAY
Let's Eat!
Today's Scripture: 1 Corinthians 11:28

Eating. Who doesn't love to eat? God designed us with appetites and we have faithfully succumbed to those appetites for thousands of years. I have no intention of stopping, do you?

Gathering around a table to partake of food is one of the great blessings of family. It isn't just about the food. It is about people, fellowship, and relationships. Some of my favorite childhood memories involve family meals. Those were special times and significant to the bond that I established with my parents and my brothers and sister.

In our passage Paul says, after one examines himself, "and so let him eat." It reminds me of Mom calling to us kids, "Let's eat!" You didn't have to call me twice! It was a call for us to all come together. During the day, our lives were scattered all over. Our activities were as different as night to day. Yet here we were, gathering together.

The Lord's Supper is a unique act of worship. It embodies a wonderful time when all of us, scattered throughout the week, come together and share this special meal. Our minds have been on so many different things during the week. Now, however, we're together. Our hearts and minds are joined in thinking about and partaking in this wonderful supper. We are God's family (1 Timothy 3:16), called to the table by our Lord and Savior Jesus Christ. It is a special group of people, partaking in a special meal.

Church historians note that some early Christian groups "barred the door" after asking visitors to depart from the assembly. They were going to partake of the Lord's Supper, and it was only to be enjoyed by God's people. While there is no such instruction in Scripture for us to do this, it does illustrate how some of our ancestors in the faith prized and valued this act of worship.

Our Lord is inviting us to His table! What a blessing it is!

Today, I will…remind myself of the blessing of being a part of God's spiritual family.

WEDNESDAY
The Bread
Today's Scripture: 1 Corinthians 11:28

Quick…name the five basic food groups. Props to you if you can. I know I couldn't. In case you're wondering, they are grouped into the following: (1) Vegetables and fruits, (2) Grains and cereals, (3) Meat, poultry, fish, eggs, legumes, nuts, seeds, (4) Milk, cheese, yogurt, dairy alternatives, and (5) Fats, oils, and sweets.

When we look over that list, we can see how the basic groups enable us to enjoy a wide variety of food experiences. The very best meals (Italian, of course) derive from these food categories. Some meals, however, can be pretty plain. They may not be the pride and joy of executive chefs, but they may be staple meals for generations of people.

When Jesus instituted the Lord's Supper, two foods took center stage. Those two foods were simple and basic. Why? Because it wasn't about the food itself, but what it represented. Consider the bread. We learn from Scripture that this bread was made from flour and water and baked before it would rise minimally. This unleavened bread had special significance as given in Deuteronomy 16:3 (cf. 1 Corinthians 5:8). It was not meant to be a specialty bread with fruits, nuts, and spices added to it. It was simple and basic. Why? Because it represented "the bread of affliction."

When Jesus instituted the Lord's Supper (cf. Matthew 26:26), He took some bread and said to the disciples, "Take, eat, this is My body" (ESV). Thus, when we partake of the bread, our minds should focus on what it represents—the body of Jesus! We are reminded of what happened to Jesus' body—the beating, the crown of thorns, the pierced side, and the nailing to the cross. What His body endured!

The bread we eat at the Lord's Supper isn't much. It won't fill us up and isn't supposed to. It is designed to fill us up spiritually!

Today, I will…appreciate the meaning of the bread and the body of our Lord Jesus.

THURSDAY
The Fruit of the Vine
Today's Scripture: Matthew 26:26-29

It might have been 8th-grade biology. The teacher was talking about blood. We had to learn "twelve important facts about blood." I don't remember any of them except that not all blood is red (some creatures have blue blood!). The overriding point, however, was that blood is essential to life. As time went on, I've learned just how true that is. Modern medicine has established the following functions of blood: (1) It carries oxygen and nutrients throughout your body, (2) forms blood clots to manage bleeding, (3) protects your body from infections, (4) carries waste products, and (5) regulates body temperature.

Many are unaware that the first President of the United States, George Washington, also went through a process called "bloodletting." This is where the patient is intentionally bled with the hope of curing his illness. It didn't work. Amazingly, the practice of bloodletting continued through the 19th century!

The Bible established the importance of blood during the time of Moses. God had Moses write, "For the life of every creature is its blood: its blood is its life" (Leviticus 17:14, ESV). Again, notice…"Its blood is its life."

This understanding of blood magnifies the importance of the fruit of the vine, of which Jesus said: "This is My blood of the covenant, which is poured out for many for the forgiveness of sins" (Matthew 26:28, ESV). Notice two aspects of Jesus' words. First, His blood was to be "poured out." Certainly, the brutality of crucifixion would cause Jesus to bleed profusely. Since "life is in the blood," Jesus' very life was being poured out on the cross. Secondly, Jesus says that His blood is "for the forgiveness of sins." Notice the irony. Jesus lost his life when His blood "poured out." We have spiritual life—the forgiveness of sins— by that same blood!

Knowing this truth about the blood has changed me. I've never thought of the fruit of the vine the same since.

Today, I will…thank God for the blood that Jesus shed so I could live.

FRIDAY
Discern the Body
Today's Scripture: 1 Corinthians 11:29

There is a risk in doing the same thing over and over again. It can become boring and monotonous. Jesus saw this with the "meaningless repetition" of the Gentile's prayers (Matthew 6:7). This could also become a problem with the Lord's Supper. It is God's plan that we partake every first day of the week (Acts 20:7). This means that we are partaking 52 times a year. If you've been a Christian for ten years and haven't missed a Sunday, you've taken it 520 times. How about those who have been Christians for, say, 40 years? They are now looking at around 2,080 times! Talk about repetition!

Paul warns the Corinthian Christians (and us) to not allow the Lord's Supper to become something that loses its significance. It is conceivable that because we've done it so many times, it is rote, robotic, and—yes, meaningless. However, Paul's warning alone proves that we do not have to fall into the trap of the mundane.

How can we keep the Lord's Supper fresh and relevant? Paul offers two suggestions. First, each must "examine himself" (1 Corinthians 11:28). We engage our hearts and minds in what we're doing. We're thinking about it, and we're reminding ourselves of the great cost Jesus paid to give us this privilege. We do not forget that without the gift of His body and blood, we would have no chance of heaven! Second, each must "discern the body." Some believe that Paul has in mind the body of Jesus. If this is the meaning, it would go back to verse 24, where Jesus applies the elements to His body and blood. Others see Paul referring to one discerning his own body or the church. This would go along with what Paul says in verses 30-33. Either way, the point should remind us of the importance of this act of worship.

Today, I will…thank God for the privilege of gathering around His table each week.

Table Meditation
Scripture: Mark 8:34-35

Mark 8:34-35 says, "And He summoned the crowd with His disciples, and said to them, "If anyone wishes to come after Me, he must deny himself, and take up his cross and follow Me. For whoever wishes to save his life will lose it, but whoever loses his life for My sake and the gospel's will save it" (NASB 1995).

"Take up your cross and follow Me" is a call to self-sacrifice. One must be willing to deny themselves to follow Jesus. Dying to self is an absolute surrender to God. Simply put, if faced with a choice—Jesus or the comforts of this life— which will we choose?

If you read the book of Mark like you would read a novel, you could see how this is foreshadowing. Later in Mark 15, we learn of this man, Simon of Cyrene. The soldiers press Simon into service to bear the cross of Jesus.

There are two idioms we use in speech: "the hill you're willing to die on," and "stake in the ground." They both highlight determination. When I see a cross, I am reminded of these idioms and the determination of God and His Son Jesus. God put a stake in the ground. It was the cross of Jesus. God showed each one of us how much he loves us by letting His only Son die on that cross. Golgotha was the hill Jesus died on. Jesus demonstrated His absolute surrender to God.

MONDAY
Encourage One Another
Today's Scripture: Hebrews 10:24-25

The great Hebrew writer addressed people who were experiencing challenges as followers of Jesus. These challenges were largely originating from those outside of Christ. But an element within believed a person must hold to the teachings of the Law of Moses as well as follow Christ. With that in view, it is not difficult to see why the Hebrew writer made it the major goal to express the superiority of Christ in multiple areas: Christ is superior to prophets, angels, Moses, Joshua's rest, the other High Priests; and Christ's covenant and sacrifice are superior to all others. With great clarity, Hebrews helps the reader understand that Christ stands above all else.

The concept of encouragement runs throughout the letter. In Hebrews 10:24–25, we read, "And let us consider how to stir up one another to love and good works, not neglecting to meet together, as is the habit of some, but encouraging one another, and all the more as you see the Day drawing near" (ESV). Twice in this short sentence, the writer calls for us to encourage one another. The first is the phrase, "stir up one another." The word used here means "an incitement to good." There is also a negative sense of this word, but the context clearly indicates that the Hebrew writer intends the positive nature of the word. We ought to incite, or encourage, one another to love and good works.

The second call is seen in the plainly stated, "encourage one another," in verse 25. This word means "to encourage, exhort, strengthen, comfort, or console." It is an interesting word used in this passage because of the context. As we face challenging moments in life, we know that we are not alone. The recipients of the Hebrew letter also faced great challenges. But the writer calls for intentionality and commitment to one another—to encourage one another. That is our calling as well. Encourage one another!

Today, I will…seek to encourage others.

TUESDAY
A Timely Word
Today's Scripture: Hebrews 10:24-25

With the call of the Hebrew writer for his readers to "stir up one another" and "encourage one another" (Hebrews 10:24–25, ESV), we cannot help but ask ourselves, "In what ways am I accomplishing this task?" Certainly, the import of this passage is upon the gathering together of the saints. Perhaps one of the greatest blessings we have been given by God is the opportunity each week to assemble *together*, worship God *together*, and participate in the Lord's Supper *together*. What a blessing!

In many congregations, someone will stand before the church and share a thought or message that intends to focus minds on the great sacrifice of Jesus. As we prepare to commune together, our hearts are collectively brought to the foot of the cross, where we contemplate the wonderful gift of God in Christ. These words spoken by the person presiding over the Supper encourage us to reflect on what God has done for us, the love of Christ displayed in His selfless sacrifice, and the responsibility that we have toward our brothers and sisters in Christ. Not only are we communing with God, but we are communing with one another, sharing the body and blood of our Savior *together*.

Proverbs 15:23 says, "To make an apt answer is a joy to a man, and a word in season, how good it is!" How good it is! How good what is? A word in season. This phrase is from a word that implies timeliness. We might render this phrase as "a timely word." As we gather each Lord's Day to celebrate and participate in the Lord's Supper, my prayer is that we will recognize the importance of a timely word and that we will allow the simple message of Jesus' gracious death on the cross to encourage us. May we seek to encourage one another as we share the Supper *together*.

Today, I will…share a timely word with others.

Taking Advantage of Opportunities
Today's Scripture: Hebrews 10:24-25

The wise man wrote, "For lack of wood the fire goes out, and where there is no whisperer, quarreling ceases. As charcoal to hot embers and wood to fire, so is a quarrelsome man for kindling strife. The words of a whisperer are like delicious morsels; they go down into the inner parts of the body" (Proverbs 26:20-22, ESV). Our words and actions can have a powerful impact on others—positively and negatively. Oh, how important are our words!

One writer pointed out, "One of the highest of human duties is the duty of encouragement. It is easy to laugh at men's ideals; it is easy to pour cold water on their enthusiasm; it is easy to discourage others. The world is full of discouragers. We have a Christian duty to encourage one another. Many a time a word of praise or thanks or appreciation or cheer has kept a man on his feet. Blessed is the man who speaks such a word."[1] This truth is rooted in what the Hebrew writer exhorted, "And let us consider how to stir up one another to love and good works, not neglecting to meet together, as is the habit of some, but encouraging one another, and all the more as you see the Day drawing near" (Hebrews 10:24–25, ESV). We ought to always seek ways that we can encourage those around us.

As we assemble each first day of the week, we have the great opportunity to commune together with the Lord and one another. The Hebrew writer acknowledges that some were in the habit of not assembling with the Body. They were not recognizing the great benefit, blessing, and encouragement that accompanies the gathering of God's people. As followers of Jesus, we ought to encourage each other to take full advantage of every opportunity afforded to us to gather around the Lord's Table.

Today, I will…encourage brothers and sisters in Christ to make gathering together a priority.

---

[1] Barclay, William. *The New Daily Study Bible: The Letter to the Hebrews.* Westminster John Knox, 2001.

There's a Great Day Coming
Today's Scripture: Hebrews 10:24-25

The writer of Hebrews wants the reader to understand the importance of being steadfast in faith and committed to one another. With the call to "stir up one another" and "encourage one another" comes the exhortation to do so "all the more as you see the Day drawing near" (Hebrews 10:24–25, ESV). All of this lies within his call to hold fast to the faith and to see the importance of meeting together as followers of Jesus. The writer encourages readers to understand the powerful nature of the encouragement that results from being together with people of like-precious faith. In the face of challenging circumstances, meeting together, communing together, and worshiping God together motivates and encourages one another to stay the course.

Individually, we ought to continually encourage one another. But we need to make sure our words are appropriate. One little boy loved his mother and loved to sit on her lap. One day, the boy was sitting on his mother's lap while she was reading a book to him. After she finished the book, he cuddled up close to her and said, "I love you, Mommy!" His mother was grateful for his love but questioned, "Oh son, how could you love a mother who's so fat and ugly?" The little boy offered a word of encouragement when he responded, "Oh no, Mommy. You're not fat and ugly. You're fat and pretty!"

When it comes to the people of God, the Church, we must remember that there is a great day coming. We are blessed to assemble and surround the Table of the Lord each week. We will one day gather with ALL of God's people and surround the Heavenly Table to share a great feast. The Apostle John was told, "Come, gather for the great supper of God ..." (Revelation 19:17, ESV). There's a great day coming! Let's remind and encourage one another with these words!

Today, I will…remember and look forward to the great supper of God.

FRIDAY
How to Be Encouragers
Today's Scripture: Hebrews 10:24-25

Charles Swindoll wrote, "The lack of encouragement is almost an epidemic. To illustrate this point, when did you last encourage someone else? I firmly believe that an individual is never more Christlike than when full of compassion for those who are down, needy, discouraged, or forgotten. How terribly essential is our commitment to encouragement! Is there some soul known to you in need of encouragement? A student off at school, a young couple up against it, a divorcée struggling to gain back self-acceptance, a forgotten servant of God laboring in an obscure and difficult ministry, a widow who needs your companionship, someone who tried something new and failed? Encourage generously. Encouragement! A new watchword for our times. Shout it out. Pass it around."[2]

I am convinced that we can never have too much encouragement. Imagine if everyone truly committed themselves to encouraging everyone they encountered throughout the day: What do you think that day would be like? What do you suppose would be the attitude and spirit of people on that day?

Imagine if we committed ourselves to letting this be our daily lives. Imagine if we were the kind of people who lived by the adage, "If you don't have something nice to say, don't say anything at all."

How can we be encouragers? Here are some simple ways: let people know you are praying for them—and actually pray for them; let people know what you appreciate, respect, like, and enjoy about them; let people know they are a great example to you and thank them for that; let people know you care by sending a card, giving them a call, or visiting them; let people know how you see God at work in their lives; and let people know the ways they encourage you.

Perhaps one more way to be an encourager is in order: Smile a lot!

Remember the call of the Hebrew writer: "stir up one another" and "encourage one another" (Hebrews 10:24–25). Let's be encouragers!

Today, I will…speak words of encouragement.

---

[2] *Swindoll's Ultimate Book of Illustrations and Quotes.* Thomas Nelson, 1998.

Additional TJI Titles Available

NEW! Weekly Hope for Senior Saints
Weekly Peace for Senior Saints
Weekly Joy for Senior Saints

The Church Matters: A Book for Young Adults
Reviving the Revival (Chad Ramsey)

The Living Word: Sermons of Jerry A. Jenkins
Before I Go: Notes from Older Preachers

Thoughts from the Mound (Jeff Jenkins)
More Thoughts from the Mound (Jeff Jenkins)

Beyond the Valley of Death (Jeff Jenkins)

All I Ever Wanted to Do Was Preach (Dale Jenkins)
I Hope You Have to Pinch Yourself (Dale Jenkins)

The Preacher as Counselor (Dale Jenkins and others)

Don't Quit on a Monday (Jeff & Dale Jenkins)
Don't Quit on a Tuesday (Jeff & Dale Jenkins)
Don't Quit on a Wednesday (Jeff & Dale Jenkins)
Don't Quit on a Thursday (Jeff & Dale Jenkins)
Don't Quit on a Friday (Jeff & Dale Jenkins)
Don't Quit on a Saturday (Jeff & Dale Jenkins)
Don't Quit on a Sunday (Jeff & Dale Jenkins)

Five Secrets and a Decision (Dale Jenkins)
Centered: Marking Your Map in a Muddled World
(Dale Jenkins)
On Moving Well: The Scoop-Meister's Thoughts on Ministry Transitions (Dale Jenkins)
Praying Always: Prayers for Preachers (gift book)
(Jeff & Dale Jenkins)
You're Fired! Now What? (Dale Jenkins)

Keys to Effective Ministry (Jeff & Dale Jenkins)
A Minister's Heart (Jeff & Dale Jenkins)
A Youth Minister's Heart (Jeff & Dale Jenkins)
A Mother's Heart (Jeff & Dale Jenkins)
A Father's Heart (Jeff & Dale Jenkins)

Immerse: A Simple Look at Baptism (Dale Jenkins)

We Think You'll Love It Here (personalized for guests)

His Word (Daily devotionals from the New Testament)
His Life (Daily devotionals from Jesus' life & ministry)
My Life (Daily devotionals covering the Christian life)
His Family (Daily devotionals studying the church)
My Family (Daily devotionals studying the home)
Meeting God's People (Daily devotionals on Bible lives of faith)
His Table (Daily devotionals for the Lord's Supper)

The Glory of Preaching (Jay Lockhart &
Clarence DeLoach)
Profiles of Faith & Courage: Interviews with Gospel Preachers
(Dennis Gulledge)
Me, You, and the People in the Pews (Tracy Moore)
From Mother's Day to Father's Day (Paul Shero)
Little Fish, Big Splash (Mark Neaves &
Shawn Weaver)
The Three Little Ministers (Philip Jenkins)
Choice Over Circumstance (Drake Jenkins)
Pocket Guide for Preachers: 1 Timothy
(Joey Sparks & Cole Wade)

Free Evangelism Resources by Jerry Jenkins:
God Speaks Today
Lovingly Leading Men to the Savior

To order, visit *thejenkinsinstitute.com/shop*

Made in the USA
Columbia, SC
26 November 2024

46986710R00202